Red Hat® Linux®
POCKET ADMINISTRATOR

Richard Petersen
Ibrahim Haddad

McGraw-Hill/Osborne

New York   Chicago   San Francisco
Lisbon   London   Madrid   Mexico City   Milan
New Delhi   San Juan   Seoul   Singapore   Sydney   Toronto

The McGraw·Hill Companies

McGraw-Hill/Osborne
2100 Powell Street, 10th Floor
Emeryville, California 94608
U.S.A.

To arrange bulk purchase discounts for sales promotions,
premiums, or fund-raisers, please contact **McGraw-Hill**/Osborne
at the above address. For information on translations or book
distributors outside the U.S.A., please see the International
Contact Information page immediately following the index of
this book.

Red Hat® Linux® Pocket Administrator

Publisher   Brandon A. Nordin
Vice President & Associate Publisher   Scott Rogers
Acquisitions Editor   Francis Kelly
Project Editor   Julie M. Smith
Acquisitions Coordinator   Jessica Wilson
Technical Editor   Ibrahim Haddad
Copy Editor   Brian MacDonald
Proofreader   Susie Elkind
Indexer   Richard Shrout
Composition   Tara A. Davis, Lucie Ericksen
Illustrator   Lyssa Wald
Series Design   Peter F. Hancik, Lucie Ericksen, Elizabeth Jang
Cover Series Design   Jeff Weeks

1234567890 DOC DOC 019876543

ISBN 0-07-222974-8

This book was composed with Corel VENTURA™ Publisher.

To my nephew Christopher
Richard Petersen

*to my wonderful family, for their love and support, and
to the love of my life, who brings me happiness every day*
Ibrahim Haddad

About the Authors

Richard Petersen teaches UNIX and C/C++ courses at the University of California at Berkeley. He is the author of four editions of *Linux: The Complete Reference* and many other books.

Ibrahim Haddad is a Researcher at the Ericsson Corporate Research division's Open System Lab, located in Montreal, Canada. Mr. Haddad is involved with the system architecture of third generation wireless IP networks and guiding Ericsson Open Source contributions, which promote and advance the use of Linux in the area of telecommunication.

Mr. Haddad represents Ericsson on the Technical Board of the Open Source Development Lab and serves as Contributing Editor to the *Linux Journal*. In addition to his contributions to the *Linux Journal*, Mr. Haddad writes for *Linux User & Developer* in the areas of IPv6 and telecommunications and has delivered a number of presentations and tutorials at local universities, IEEE and ACM conferences, Open Source forums, and international conferences.

Mr. Haddad received his Bachelor and Master degrees in Computer Science from the Lebanese American University, charted by the University of the State of New York. He is currently a Dr. Sc. Candidate at Concordia University in Montreal researching Next Generation Internet Servers. Academic awards include the "J. W. McConnell Memorial Graduate Fellowship" and the "Concordia University 25th Anniversary Fellowship," received in 2000.

CONTENTS

INTRODUCTION

With its up-to-date coverage of Red Hat and Linux kernel, the Red Hat Linux Administrator's Pocket Reference is just what you need to master administration fundamentals and commands. This book provides all the basic aspects of the Red Hat Linux administration, with particular attention to users, devices, software, file systems, printer management, kernel administration, and system management

The book is also for people who want to learn how to manage their Linux machines and become more efficient with their administration tasks using the best commands and options for their specific tasks. It covers a wide range of topics such as system configuration, users and groups management, software management, file system management, devices, print servers, kernel administration, and various system administrator tasks. It teaches readers how to manage user accounts, customize their Linux kernel, configure RAID devices, access file systems, schedule and monitor system tasks secure passwords, and much more. The book provides a lot of examples and tips to help readers experiment with all the discussed administration commands.

If you are learning to administer Linux, looking for new commands and options that will help you do your administration tasks faster and more efficiently, or wishing you had a pocket-sized book with your need-to-know information at your fingertips, this book is right for you.

Chapter 1

Basic System Administration

Linux is designed to serve many users at the same time,
and to provide an interface between the users and the
computer with its storage media, such as hard disks and
tapes. Users have their own shells through which they
interact with the operating system, but you may need
to configure the operating system itself in different ways.
You may need to add new users, devices like printers and
scanners, and even file systems. Such operations come
under the heading of system administration. The person
who performs such actions is referred to as either a *system
administrator* or a *superuser*. In this sense, there are two
types of interaction with Linux: regular users' interaction,
and the superuser, who performs system administration
tasks. The chapters in this book cover operations such as
changing system runlevels, managing users, configuring
printers, adding file systems, and compiling the kernel.
You perform most of these tasks only rarely, such as adding
a new printer or mounting a file system. Other tasks, such
as adding or removing users, you perform on a regular
basis. Basic system administration covers topics such
as system access by superusers, selecting the run level
to start, system configuration files, and performance
monitoring.

Superuser Control: the root user

To perform system administration operations, you must
first have access rights such as the correct password that
enables you to log in as the root user, making you the
superuser. Because a superuser has the power to change
almost anything on the system, such a password is usually
a carefully guarded secret, changed very frequently, and
given only to those whose job is to manage the system. With
the correct password, you can log in to the system as

a system administrator and configure the system in different ways. You can start up and shut down the system, as well as change to a different operating mode, such as a single-user mode. You can also add or remove users, add or remove whole file systems, back up and restore files, and even designate the system's name and address.

To become a superuser, you log in to the *root user account*. This is a special account reserved for system management operations with unrestricted access to all components of your Linux operating system. You can log in as the root user from either the GUI (Graphical User Interface) login screen, or from the command line login prompt. You then have access to all administrative tools. Using a GUI interface like Gnome, the root user has access to a number of Red Hat GUI administrative tools, such as redhat-config-packages for installing software or redhat-config-users for managing users. If you log in from the command line interface, you can run corresponding administrative command like `rpm` to install packages or `useradd` to add a new user. From your GUI desktop, you can also run command-line administrative tools using a terminal window. The command line interface for the root user uses a special prompt, the sharp sign, #. In the next example, the user logs in to the system as the root user and receives the # prompt.

```
login: root
password:
#
```

Root User Password

As the root user, you can use the `passwd` command to change the password for the root login, as well as for any other user on the system. The `passwd` command will check your password with Pluggable Authentication Modules (PAM), as discussed in Chapter 2, to see if you've selected one that can be easily cracked. To more easily change your root password from a GUI interface, you can use the redhat-config-rootpassword tool.

```
# passwd root
New password:
Re-enter new password:
#
```

You must take precautions to protect your root password. Anyone who gains access as the root user will have complete control over your system. The online manual for the `passwd` command provides detailed recommendations for handling and choosing your password. For example, never store your password in a file on your system, and never choose one based on any accessible information, such as your phone number or date of birth. A basic guideline is to make your password as complex as possible using a phrase of several words with numbers and upper and lower case, yet something you can still remember easily so you never have to write it down. You can access the `passwd` online manual page with the command:

```
# man passwd
```

Root User Access: su

While you are logged in to a regular user account, it may be necessary for you to log in as the root and become a superuser. Ordinarily, you would have to log out of your user account first, and then log in to the root. Instead, you can use the `su` command (switch user) to log in directly to the root while remaining logged in to your user account. If you are using a GUI desktop like Gnome, you can enter the `su` command from a terminal window, or use ALT-CTRL-F1 to switch to a command line interface (ALT-CTRL-F10 returns you back to the GUI interface). A CTRL-D or `exit` command returns you to your own user login. When you are logged in as the root, you can use `su` to log in as any user, without providing the password. In the next example, the user is logged in already. The `su` command then logs in as the root user, making the user a superuser. Some basic superuser commands are shown in Table 1-1.

```
$ pwd
/home/chris
```

```
$su
 password:
# cd
# pwd
/root
# exit
$
```

SECURITY SCAN *For security reasons, Linux distributions do not allow the use of* su *in a telnet session to access the root user. For SSH and Kerberos enabled systems, Red Hat provides secure login access using slogin (SSH) and rlogin (Kerberos version).*

Command	Description
su root	Logs a superuser into the root from a user login; the superuser returns to the original login with a CTRL-D.
passwd *login-name*	Sets a new password for the login name.
crontab *options file-name*	With *file-name* as an argument, installs crontab entries in the file to a crontab file; these entries are operations executed at specified times (see later section): -e Edits the crontab file -l Lists the contents of the crontab file -r Deletes the crontab file
telinit *runlevel*	Changes the system runlevels.
shutdown *options time*	Shuts down the system.
date	Sets the date and time for the system.
Red Hat Date and Time Properties tool, redhat-config-date	GUI tool to set system time and date (System Settings | Date & Time).
Kcron	KDE GUI interface cron management tool (System Tools | Task Scheduler).

Table 1-1. Basic System Administration tools

Command	Description
redhat-config-rootpassword	GUI tool to change the root user (administrator) password. (System Settings | Root Password).
redhat-logviewer	GUI tool to view system logs the root user. (System Settings | Root Password).

Table 1-1.   Basic System Administration tools *(continued)*

System Time and Date

You can set the system time and date, using the shell `date` command or the Red Hat GUI tool redhat-config-date. You probably set the time and date when you first installed your system. You should not need to do so again. If you entered the time incorrectly or moved to a different time zone, though, you could use this utility to change your time.

Using the redhat-config-date Utility

The preferred way to set the system time and date is to use the Red Hat Date and Time Properties utility (redhat-config-date). Select it on the System Settings window accessible from the Start Here window. There are two panels, one for the date and time and one for the time zone (see Figure 1-1). Use the calendar to select the year, month, and date. Then, use the Time box to set the hour, minute, and second. The Time Zone panel shows a map with locations. Select the one nearest you to set your time zone.

Red Hat also supports the Network Time Protocol (NTP), which allows a remote server to set the date and time. NTP allows for the most accurate synchronization of your system's clock. It is often used to manage the time and date for networked systems, freeing the administrator from having to synchronize clocks manually. The date and time panel is obtained from an NTP server. Your network may have its own, or you can use one of the public NTP servers listed at www.ntp.org. You can also download current documentation and NTP software from the www.ntp.org site.

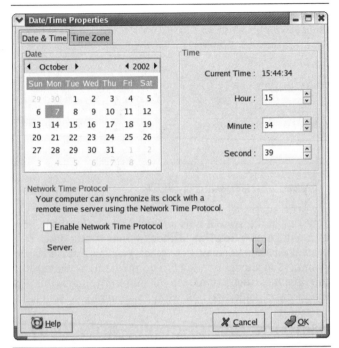

Figure 1-1 redhat-config-date

Using the date Command

You can also use the date command on your root user command line to set the date and time for the system. As an argument to date, you list (with no delimiters) the month, day, time, and year. In the next example, the date is set to 2:59 P.M., April 6, 2003 (04 for April, 06 for the day, 1459 for the time, and 03 for the year 2003):

```
# date 0406145903
Sun Mar 6 02:59:27 PST 2003
```

NOTE *You can also set the time and date with the Date & Time tool in the KDE Control Center.*

| Scheduling Tasks: cron | 1 |

 Scheduling regular maintenance tasks, such as backups, is managed by the `cron` service on Linux, implemented by a `cron` daemon. A *daemon* is a continually running server that constantly checks for certain actions to take. These tasks are listed in the `crontab` file. The `cron` daemon constantly checks the user's `crontab` file to see if it is time to take these actions. Any user can set up a `crontab` file of his or her own. The root user can set up a `crontab` file to take system administrative actions, such as backing up files at a certain time each week or month.

TIP   *For a system that may normally be shut down during times that `cron` is likely to run, you may want to supplement `cron` with `anacron`. For example, if a system is shutdown on a weekend when `cron` jobs are scheduled, then the jobs will not be performed. `anacron`, however, checks to see what jobs need to be performed when the system is turned on again, and then runs them. It is designed only for jobs that run daily or weekly. For `anacron` jobs, you place `crontab` entries in the `/etc/anacrontab` file.*

The crond Service

The name of the `cron` daemon is `crond`. Normally, it is started automatically when your system starts up. You can set this feature using redhat-config-services or `chkconfig`, as described in Chapter 10. The following example starts the `crond` service automatically whenever you boot the system:

```
chkconfig crond on
```

You can also start and stop the `crond` service manually, which you may want to do for emergency maintenance or during upgrades. Use the `service` command and the `stop` option to shut down the service, and the `start` option to run it again:

```
service crond stop
```

crontab Entries

A `crontab` entry has six fields: the first five are used to specify the time for an action, while the last field is the action itself. The first field specifies minutes (0–59), the second field specifies the hour (0–23), the third field specifies the day of the month (1–31), the fourth field specifies the month of the year (1–12, or month prefixes like *Jan* and *Sep*), and the fifth field specifies the day of the week (0–6, or day prefixes like *Wed* and *Fri*), starting with 0 as Sunday. In each of the time fields, you can specify a range, a set of values, or use the asterisk to indicate all values. For example, 1–5 for the day-of-week field specifies Monday through Friday. In the hour field, 8, 12, 17 would specify 8 A.M., 12 noon, and 5 P.M. An * in the month-of-year field indicates every month. The format of a `crontab` field follows:

```
minute   hour   day-month   month   day(s)-week   task
```

The following example backs up the `projects` directory at 2:00 A.M. every weekday:

```
0 2 * * 1-5   tar cf /home/ backp /home/projects
```

The same entry is listed here again using prefixes for the month and weekday:

```
0 2 * * Mon-Fri tar cf /home/backp /home/projects
```

To specify particular months, days, weeks, or hours, you can list them individually, separated by commas. For example, to perform the previous task on Sunday, Wednesday, and Friday, you could use `0,3,5` in the day-of-week field, or their prefix equivalents, `Sun,Wed,Fri`.

```
0 2 * * 0,3,5   tar cf /home/backp /home/projects
```

Cron also supports comments. A comment is any line beginning with a # sign.

```
# Weekly backup for Chris's projects
0 2 * * Mon-Fri  tar cf /home/backp /home/projects
```

cron Environment Variables

`cron` also lets you define environment variables for use with tasks performed. Red Hat defines variables for SHELL, PATH, HOME, and MAILTO. SHELL designates the shell to use tasks; in this case, the bash shell. PATH lists the directories where programs and scripts can be found. This example lists the standard directories, /usr/bin and /bin, as well as the system directories reserved for system applications, /usr/sbin and /sbin. MAILTO designates to whom the results of a task are to be mailed. By default, these are mailed to the user who schedules it, but you can have the results sent to a specific user, like the administrator's e-mail address, or an account on another system in a network. HOME is the home directory for a task; in this case, the top directory.

```
SHELL=/bin/bash
PATH=/sbin:/bin:/usr/sbin:/usr/bin
MAILTO=root
HOME=/
```

cron.d Directory

On a heavily used system, the /etc/crontab file can become crowded easily. There may also be instances where certain entries require different variables. For example, you may need to run some task under a different shell. To help better organize your crontab tasks, you can place crontab entries in files within the cron.d directory. The files in the cron.d directory all contain crontab entries of the same format as /etc/crontab. They may be given any name. They are treated as added crontab files, with cron checking them for task to run. For example, Red Hat installs a sysstat file in the cron.d that contains crontab entries to run tools to gather system statistics.

crontab Command

You use the `crontab` command to install your entries into
a `crontab` file. To do this, first create a text file and type
your `crontab` entries. Save this file with any name you
want, such as `mycronfile`. Then, to install these entries,
enter `crontab` and the name of the text file. The `crontab`
command takes the contents of the text file and creates a
`crontab` file in the `/var/spool/cron` directory, adding
the name of the user who issued the command. In the
following example, the root user installs the contents of
the `mycronfile` as the root's `crontab` file. This creates
a file called `/var/spool/cron/root`. If a user named
justin installed a `crontab` file, it would create a file
called `/var/spool/cron/justin`. You can control
use of the `crontab` command by regular users with the
`/etc/cron.allow` file. Only users with their names in
this file can create `crontab` files of their own. Conversely,
the `/etc/cron.deny` file lists those users denied use
of the `cron` tool, preventing them for scheduling tasks.
If neither file exists, access is denied to all users. If a
user is not in a `/etc/cron.allow` file, access is denied.
However, if the `/etc/cron.allow` file does not exist,
and the `/etc/cron.deny` file does, then all users not listed
in `/etc/cron.deny` are automatically allowed access.

```
# crontab mycronfile
```

cron Editing

Never try to edit your `crontab` file directly. Instead, use
the `crontab` command with the `-e` option. This opens your
`crontab` file in the `/var/spool/cron` directory with the
standard text editor, such as vi. `crontab` uses the default
editor as specified by the `EDITOR` shell environment
variable. To use a different editor for `crontab`, change
the default editor by assigning the editor's program
name to the `EDITOR` variable and exporting that variable.
Normally, the editor variable is set in the `/etc/profile`
script. Running `crontab` with the `-l` option displays the
contents of your `crontab` file, and the `-r` option deletes
the entire file. Invoking `crontab` with another text file of
`crontab` entries overwrites your current `crontab` file,
replacing it with the contents of the text file.

Organizing Scheduled Tasks

1

You can organize administrative `cron` tasks into two general groups: common administrative tasks that can be run at regular intervals, or specialized tasks that need to be run at a unique time. Unique tasks can be run as entries in the `/etc/crontab` file, as described in the next section. Common administrative tasks, though they can be run from the `/etc/crontab` file, are better organized into specialized `cron` directories. Within such directories, each task is placed in its own shell script that will invoke the task when run. For example, there may be several administrative tasks that all need to be run each week on the same day, say if maintenance for a system is scheduled on a Sunday morning. For these kinds of task, `cron` provides several specialized directories for automatic daily, weekly, monthly, and yearly tasks. Each contains a `cron` prefix and a suffix for the time interval. The `/etc/cron.daily` directory is used for tasks that need to be performed every day, whereas weekly task can be placed in the `/etc/cron.weekly` directory. The `cron` directories are listed in Table 1-2.

cron files and directories	Description
/etc/crontab	System `crontab` file, accessible only by the root user
/etc/cron.d	Directory containing multiple `crontab` files, accessible only by the root user
/etc/cron.hourly	Directory for tasks performed hourly
/etc/cron.daily	Directory for tasks performed daily
/etc/cron.weekly	Directory for tasks performed weekly
/etc/cron.monthly	Directory for tasks performed monthly
/etc/cron.yearly	Directory for tasks performed yearly
/etc/cron.hourly	Directory for tasks performed hourly
/etc/cron.allow	Users allowed to submit `cron` tasks
/etc/cron.deny	Users denied access to `cron`

Table 1-2. Cron files and directories

Running cron Directory Scripts

Each directory contains scripts that are all run at the same time. The scheduling for each group is determined by an entry in the /etc/crontab file. The actual execution of the scripts is performed by the /usr/bin/run-parts script, which runs all the scripts and programs in a given directory. Scheduling for all the tasks in a given directory is handled by an entry in the /etc/crontab file. Red Hat provides entries with designated times, which you may change for your own needs. The default Red Hat crontab file is shown here, with times for running scripts in the different cron directories. Here, you can see that most scripts are run at about 4 A.M., either daily (4:02), Sunday (4:22), or on the first day of each month (4:42). Hourly ones are run one minute after the hour.

```
SHELL=/bin/bash
PATH=/sbin:/bin:/usr/sbin:/usr/bin
MAILTO=root
HOME=/
# run-parts
01 * * * * root run-parts /etc/cron.hourly
02 4 * * * root run-parts /etc/cron.daily
22 4 * * 0 root run-parts /etc/cron.weekly
42 4 1 * * root run-parts /etc/cron.monthly
```

TIP *Scripts within a* cron *directory are run alphabetically. If you need a certain script to run before any others, you may have to alter its name. One method is to prefix the name with a numeral. For example, in the* /cron.weekly *directory, the* anacron *script is named* 0anacron *so that it will run before any others.*

Keep in mind, though, that these are simply directories that contain executable files. The actual scheduling is performed by the entries in the /etc/crontab file. For example, if the weekly field in the cron.weekly crontab entry is changed to * instead of 0, and the monthly field to 1 (22 4 1 * * instead of 22 4 * * 0), tasks in the cron.weekly file would end up running monthly instead of weekly.

Cron Directory Names

The names used for these directories are merely conventions. They have no special meaning to the `cron` daemon. You could, in fact, create your own directory, place scripts within it, and schedule run-parts to run those scripts at a given time. In the next example, scripts placed in the `/etc/cron.mydocs` directory will run at 12 noon every Wednesday.

```
* 12 * * 3 root run-parts /etc/cron.mydocs
```

System Runlevels: telinit, initab, and shutdown

A Linux system can run in different levels, depending on the capabilities you want to give it. For example, you can run your system at an administrative level, locking out user access. Normally, full operations are activated by simply running your system at a certain level of operational capability, such as supporting multiuser access or graphical interfaces. These levels (also known as states or modes) are referred to as *runlevels*, the level of support that you are running your system at.

runlevels

A Linux system has several runlevels, numbered from 0 to 6. When you power up your system, you enter the default runlevel. Runlevels 0, 1, and 6 are special runlevels that perform specific functions. Runlevel 0 is the power-down state and is invoked by the `halt` command to shut down the system. Runlevel 6 is the reboot state—it shuts down the system and reboots. Runlevel 1 is the single-user state, which allows access only to the superuser, and does not run any network services. This enables you, as the administrator, to perform administrative actions without interference from others.

Other runlevels reflect how you want the system to be used. Runlevel 2 is a partial multiuser state, allowing

access by multiple users, but without network services
like NFS or xinetd (eXtended InterNET services daemon).
This level is useful for a system that is not part of a network.
Both runlevel 3 and runlevel 5 run a fully operational Linux
system, with multiuser support and remote file sharing
access. They differ in terms of the interface they use.
Runlevel 3 starts up your system with the command
line interface (also known as the text mode interface).
Runlevel 5 starts up your system with an X session,
running the X Window System server and invoking a
graphical login, using display managers, such as gdm
or xdm. If you choose to use graphical logins during
installation, runlevel 5 will be your default runlevel.
Linux provides two keyboard sequences to let you switch
between the two during a login session: CTRL-ALT-F1
changes from the graphical interface (runlevel 5) to the
command line interface (runlevel 3) and CTRL-ALT-F7
changes from the command line interface to the graphical
interface. The runlevels are listed in Table 1-3.

Changing runlevels can be helpful if you have problems
at a particular runlevel. For example, if your video card
is not installed properly, then any attempt to start up in
runlevel 5 will likely fail, as this level immediately starts
your graphical interface. Instead you should use the
command line interface, runlevel 3, to fix your video card
installation.

TIP *You can use the single-user runlevel (1) as a recovery
mode state, allowing you to start up your system without
running startup scripts for services like DNS. This is helpful
if your system hangs when you try to start such services.
Networking is disabled, as well as any multiuser access.
You can also use* linux -s *at the boot prompt to enter
runlevel 1. If you want to enter the single-user state and
also run the startup scripts, you can use the special* s *or*
s *runlevels.*

initab runlevels

When your system starts up, it uses the default
runlevel as specified in the default init entry in the

State	Description
System Runlevels (states)	
0	Halt (do *not* set the default to this level); shuts down the system completely.
1	Administrative single-user mode; denies other users access to the system, but allows root access to the entire multiuser file system. Startup scripts are not run. (Use s or S to enter single-user mode with startup scripts run.)
2	Multiuser, without network services like NFS, xinetd, and NIS (the same as 3, but you do not have networking).
3	Full multiuser mode with login to command-line interface; allows remote file sharing with other systems on your network. Also referred to as the *text mode state*.
4	Unused.
5	Full multiuser mode that starts up in an X session, initiating a graphical login; allows remote file sharing with other systems on your network (same as 3, but with graphical login).
6	Reboots; shuts down and restarts the system (do *not* set the default to this).

Table 1-3.   System Runlevels (states)

/etc/inittab file. For example, if your default init runlevel is 5 (the graphical login), the default init entry in the /etc/inittab file would be

```
init:5:default:
```

You can change the default runlevel by editing the /etc/ inittab file and changing the init default entry. Editing the /etc/inittab file can be dangerous. You should do this with great care. As an example, if the default runlevel is 3 (command line), the entry for your default runlevel in the /etc/inittab file should look like the following:

```
id:3:initdefault:
```

You can change the 3 to a 5 to change your default runlevel from the command line interface (3) to the graphical login (5). Change only this number and nothing else.

```
id:5:initdefault:
```

TIP *If your* `/etc/inittab` *file becomes corrupted, you can reboot and enter* `linux single` *at the boot prompt to start up your system, bypassing the* `inittab` *file. You can then edit the file to fix it.*

Changing runlevels with telinit

No matter what runlevel you start in, you can change from one runlevel to another with the `telinit` command. If your default runlevel is 3, you power up in runlevel 3, but you can change to, say, runlevel 5 with `telinit 5`. The command `telinit 0` shuts down your system. In the next example, the `telinit` command changes to runlevel 1, the administrative state:

```
# telinit 1
```

`telinit` is really a symbolic link (another name for a command) to the `init` command. The `init` command performs the actual startup operations and is automatically invoked when your system starts up. Though you could use `init` to change runlevels, it is best to use `telinit`. When invoked as `telinit`, `init` merely changes runlevels.

runlevel Command

Use the `runlevel` command to see what state you are currently running in. It lists the previous state followed by the current one. If you have not changed states, the previous state will be listed as N, indicating no previous state. This is the case for the state you boot up in. In the next example, the system is running in state 3, with no previous state change.

```
# runlevel
N 3
```

shutdown

Although you can power down the system with the telinit command and the 0 state, you can also use the shutdown command. The shutdown command has a time argument that gives users on the system a warning before you power down. You can specify an exact time to shut down, or a period of minutes from the current time. The exact time is specified by *hh:mm* for the hour and minutes. The period of time is indicated by a + and the number of minutes. The shutdown command takes several options with which you can specify how you want your system shut down. The -h option, which stands for halt, simply shuts down the system, whereas the -r option shuts down the system and then reboots it. In the next example, the system is shut down after ten minutes.

```
# shutdown -h +10
```

To shut down the system immediately, you can use +0 or the word now. The following example shuts down the system immediately, and then reboots.

```
# shutdown -r now
```

With the shutdown command, you can include a warning message to be sent to all users currently logged in, giving them time to finish what they are doing before you shut them down.

```
# shutdown -h +5 "System needs a rest"
```

If you do not specify either the -h or the -r options, the shutdown command shuts down the multiuser mode and shifts you to an administrative single-user mode. In effect, your system state changes from 3 (multiuser state) to 1 (administrative single-user state). Only the root user is active, allowing the root user to perform any necessary system administrative operations with which other users might interfere.

TIP   *You can also shut down your system from the Gnome or KDE desktops.*

The shutdown options are listed in Table 1-4.

Command	Description
`shutdown [-rkhncft]` `time [warning-message]`	Shuts the system down after the specified time period, issuing warnings to users; you can specify a warning message of your own after the time argument; if neither `-h` nor `-r` is specified to shut down the system, the system sets to the administrative mode, runlevel state 1.
Argument	
`Time`	Has two possible formats: it can be an absolute time in the format *hh*:*mm*, with *hh* as the hour (one or two digits) and *mm* as the minute (in two digits); it can also be in the format +*m*, with *m* as the number of minutes to wait; the word `now` is an alias for +0.
Option	
`-t sec`	Tells `init` to wait *sec* seconds between sending processes the warning and the kill signals, before changing to another runlevel.
`-k`	Doesn't actually shut down; only sends the warning messages to everybody.
`-r`	Reboots after shutdown, runlevel state 6.
`-h`	Halts after shutdown, runlevel state 0.
`-n`	Doesn't call `init` to do the shutdown; you do it yourself.
`-f`	Skips file system checking (fsck) on reboot.
`-c`	Cancels an already running shutdown; no time argument.

Table 1-4.   System Shutdown Options

Managing Services

As noted previously for the `crond` service, you can select certain services to run and the runlevel at which to run them. Most services are servers like a web server or proxy server. Other services provide security, such as SSH or Kerberos. You can decide which services to use with the `chkconfig`, `service`, or redhat-config-services tools. These are described here briefly, and in more detail in Chapter 10.

chkconfig

To configure a service to start up automatically, you can use the redhat-config-services tool available on the desktop or the `chkconfig` tool which is run on a command line. redhat-config-services will display a list of available services, letting you choose the ones you want to start and de-select. The `chkconfig` command uses the `on` and `off` options to select and de-select services for startup (see Chapter 10 for more details).

```
chkconfig httpd on
```

service Command

To start and stop services manually, you can user either redhat-config-services or the `service` command. With the `service` command, you list the service with the `stop` argument to stop it, the `start` argument to start it, and the `restart` argument to restart it.

```
service httpd start
```

redhat-config-services

Most administration tools provide interfaces displaying a simple list of services from which you can select the ones you want to start up. On the redhat-config-services tool, the main panel lists different daemons and servers that you can have start by just clicking a check box.

Red Hat Administration Tools

On Red Hat, most administration tasks can be handled by a set of separate, specialized administrative tools developed and supported by Red Hat, such as those for user management and display configuration. Many of these are GUI-based and will work on any X Window System environment, such as Gnome or KDE. To access the GUI-based Red Hat tools, you log in as the root user to the Gnome desktop and open the Start Here window or select the main menu. System administrative tools are listed in the System Settings folder, and on the System Settings menu listed in the main menu. Here you will find tools to set the time and date, manage users, configure printers, and update software. Users & Groups lets you create and edit users. Printing lets you install and reconfigure printers. All tools provide very intuitive GUI interfaces that are easy to use. In the System Settings folder and menu, tools are identified by simple descriptive terms, whereas their actual name normally begins with the term redhat-config. For example, the printer configuration tool is listed as Printing, but its actual name is redhat-config-printer. You can separately invoke any tool by entering its name in a terminal window. Table 1-5 provides a complete listing of Red Hat administration tools.

Red Hat Administration Tools	Description
System Settings	Red Hat window and menu for accessing administrative tools
redhat-config-users	User and Group configuration tool
redhat-config-printer	Printer configuration tool
redhat-config-xfree86	Red Hat display configuration tool (video card and monitor)
redhat-config-packages	Software management
redhat-config-rootpassword	Changes the root user password
redhat-config-keyboard	Changes the keyboard configuration
redhat-config-date	Changes system time and date

Table 1-5. Red Hat Configuration Tools

Red Hat Administration Tools	Description
redhat-config-mouse	Configures your mouse
redhat-config-language	Selects a language to use
redhat-config-soundcard	Configures your sound card

Table 1-5. Red Hat Configuration Tools *(continued)*

System Directories

Your Linux file system is organized into directories whose files are used for different system functions (see Table 1-6). For basic system administration, you should be familiar with the system program directories where applications

Directories	Description
/bin	System-related programs
/sbin	System programs for specialized tasks
/lib	System libraries
/etc	Configuration files for system and network services and applications
/home	The location of user home directories and server data directories, such as Web and FTP site files
/mnt	The location where CD-ROM and floppy disk files systems are mounted (Chapter 4)
/var	The location of system directories whose files continually change, such as logs, printer spool files, and lock files (Chapter 4)
/usr	User-related programs and files. Includes several key subdirectories, such as /usr/bin, /usr/X11, and /usr/doc
/usr/bin	Programs for users
/dev	Device files (Chapter 7)
/usr/X11	X Window System configuration files
/usr/share	Shared files
/usr/share/doc	Documentation for applications
/tmp	Directory for system temporary files

Table 1-6. System Directories

are kept, the system configuration directory (/etc) where
most configuration files are placed, and the system log
directory (/var/log) that holds the system logs, recording
activity on your system. Other system directories are
covered in their respective chapters, with many discussed
in Chapter 4.

Program Directories

Directories with "bin" in the name are used to hold
programs. The /bin directory holds basic user programs,
such as login, shells (bash, tcsh, and zsh), and file
commands (cp, mv, rm, ln, and so on). The /sbin directory
holds specialized system programs for such tasks as file
system management (fsck, fdisk, mkfs) and system
operations like shutdown and startup (init). The /usr/bin
directory holds program files designed for user tasks. The
/usr/sbin directory holds user-related system operations,
such as useradd to add new users. The /lib directory
holds all the libraries your system makes use of, including
the main Linux library, libc, and subdirectories such as
modules, which holds all the current kernel modules.

Configuration Directories and Files

When you configure different elements of your system,
like users, applications, servers, or network connections,
you make use of configuration files kept in certain system
directories. On Red Hat, configuration files are placed in
the /etc directory, with more specific device and service
configurations located in the /etc/sysconfig directory .

Configuration Files: /etc

The /etc directory holds your system, network, server,
and application configuration files. Here, you can find the
fstab file listing your file systems, the hosts file with IP
addresses for hosts on your system, and grub.conf for
the boot systems supported by the GRUB boot loader.
This directory includes various subdirectories, such as
/apache for the Apache web server configuration files

1

and /X11 for the X Window System and window manager
configuration files. You can configure many applications
and services by directly editing their configuration files,
though it is best to use a corresponding administration
tool, like those provided by Red Hat. Table 1-7 lists
several commonly used configuration files found in
the /etc directory.

File	Description
/etc/inittab	Sets the default state, as well as terminal connections
/etc/passwd	Contains user password and login configurations
/etc/shadow	Contains user-encrypted passwords
/etc/group	Contains a list of groups with configurations for each
/etc/fstab	Automatically mounts file systems when you start your system
/etc/grub.conf	The GRUB configuration file for the GRUB boot loader
/etc/modules.conf	Modules on your system to be automatically loaded
/etc/printcap	Contains a list of each printer and its specifications
/etc/termcap	Contains a list of terminal type specifications for terminals that could be connected to the system
/etc/skel	Directory that holds the versions of initialization files, such as .bash_profile, which are copied to new users' home directories
/etc/services	Services run on the system and the ports they use
/etc/profile	Default shell configuration file for users
/etc/shells	Shells installed on the system that users can use
/etc/motd	System administrator's message of the day

Table 1-7. Configuration Files

/etc/sysconfig

On Red Hat systems, configuration and startup information is also kept in the `/etc/sysconfig` directory. Here you will find files containing definitions of system variables used to configure devices such as your keyboard and mouse. These entries were defined for you when you configured your devices during installation. You will also find network definitions as well as scripts for starting and stopping your network connections.

A sample of the keyboard file `/etc/sysconfig/keyboard` is shown here:

```
KEYBOARDTYPE="pc"
KEYTABLE="us"
```

Several of these files are generated by Red Hat administration tools such as redhat-config-mouse, redhat-config-keyboard, or redhat-config-network. Table 1-8 lists several commonly used tools and the sysconfig files they control. For example, redhat-config-mouse generates configuration variables for the mouse device name, type, and certain features, placing them in the `/etc/sysconfig/mouse` file, as shown here:

```
FULLNAME="Generic - 3 Button Mouse (PS/2)"
MOUSETYPE="PS/2"
XMOUSETYPE="PS/2"
XEMU3="no"
DEVICE=/dev/mouse
```

Other files, like `hwconf`, list all your hardware devices, defining configuration variables such as its class (video, CD-ROM, hard drive), the bus it uses (PCI, IDE), its device name (such as `hdd` or `st0`), the drivers it uses, and a description of the device. A CD-ROM entry is shown here:

```
class: CDROM
bus: IDE
detached: 0
device: hdd
driver: ignore
desc: "TOSHIBA DVD-ROM SD-M1402"
```

Tools	Configuration files	Description
authconfig-gtk	`/etc/sysconfig/ authconfig` `/etd/sysconfig/ network`	Authentication options, such as enabling NIS, shadow passwords, Kerberos, and LDAP.
redhat-config-securitylevel	`/etc/sysconfig/ iptables`	Selects the level of firewall protection: High, Medium, and None.
redhat-config-keyboard	`/etc/sysconfig/ keyboard`	Selects the keyboard type.
redhat-config-mouse	`/etc/sysconfig/ mouse`	Selects the mouse type.
redhat-config-network	`/etc/sysconfig/ network` `/etc/sysconfig/ network-scripts/ ifcfg-ethN`	Sets your network settings.
redhat-config-date	`/etc/sysconfig/ clock`	Sets the time and date.
redhat-logviewer	`/etc/sysconfig/ redhat-logviewer`	Red Hat Log Viewer views and searches system logs.

Table 1-8. Sysconfig files with corresponding Red Hat System Administration Tools

Several directories are included, such as `network-scripts`, which list several startup scripts for network connections— such as `ifup-ppp`, which starts up PPP connections.

Some administration tools use more than one `sysconfig` file. redhat-config-network places its network configuration information like the hostname and gateway in the `/etc/sysconfig/network` file. Specific Ethernet device configurations, which would include your IP address and netmask, are placed in the appropriate Ethernet device configuration file in the `/etc/sysconfig/ network-scripts` directory. For example, the IP address and netmask used for the `eth0` Ethernet device can be found in `/etc/sysconfig/network-scripts/ifcfg-eth0`. Local host settings are in `/etc/sysconfig/ network-scripts/ifcfg-lo`.

TIP   *Some administration tools, like authconfig-gtk, will further configure configuration files for the services selected. The authconfig-gtk tool configures* /etc/ sysconfig/authconfig *as well as* /etc/krb5.conf *for Kerberos authentication,* /etc/yp.conf *for NIS support, and* /etc/openldap/ldap.conf *for LDAP authentication.*

System Logs: /var/log and syslogd

Various system logs for tasks performed on your system are stored in the /var/log directory. Here, you can find logs for mail, news, and all other system operations, such as web server logs. The /var/log/messages file is a log of all system tasks not covered by other logs. This usually includes startup tasks, such as loading drivers and mounting file systems. If a driver for a card failed to load at startup, you find an error message for it here. Logins are also logged in this file, showing you who attempted to log in to what account. The /var/log/maillog file logs mail message transmissions and news transfers.

redhat-logviewer

You can manage and view logs with the Red Hat Log Viewer, redhat-logviewer (System Tools | System Logs). The Red Hat Log Viewer displays a list of all current system logs in a left pane (see Figure 1-2). Clicking a log displays the contents of that log in the left pane. Use the Filter box to enter patterns you wish to look for, and click the Filter button to perform the match. Reset restores the complete listing. In the Preferences dialog, the Log Files panel lets you select a different location for a log file. The Alerts panel lets you create alert words. An alert icon is displayed next to any entry containing an alert word. Configuration settings, such as log file locations and alert words, are kept in the /etc/sysconfig/redhat-logviewer file.

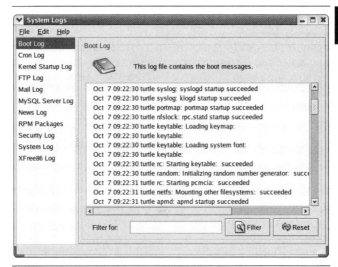

Figure 1-2. Red Hat Log Viewer

syslogd and syslog.conf

The `syslogd` daemon manages all the logs on your
system, as well as coordinating with any of the logging
operations of other systems on your network. Configuration
information for `syslogd` is held in the `/etc/syslog.conf`
file, which contains the names and locations for your system
log files. Here you find entries for `/var/log/messages`
and `/var/log/maillog`, among others. Whenever you
make changes to the syslog.conf file, you need to restart
the `syslogd` daemon using the following command (or
use redhat-config-services, Server Settings | Services):

```
service syslog restart
```

syslogd.conf Entries

An entry in syslog.conf consists of two fields: a *selector* and an *action*. The selector is the kind of service to be logged, such as mail or news, and the action is the location where messages are to be placed. The action is usually a log file, but it can also be a remote host or a pipe to another program. This kind of service is referred to as a *facility*. syslogd has several terms it uses to specify certain kinds of service (see Table 1-9). A facility can be further qualified by a priority. A *priority* specifies the kind of message generated by the facility. syslogd uses several designated terms to indicate different priorities. A *sector* is constructed from both the facility and priority, separated by a period. For example, to save error messages generated by mail systems, you use a sector consisting of the mail facility and the err priority, as shown here:

```
mail.err
```

To save these messages to the /var/log/maillog file, you specify that file as the action, giving you the following entry:

```
mail.err /var/log/maillog
```

syslogd also supports the use of * as a matching character to match either all the facilities or priorities in a sector. cron.* would match on all cron messages no matter what the priority, *.err would match on error messages from all the facilities, and *.* would match on all messages. The following example saves all mail messages to the /var/log/maillog file and all critical messages to the /var/log/mycritical file:

```
mail.* /var/log/maillog
*.crit /var/log/mycritical
```

Priorities

When you specify a priority for a facility, all messages with a higher priority are also included. So the err priority also includes the crit, alert, and emerg priorities. If you just want to select the message for a specific priority, you qualify the priority with the = operator. For example, mail.=err

Facilities	Description
auth-priv	Security/authorization messages (private)
cron	Clock daemon (**cron** and **at**) messages
daemon	Other system daemon messages
kern	Kernel messages
lpr	Line printer subsystem messages
mail	Mail subsystem messages
mark	Internal use only
news	Usenet news subsystem messages
syslog	Syslog internal messages
user	Generic user-level messages
uucp	UUCP subsystem messages
local0 through local7	Reserved for local use

Priorities	Description
debug	7, Debugging messages, lowest priority
info	6, Informational messages
notice	5, Notifications, normal, but significant, condition
warning	4, Warnings
err	3, Error messages
crit	2, Critical conditions
alert	1, Alerts, action must be taken immediately
emerg	0, Emergency messages, system is unusable , highest priority

Operators	Description
*	Matches all facilities or priorities in a sector
=	Restrict to a specified priority
!	Exclude specified priority and higher ones
/	A file to save messages to
@	A host to send messages to
|	FIFO pipe to send messages to

Table 1-9. Syslogd Facilities, Priorities, and Operators

will select only error messages, not `crit`, `alert`, and
`emerg` messages. You can also restrict priorities with
the `!` operator. This will eliminate messages with the
specified priority and higher. For example, `mail.!crit`
will exclude `crit` messages, and the higher `alert` and
`emerg` messages. To specifically exclude all the messages
for an entire facility, you use the `none` priority. `mail.none`
excludes all mail messages. This is usually used when
you're defining several sectors in the same entry.

You can list several priorities or facilities in a given
sector by separating them with commas. You can also
have several sectors in the same entry by separating
them with semicolons. The first example saves to the
`/var/log/messages` file all messages with `info` priority,
excluding all mail, and authentication messages (`authpriv`).
The second saves all `crit` messages and higher for the
`uucp` and `news` facilities to the `/var/log/spooler` file:

```
*.info;mail.none;authpriv.none /var/log/messages
uucp,news.crit /var/log/spooler
```

actions and users

In the action field, you can specify files, remote systems,
users, or pipes. An action entry for a file must always
begin with a `/` and specify its full path name, such as
`/var/log/messages`. To log messages to a remote host,
you simply specify the hostname preceded by an `@` sign.
The following example saves all kernel messages on
rabbit.trek.com:

```
kern.* @rabbit.trek.com
```

To send messages to users, you list their login names.
The following example will send critical news messages
to the consoles for the users `chris` and `aleina`:

```
news.=crit chris,aleina
```

You can also output messages to a named pipe (FIFO).
The pipe entry for the action field begins with a `|`. The
following example pipes kernel debug messages to
the named pipe `|/usr/adm/debug`:

```
kern.=debug |/usr/adm/debug
```

/etc/syslog.conf Example

1

The default `/etc/syslog.conf` file for Red Hat systems is shown here. Messages are logged to various files in the `/var/log` directory.

```
# Log all kernel messages to the console.
#kern.*                                 /dev/console
# Log anything (except mail) info or higher.
*.info;mail.none;news.none /var/log/messages
# Don't log private authentication messages!
*.info;authpriv.none;cron.none /var/log/messages

# The authpriv file has restricted access.
authpriv.*                      /var/log/secure
# Log all the mail messages in one place.
mail.*                          /var/log/maillog
# Log cron stuff.
cron.*                          /var/log/cron
# Everybody gets emergency messages
*.emerg                                 *
# Save mail and news errors of level err
# and higher in a special file.
uucp,news.crit                  /var/log/spooler
# Save boot messages also to boot.log
local7.*            /var/log/boot.log
# INN
news.=crit          /var/log/news/news.crit
news.=err           /var/log/news/news.err
news.notice         /var/log/news/news.notice
```

Performance Analysis Tools and Processes

Linux treats each task performed on your system as a process, and assigns a number and a name. You can examine these processes and even stop them. Red Hat provides several tools for examining processes as well as your system performance. Easy monitoring is provided by several GUI tools, like Red Hat's Procman System Monitor.

ps Command

From the command line, you can use the `ps` command to list processes. With the `-aux` option, you can list all processes. Piping the output to a `grep` command with a pattern enables you to search for a particular process. A pipe funnels the output of a preceding command as input to a following command. The following command lists all X Window System processes:

```
ps -aux | grep 'X'
```

A number of utilities on your system provide detailed information on your processes, as well as other system information such as CPU and disk use (see Table 1-10). Although these tools were designed to be used on a shell command line, displaying output in text lines, several now have KDE and Gnome versions that provide a GUI interface for displaying results and managing processes.

vmstat, free, top, iostat, Xload, and sar

The `vmstat` command outputs a detailed listing indicating the performance of different system

Performance Tool	Description
vmstat	Performance of system components
top	Listing of most CPU intensive processes
free	Listing of free RAM memory
sar	System activity information
iostat	Disk usage
Procman System Monitor	Red Hat system monitor for processes and usage monitoring (System Monitor on System Tools menu)
KDE Task Manager and Performance Monitor	KDE system monitor for processes and usage monitoring

Table 1-10. Performance Tools

components, including CPU, memory, I/O, and swap operations. A report is issued as a line with fields for the different components. If you provide a time period as an argument, it repeats at the specified interval—usually a few seconds. The `top` command provides a listing of the processes on your system that are the most CPU intensive, showing what processes are using most of your resources. The listing is in real time and updated every few seconds. Commands are provided for changing a process's status, such as its priority.

The `free` command lists the amount of free RAM memory on your system, showing how much is used and how much is free, as well as what is used for buffers and swap memory. `Xload` is an X Window System tool showing the load, CPU, and memory. `iostat` displays your disk usage, and `sar` shows system activity information.

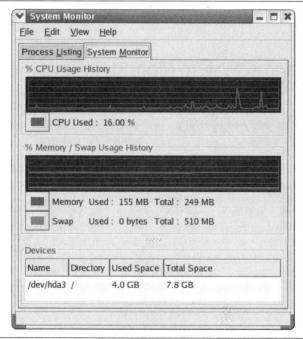

Figure 1-3. Procman System Manager

Procman System Manager

The current version of Red Hat provides the Procman
System Manager for displaying system information and
managing system processes, accessible from System
Tools | System Monitor. There are two panels, one for
processes and one for system information. The System
Monitor panel displays graphs for CPU, Memory, and
Swap memory usage (see Figure 1-3). Your disk devices
are also listed, showing the amount of disk space used
and how much is free. The Process Listing panel lists your
processes, letting you sort or search for processes. You can
use field buttons to sort by name, process id, user, memory,
and even percentage of CPU time used. The View pop-up
menu lets you select all processes, just your own, or active
processes. You can easily stop any process by selecting it
and then clicking the End Process button. Right-clicking
an item displays actions you can take on the process such
as stopping or hiding it. The Memory Maps display, selected
from the View menu, shows information on virtual memory,
inodes, and flags.

Gnome System Manager (GTop)

With the Gnome System Manager (GTop), you can sort the
processes according to their fields by clicking the field's
button at the top of the process list. If you right-click an
entry, a pop-up menu displays actions you can perform on
that entry. System statistic summary graphs are displayed
at the top of the window, showing the CPU load, memory
use, and disk use. You can add more graphs or change
their display features, such as the colors used. The GTop
window displays three tabbed panels for detailed reports
showing processes, memory use, and file system use. You
can add more, showing customized reports such as only
the user processes. Process lists can be further refined to
show user, system, or all processes. To configure GTop,
select the Settings | Preferences to display a menu with
tabbed panels for specifying the update frequency for
different statistics, determining the summaries you want
displayed, and which process fields to show. You can find
the Gnome System Manager in the Utilities menu.

KDE Process Manager (kpm)

The K Desktop provides the KDE Process Manager (kpm) for viewing and managing your processes. You can sort the processes according to their fields by clicking the field's button at the top of the process list. If you select a process, you can then choose to perform several different actions on it, such as ending it (killing the process) or suspending it (putting it to sleep). A right-click on a process entry displays a pop-up menu with the different actions you can take. You can further refine your process list by choosing to view only your own processes, system processes, or all processes.

KDE Task Manager and Performance Monitor (KSysguard)

Red Hat also provides the KDE Task Manager and Performance Monitor, KSysguard, accessible from the Extras System Tools menu as KDE System Guard. This tools allows you to monitor the performance of your own system as well as remote systems. KSysguard can provide simple values or detailed tables for various parameters. A System Load panel provides graphical information about CPU and memory usage, and a Process Table lists current processes using a tree format to show dependencies. You can design your own monitoring panels with worksheets, showing different types of values you want to display and the form you want to display them in, like a bar graph or digital meter. The Sensor Browser pane is an expandable tree of sensors for information like CPU System Load or Memory's Used Memory. There is a top entry for each host you are connected to, including your own, localhost. To design your own monitor, create a worksheet and drag and drop a sensor onto it.

Chapter 2

Managing Users

As a system administrator, you must manage the users of your system. You can add or remove users, as well as add and remove groups, and you can modify access rights and permissions for both users and groups. You also have access to system initialization files you can use to configure all user shells. And you have control over the default initialization files copied into a user account when it is first created. You can decide how new user accounts should be configured initially by configuring these files.

SECURITY SCAN *Every file is owned by a user who can control access to it. System files are owned by the root user and accessible by the root only. Services like FTP are an exception to this rule. Though accessible by the root, a service's files are owned by their own special user. For example, FTP files are owned by an* ftp *user. This provides users with access to a service's files without also having root user access.*

User Configuration Files

Any utility to manage a user, such as the Red Hat User Manager, makes use of certain default files, called *configuration files*, and directories to set up the new account. A set of pathnames is used to locate these default files or to indicate where to create certain user directories. For example, /etc/skel holds initialization files for a new user. A new user's home directory is created in the /home directory. Table 2-1 has a list of the pathnames.

Directory and Files	Description
/home	Location of the user's own home directory.
/etc/skel	Holds the default initialization files for the login shell, such as .bash_profile, .bashrc, and .bash_logout. Includes many user setup directories and files such as .kde for KDE and Desktop for Gnome.
/etc/shells	Holds the login shells, such as bash or tcsh.
/etc/passwd	Holds the password for a user.
/etc/group	Holds the group to which the user belongs.
/etc/shadow	Encrypted password file.
/etc/gshadow	Encrypted password file for groups.
/etc/login.defs	Default login definitions for users.

Table 2-1. Paths for User Configuration Files

TIP *You can find out which users are currently logged in with the* w *or* who *commands. The* w *command displays detailed information about each connected user, such as from where they logged in and how long they have been inactive, and the date and time of login. The* who *command provides less detailed data.*

The Password Files

A user gains access to an account by providing a correct login and password. The system maintains passwords in password files, along with login information like the user name and id. Tools like the passwd command let users change their passwords by modifying these files. /etc/passwd is the file that traditionally held user passwords, though in encrypted form. However, all users are allowed to read the /etc/passwd file, which would have allowed access by users to the encrypted passwords. For better security, password entries are kept in the /etc/shadow file, which is restricted to the root user.

/etc/passwd

When you add a user, an entry for that user is made in the `/etc/passwd` file, commonly known as the *password file*. Each entry takes up one line that has several fields separated by colons. The fields are as follows:

- **Username**   Login name of the user

- **Password**   Encrypted password for the user's account

- **User ID**   Unique number assigned by the system

- **Group ID**   Number used to identify the group to which the user belongs

- **Comment**   Any user information, such as the user's full name

- **Home directory**   The user's home directory

- **Login shell**   Shell to run when the user logs in; this is the default shell, usually `/bin/bash`

Depending on whether or not you are using shadow passwords, the password field (the second field) will be either an `x` or an encrypted form of the user's password. Red Hat implements shadow passwords by default, so these entries should have an `x` for their passwords. The following is an example of an `/etc/passwd` entry. For such entries, you must use the `passwd` command to create a password. Notice also that user IDs in this particular system start at 500 and increment by one.

```
dylan:x:500:500:User:/home/dylan:/bin/bash
chris:x:501:501:User:/home/chris:/bin/bash
```

 **SECURITY SCAN** *If you turn off shadow password support, entries in your passwd file will display encrypted passwords. Because any user can read the /etc/passwd file, intruders can access and possibly crack the encrypted passwords.*

 **SECURITY SCAN** *Although it is technically possible to edit entries in the* /etc/passwd *file directly, it is not recommended. In particular, deleting an entry does not remove any other information, permissions, and data associated with a user, which opens a possible security breach whereby an intruder could take over the deleted user's id or disk space.*

/etc/shadow and /etc/gshadow

The /etc/passwd file is a simple text file, and is vulnerable to security breaches. If anyone gains access to the /etc/ password file, they might be able to decipher or crack the encrypted passwords through brute force crack. The shadow suite of applications implements a greater level of security. These include versions of useradd, groupadd, and their corresponding update and delete programs. Most other user configuration tools, including redhat-config-users, support shadow security measures. With shadow security, passwords are no longer kept in the /etc/password file. Instead, passwords are kept in a separate file called /etc/shadow. Access is restricted to the root user.

The following example shows the /etc/shadow entries for two users, listing their encrypted passwords. The entry for chris has an * in its Password field, indicating that a password has not yet been created for this user.

```
dylan:YOTPdPyyc:500:500:User:/home/dylan:/bin/bash
chris:*:501:501:User:/home/chris:/bin/bash
```

A corresponding password file, called /etc/gshadow, is also maintained for groups that require passwords. Red Hat supports shadow passwords by default. You can manually specify whether you want to use shadow passwords with the Red Hat authentication tool.

Password Tools

To change any particular field for a given user, you should use the user management tools provided, such as the passwd command, redhat-config-users, adduser, usermod, useradd, and chage, discussed in this chapter. The passwd command lets you change the password only. Other tools, like redhat-config-users, not only make entries in the /etc/passwd file, but also create the home directory for the user and install initialization files in the user's home directory.

These tools also let you control a user's access to their accounts. You can set expiration dates for users or lock them out of their accounts. Users locked out of their accounts will have their password in the /etc/shadow file prefixed by the invalid string, !!. Unlocking the account removes this prefix.

SECURITY SCAN *With the Red Hat Authentication tool (authconfig-gtk) you can enable and configure various authentication tools such as NIS and LDAP servers, as well as enabling shadow passwords, LDAP, and Kerberos authentication (accessible as Authentication on the System Settings menu and windows).*

Managing User Environments

Each time a user logs in, two profile scripts are executed, a system profile script that is the same for every user, and a user login profile script that can be customized to each user's needs. When the user logs out, a user logout script is run. In addition, each time a shell is generated, including the login shell, a user shell script is run. There are different kinds of scripts used for different shells. On Red Hat, the default shell commonly used is the bash shell. As an alternative, users could use different shells such as tcsh or the Z shell, both installed with Red Hat Linux.

Profile Scripts

For the bash shell, each user has their own bash login profile script named .bash_profile in their home directory. The system profile script is located in the /etc

directory and named `profile` with no preceding period.
The bash shell user shell script is called `.bashrc`. The
`.bashrc` file also runs the `/etc/bashrc` file to implement
any global definitions such as the `PS1` and `TERM` variables.
The `/etc/bashrc` file also executes any specialized
initialization file in the `/etc/profile.d` directory, such
as those used for KDE and Gnome. The `.bash_profile`
file runs the `.bashrc` file, and through it, the `/etc/bashrc`
file, implementing global definitions.

As a superuser, you can edit any of these profile or shell
scripts and put in any commands you want executed for
each user when they log in. For example, you may want to
define a default path for commands, in case the user has
not done so. Or, you may want to notify the user of recent
system news or account changes.

/etc/skel

When you first add a user to the system, you must provide
the user with a skeleton version of their login, shell, and
logout initialization files. For the bash shell, this would be
the `.bash_profile`, `.bashrc`, and `.bash_logout` files.
The `useradd` command and other user management tools
like Red Hat User Manager add these files automatically,
copying any files in the directory `/etc/skel` to the user's
new home directory. The `/etc/skel` directory contains a
skeleton initialization file for the `.bash_profile`, `.bashrc`,
and `.bash_logout` files or, if you are using the tcsh
shell as your login shell, the `.login`, `.tcshrc`, and
`.logout` files. The `/etc/skel` directory also contains
default files and directories for your desktops. These
include a `.screenrc` file for the X Window System,
a `.kde` directory for the KDE desktop, and a `Desktop`
directory that contains default configuration files for the
Gnome desktop.

As a superuser, you can configure the `.bash_profile`
or `.bashrc` file in the `/etc/skel` directory any way
you want. Usually, basic system variable assignments
are included that define pathnames for commands and
command aliases. The `PATH` and `BASH_ENV` variables are
defined in `.bash_profile`. Once users have their own

`.bash_profile` or `.bashrc` file, they can redefine variables or add new commands as they choose.

/etc/login.defs

Systemwide values used by user and group creation utilities such as `useradd` and `usergroup` are kept in the `/etc/login.defs` file. Here you will find the range of possible user and group IDs listed. `UID_MIN` holds the minimum number for user IDs, and `UID_MAX` the maximum number. Various password options control password controls—such as `PASS_MIN_LEN`, which determines the minimum number of characters allowable in a password. Options such as `CREATE_HOME` can be set to tell user tools like `useradd` to create home directories for new accounts by default. Samples of these entries are shown here.

```
MAIL_DIR /var/spool/mail
PASS_MIN_LEN          5
CREATE_HOME yes
```

/etc/login.access

You can control user login access by remote users to your system with the `/etc/login.access` file. The file consists of entries listing users, whether they are allowed access, and from where they can access the system. A record in this file consists of three colon-delimited fields: a plus (+) or minus (–) sign indicating whether users are allowed access, user login names allowed access, and the remote system (host) or terminal (tty device) from which they are trying to log in. The following enables the user `chris` to access the system from the rabbit.mytrek.com remote system:

```
+:chris:rabbit.mytrek.com
```

You can list more than one user or location, or use the `ALL` option in place of either users or locations to allow access by all users and locations. The `ALL` option can be qualified with the `EXCEPT` option to allow access by all users except certain specified ones. The following entry allows any valid user to log in to the system using the console, except for the users `larisa` and `aleina`:

```
+:ALL EXCEPT larisa aleina:console
```

Other access control files are used to control access for specific services, such as the `hosts.deny` and `hosts.allows` files used with the `tcpd` daemon for xinetd-supported servers.

Controlling User Passwords

Once you have created a user account, you can control the user's access to it. Both the Red Hat User Manager and the `passwd` tool let you lock and unlock a user's account. You use the `passwd` command with the `-1` option to lock an account, invalidating its password, and you use the `-u` option to unlock it.

You can also force a user to change his or her password at given intervals by setting an expiration date for that password. Both the Red Hat User Manger and the `chage` command let you specify an expiration limit for a user's password. A user could be required to change his or her password every month, every week, or at a given date. Once the password expires, the user will be prompted to enter a new one. You can issue a warning beforehand, telling the user how much time is left before the password expires. For accounts that you want to close, you can permanently expire a password. You can even shut down accounts that are inactive too long. In the next example, the password for the `chris` account will stay valid for only 7 days. The `-M` option with the number of days sets the maximum time that a password can be valid.

```
chage -M 7  chris
```

To set a particular date for the account to expire, use the `-E` option with the date specified mm/dd/yyyy.

```
chage -E 07/30-/2003  chris
```

To find out what the current expiration settings are for a given account, use the `-1` option.

```
chage -1 chris
```

Option	Description
-m	Minimum number of days a user must go before being able to change his password
-M	Maximum number of days a user can go without changing his password
-d	The last day the password was changed
-E	Specific expiration date for a password, date in format in yyyy-mm-dd or in commonly used format like mm/dd/yyyy
-I	Allowable account inactivity period (in days), after which password will expire
-W	Warning period, number of days before expiration when the user will be sent a warning message
-l	Display current password expiration controls

Table 2-2. Options for the chage Command

You can also combine your options into one command,

```
chage -M 7 -E 07/30-/2003  chris
```

A listing of the `chage` options is in Table 2-2:

Red Hat User Manager

For Red Hat distributions, you should use the Red Hat User Manager (redhat-config-users) to manage user accounts (see Figure 2-1). You can access the Red Hat User Manager from the System Settings window and menu. It is labeled simply as Users & Groups. You can also access it from the Gnome System menu.

The Red Hat User Manager window displays panels for listing both users and groups. You use the User Manager to manage your groups, as well as users. Click the appropriate tab to display either users or groups. Within the user and group panels, field labels are displayed at the top for usernames, group, the user's full name, login shell, or home directories. A button bar lists various tasks you can perform, including creating new users or groups, editing current ones (Properties), or deleting a selected

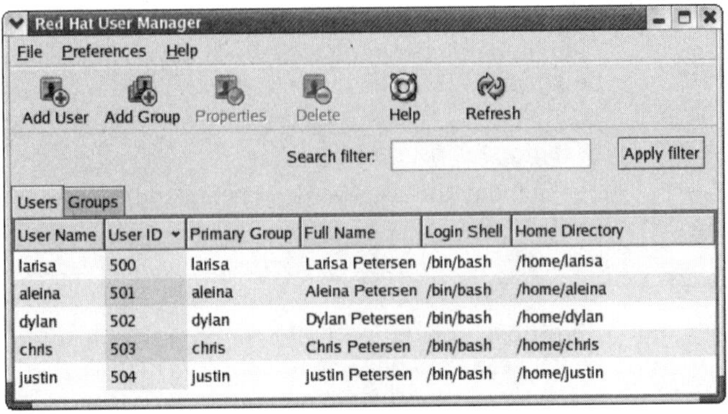

Figure 2-1. Red Hat User Manager

user or group. The number of users and groups on a system can be extensive, so the User Manager provides an easy-to-use search tool. You can enter a search string in the box labeled "Filter By." When you click the Apply Filter button, only those matching users or groups are listed. From the Preferences menu, you can elect to filter out users and groups set up by your system for administration purposes, leaving just your normal users and groups.

To create a new user, click the Add User button. This opens a window with entries for the username, password, and login shell, along with options to create a home directory and a new group for that user. Once you have created a user, you can edit its properties to add or change features. Select the user's entry and click the Properties button. This displays a window with tabbed panels for User Data, Account Info, Password Info, and Groups. You can change basic features such as the password and login shell in the User Data panel. Account Info lets you lock an account and set an expiration date for it. Password Info lets you set password expiration limits to force a user to change his or her password or to render the account inactive after a certain time. On the Groups panel, you can select the groups that the user belongs to, adding or removing group membership.

Adding and Removing Users with useradd, usermod, and userdel

2

Linux also provides the `useradd`, `usermod`, and `userdel` commands to manage user accounts. All these commands take in all their information as options on the command line. If an option is not specified, they use predetermined default values.

useradd

With the `useradd` command, you enter values as options on the command line, such as the name of a user, to create a user account. It then creates a new login and directory for that name using all the default features for a new account.

```
# useradd chris
```

The useradd utility first checks the `/etc/login.defs` file for default values for creating a new account. For those defaults not defined in the `/etc/login.defs` file, useradd supplies its own. You can display these defaults using the `useradd` command with the `-D` option. The default values include the group name, the user ID, the home directory, the `skel` directory, and the login shell. Values the user enters on the command line will override corresponding defaults. The group name is the name of the group in which the new account is placed. By default, this is `other`, which means the new account belongs to no group. The user ID is a number identifying the user account. The `skel` directory is the system directory that holds copies of initialization files. These initialization files are copied into the user's new home directory when it is created. The login shell is the pathname for the particular shell the user plans to use.

The `useradd` command has options that correspond to each default value. Table 2-3 holds a list of all the options

Options	Description
-d *dir*	Sets the home directory of the new user.
-D	Displays defaults for all settings. Can also be used to reset default settings for the home directory (-b), group (-g), shell (-s), expiration date (-e), and password expirations (-f).
-e *mm/dd/yy*	Sets an expiration date for the account (none, by default). Specified as month/day/year.
-f *days*	Sets the number of days an account remains active after its password expires.
-g *group*	Sets a group.
-m	Creates user's home directory, if it does not exist.
-m -k *skl-dir*	Sets the skeleton directory that holds skeleton files, such as .profile files, which are copied to the user's home directory automatically when it is created; the default is /etc/skel.
-M	Does not create user's home directory.
-p *password*	Supplies an encrypted password (crypt or MD5). With no argument, the account is immediately disabled.
-r	A Red Hat-specific option that creates a system account (one whose user ID is lower than the minimum set in logon.defs). No home directory is created unless specified by -m.
-s *shell*	Sets the login shell of the new user. This is /bin/bash by default, the bash shell.
-u *userid*	Sets the user ID of the new user. The default is the increment of the highest number used so far.

Table 2-3. Options for useradd and usermod

you can use with the useradd command. You can use specific values in place of any of these defaults when creating a particular account. The login is inaccessible until you do. In the next example, the group name for the `chris` account is set to `intro1` and the user ID is set to 578:

```
# useradd chris -g intro1 -u 578
```

Once you add a new user login, you need to give the new login a password. Password entries are placed in the `/etc/passwd` and `/etc/shadow` files. Use the `passwd` command to create a new password for the user, as shown here. The password you enter will not appear on your screen. You will be prompted to repeat the password. A message will then be issued indicating that the password was successfully changed.

```
# passwd chris
Changing password for user chris
New UNIX password:
Retype new UNIX password:
passwd: all authentication tokens updated successfully
#
```

usermod

The `usermod` command enables you to change the values for any of these features. You can change the home directory or the user ID. You can even change the username for the account. The `usermod` command takes the same options as `useradd`, listed in Table 2-1.

userdel

When you want to remove a user from the system, you can use the `userdel` command to delete the user's login. With the -r option, the user's home directory will also be removed. In the next example, the user `chris` is removed from the system:

```
# userdel -r chris
```

Managing Groups

You can manage groups using either shell commands or window utilities like the Red Hat User Manager.

/etc/group and /etc/gshadow

The system file that holds group entries is called /etc/group. The file consists of group records, with one record per line and its fields separated by colons. A group record has four fields: a group name, a password, its ID, and the users who are part of this group. The Password field can be left blank. The fields for a group record are as follows:

- **Group name**   The name of the group, which must be unique

- **Password**   With shadow security implemented, this field is an x, with the password indicated in the /etc/gshadow file.

- **Group ID**   The number assigned by the system to identify this group

- **Users**   The list of users that belong to the group, separated by commas

Here is an example of an entry in an /etc/group file. The group is called engines, the password is managed by shadow security, the group ID is 100, and the users who are part of this group are chris, robert, valerie, and aleina.

```
engines:x:100:chris,robert,valerie,aleina
```

As in the case of the /etc/passwd file, it is best to change group entries using a group management utility like groupmod, groupadd, or the Red Hat User Manager. All users have read access to the /etc/group file. With shadow security, secure group data like passwords are kept in the /etc/gshadow file, to which only the root user has access.

User Private Groups

A new user can be assigned to a special group set up for just that user and given the user's name. So the new user `dylan` is given a default group also called `dylan`. The group `dylan` will also show up in the listing of groups. This method of assigning default user groups is called the User Private Group (UPG) scheme. UPG is currently used on Red Hat systems. The supplementary groups are additional groups that the user may want to belong to. Traditionally, users were all assigned to one group named `users` that would subject all users to the group permission controls for the `users` group. With UPG, each user has its own group, with its own group permissions.

group directories

As with users, you can create a home directory for a group. To do so, you simply create a directory for the group in the `/home` directory and change its group to that of the group, along with allowing access by any member of the group. The following example creates a directory called `engines` and changes its group to that of the `engines` group:

```
mkdir /home/engines
chgrp engines /home/engines
```

Then the read, write, and execute permissions for the group level should be set with the chmod command, discussed later in this chapter:

```
chmod g+rwx /home/engines
```

Any member of the `engines` group can now access the `/home/engines` directory and any shared files placed therein. This directory becomes a shared directory for the group. You can, in fact, use the same procedure to make other shared directories at any location on the file system.

Files within the shared directory should also have their permissions set to allow access by other users in the group. When a user places a file in a shared directory, the user needs to set the permissions on that file to allow other members of the group to access it. A read permission will let others display it, write lets them change it, and execute lets them run it (used for scripts and programs). The following example first changes the group for the mymodel file to engines. Then it copies the mymodel file to the /home/engines directory and sets the group read and write permission for the engines group.

```
$ chgrp engines mymodel
$ cp mymodel /home/engines
$ chmod g+rw /home/engines/mymodel
```

Managing Groups with the Red Hat User Manager

You can add, remove, and modify any group easily with the Red Hat User Manager. First, access the Red Hat User Manager by clicking the User & Groups icon in the System Settings window, listed in the Start Here window. Then, click the tabbed panel labeled Groups in the Red Hat User Manager window. This will list all your current groups. There will be three fields for each entry: Group Name, Group ID, and Group Members.

To add a group, just click the Add Group button. This opens a small window where you can enter the group name. The new group will be listed in the User Manager's Groups listing. To add users as members of the group, select the group's entry and click the Properties button. This opens a window with tabbed panels for Group Data and Group Users. The Group Users panel lists all current users with check boxes. Click the check boxes for the users you want to be members of this group. If you want to remove a user as member, click the check box to remove its check. Click OK to effect your changes. If you want to remove a group, just select its entry in the User Manager's Groups panel and then click the Delete button.

Managing Groups Using groupadd, groupmod, and groupdel

You can also manage groups with the groupadd, groupmod, and groupdel commands.

groupadd and groupdel

With the groupadd command, you can create new groups. When you add a group to the system, the system places the group's name in the /etc/group file and gives it a group ID number. If shadow security is in place, changes are made to the /etc/gshadow file. The groupadd command only creates the group category. You need to add users to the group individually. In the following example, the groupadd command creates the engines group:

```
# groupadd engines
```

You can delete a group with the groupdel command. In the next example, the engines group is deleted:

```
# groupdel engines
```

groupmod

You can change the name of a group or its ID using the groupmod command. Enter groupmod -g with the new ID number and the group name. To change the name of a group, you use the -n option. Enter groupmod -n with the new name of the group, followed by the current name. In the next example, the engines group has its name changed to trains:

```
# groupmod -n trains engines
```

Controlling Access to Directories and Files: chmod

Each file and directory in Linux contains a set of permissions that determine who can access them and how. You set these permissions to limit access in one of three ways: You can restrict access to yourself alone, you can allow users in a pre-designated group to have access, or you can permit anyone on your system to have access. You can also control how a given file or directory is accessed.

Permissions

A file and directory may have read, write, and execute permissions. When a file is created, it is automatically given read and write permissions for the owner, enabling you to display and modify the file. You may change these permissions to any combination you want. A file could also have read-only permission, preventing any modifications.

Permission categories

Three different categories of users can have access to a file or directory: the owner, the group, and all others not belonging to that group. The owner is the user who created the file. Any file you create, you own. You can also permit a group to have access to a file. Often, users are collected into groups. For example, all the users for a given class or project could be formed into a group by the system administrator. A user can grant access to a file to the members of a designated group. Finally, you can also open up access to a file to all other users on the system. In this case, every user not part of the file's group could have access to that file. In this sense, every other user on the system makes up the "others" category. If you want to give the same access to all users on your system, you set the same permissions for both the group and the others. That way you include both members of the group (group permission) and all those users who are not members (others permission).

read, write, execute permissions

Each category has its own set of read, write, and execute permissions. The first set controls the user's own access to his or her files—the owner access. The second set controls the access of the group to a user's files. The third set controls the access of all other users to the user's files. The three sets of read, write, and execute permissions for the three categories—owner, group, and other—make a total of nine types of permissions.

The `ls` command with the `-l` option displays detailed information about the file, including the permissions. In the following example, the first set of characters on the left is a list of the permissions set for the `mydata` file:

```
$ ls -l mydata
-rw-r--r-- 1 chris weather 207 Feb 20 11:55 mydata
```

An empty permission is represented by a dash, `-`. The read permission is represented by `r`, write by `w`, and execute by `x`. Notice there are ten positions. The first character indicates the file type. In a general sense, a directory can be considered a type of file. If the first character is a dash, a file is being listed. If the first character is `d`, information about a directory is being displayed.

The next nine characters are arranged according to the different user categories. The first set of three characters is the owner's set of permissions for the file. The second set of three characters is the group's set of permissions for the file. The last set of three characters is the other users' set of permissions for the file.

Permissions on Gnome

On Gnome, you can set a directory or file permission using the Permissions panel in its Properties window. Right-click the file or directory entry in the file manager window and select Properties. Then, select the Permissions panel. Here you will find a table of boxes with columns for Read, Write, and Execute along with rows for Owner, Group, and Other. Check the appropriate box for the permission you want. Normally, the Read and Write boxes for owner permission will already be set. You can specify the group you want access provided to from the Group drop-down menu. This displays the groups a user belongs to.

chmod

You use the chmod command to change different permission configurations. chmod takes two lists as its arguments: permission changes and filenames. You can specify the list of permissions in two different ways. One way uses permission symbols and is referred to as the *symbolic method*. The other uses what is known as a "binary mask" and is referred to as either the *absolute* or the *relative method*. Table 2-4 lists options for the chmod command.

NOTE *When a program is owned by the root, setting the user ID permission will give the user the ability to execute the program with root permissions. This can be a serious security risk for any program that could effect changes—such as rm, which removes files.*

Command or Option	Execution
chmod	Changes the permission of a file or directory.
Options	
+	Adds a permission.
–	Removes a permission.
=	Assigns entire set of permissions.
r	Sets read permission for a file or directory. A file can be displayed or printed. A directory can have the list of its files displayed.
w	Sets write permission for a file or directory. A file can be edited or erased. A directory can be removed.
x	Sets execute permission for a file or directory. If the file is a shell script, it can be executed as a program. (A directory can be changed and entered.)
u	Sets permissions for the user who created and owns the file or directory.
g	Sets permissions for group access to a file or directory.

Table 2-4. File and Directory Permission Operations

Command or Option	Execution
o	Sets permissions for access to a file or directory by all other users on the system.
a	Sets permissions for access by the owner, group, and all other users.
s	Sets User ID and Group ID permission; program owned by owner and group.
t	Sets sticky bit permission; program remains in memory.
chgrp *groupname filenames*	Changes the group for a file or files.
chown *user-name filenames*	Changes the owner of a file or files.
ls -l *filename*	Lists a filename with its permissions displayed.
ls -ld *directory*	Lists a directory name with its permissions displayed.
ls -l	Lists all files in a directory with its permissions displayed.

Table 2-4. File and Directory Permission Operations *(continued)*

Ownership

Files and directories belong to both an owner and a group. A group usually consists of a collection of users, all belonging to the same group. In the following example, the `mydata` file is owned by the user `robert` and belongs to the group `weather`.

```
-rw-r--r-- 1 robert weather 207 Feb 20 11:55 mydat
```

A group can also consist of one user, however, normally it's the user who creates the file. Each user on the system, including the root user, is assigned their own group, of which they are the only member, ensuring access only by that user. In the next example, the report file is owned by the `robert` user and belongs to that user's single user group, `robert`.

```
-rw-r--r-- 1 robert robert 305 Mar 17 12:01 report
```

The root user, the system administrator, owns most of the system files that also belong to the root group, of which only the root user is a member. Most administration files, like configuration files in the /etc directory, are owned by the root user and belong to the root group. Only the root user has permission to modify them, whereas normal users can read, and, in the case of programs, also execute them. In the next example, root user owns the fstab file in /etc directory, which also belongs to the root user group.

```
-rw-r--r-- 1 root root 621 Apr 22 11:03 fstab
```

Certain directories and files located in the system directories are owned by a service, rather than the root user, because the services need to change those files directly. This is particularly true for services that interact with remote users, such as Internet servers. Most of these files are located in the /var directory. Here you will find files and directories managed by services like the Squid proxy server and the Domain Name Server (named). In this example, the Squid proxy server directory is owned by the squid user and belongs to the squid group.

```
drwxr-x--- 2 squid squid 4096 Jan 24 16:29 squid
```

Changing a File's Owner or Group: chown and chgrp

Although other users may be able to access a file, only the owner can change its permissions. If, however, you want to give some other user control over one of your file's permissions, you can change the owner of the file from yourself to the other user. The chown command transfers control over a file to another user. This command takes as its first argument the name of the other user. Following the username, you list the files you are transferring. In the next example, the user gives control of the mydata file to user robert:

```
$ chown robert mydata
$ ls -l mydata
-rw-r--r-- 1 robert weather 207 Feb 20 11:55 mydata
```

You can also, if you wish, change the group for a file, using the `chgrp` command. `chgrp` takes as its first argument the name of the new group for a file or files. Following the new group name, you list the files you want changed to that group. In the next example, the user changes the group name for `today` and `weekend` to the `forecast` group. The `ls -l` command then reflects the group change.

```
$ chgrp forecast today weekend
$ ls -l
-rw-rw-r-- 1 chris forecast 568 Feb 14 10:30 today
-rw-rw-r-- 1 chris forecast 308 Feb 17 12:40 weekend
```

You can combine the `chgrp` operation in the `chown` command by attaching a group to the new owner with a colon.

```
$ chown george:forecast tomorrow
-rw-rw-r-- 1 george forecast 568 Feb 14 10:30 tomorrow
```

Absolute Permissions: Binary Masks

Instead of permission symbols in Table 2-5, many users find it more convenient to use the absolute method. The *absolute method* changes all the permissions at once, instead of specifying one or the other. It uses a *binary mask* that references all the permissions in each category. The three categories, each with three permissions, conform to an octal binary format. Octal numbers have a base 8 structure. When translated into a binary number, each octal digit becomes three binary digits. A binary number is a set of 1 and 0 digits. Three octal digits in a number translate into three sets of three binary digits, which is nine altogether—and the exact number of permissions for a file.

You can use the octal digits as a mask to set the different file permissions. Each octal digit applies to one of the user categories. You can think of the digits matching up with the permission categories from left to right, beginning with the owner category. The first octal digit applies to the owner category, the second to the group, and the third to the others category. The actual octal digit you choose determines the read, write, and execute permissions for each category. At this point, you need to know how octal digits translate into their binary equivalents.

Calculating Octal Numbers

A simple way to calculate the octal number makes use of the fact that any number used for permissions will be a combination derived from adding in decimal terms the numbers 4, 2, and 1. Use 4 for read permission, 2 for write, and 1 for execute. The read, write, execute permission is simply the addition of 4 + 2 + 1 to get 7. The read and execute permission adds 4 and 1, to get 5. You can use this method to calculate the octal number for each category. To get 755, you would add 4 + 2 + 1 for the owner read, write, and execute permission; 4 + 1 for the group read and execute permission; and 4 + 1 again for the other read and execute permission.

Binary masks

When dealing with a binary mask, you need to specify three digits for all three categories, as well as their permissions. This makes a binary mask less versatile than the permission symbols. To set the owner execute permission on and the write permission off for the `mydata` file and retain the read permission, you need to use the octal digit 5 (101). At the same time, you need to specify the digits for group and other users access. If these categories are to retain read access, you need the octal number 4 for each (100). This gives you three octal digits, 544, which translate into the binary digits 101 100 100.

```
$ chmod 544 mydata
```

Execute Permissions

One of the most common uses of the binary mask is to set the execute permission. You can create files that contain Linux commands, called *shell scripts*. To execute the commands in a shell script, you must first indicate the file is executable—that it contains commands the system can execute. You can do this in several ways, one of which is to set the executable permission on the shell script file.

Suppose you just completed a shell script file and you
need to give it executable permission to run it. You
also want to retain read and write permission, but deny
any access by the group or other users. The octal digit 7
(111) will set all three permissions, including execute
(you can also add 4-read, 2-write, and 1-execute to get 7).
Using 0 for the group and other users denies them
access. This gives you the digits 700, which are
equivalent to the binary digits 111 000 000. In this
example, the owner permission for the `myprog` file is
set to include execute permission:

```
$ chmod 700 myprog
```

If you want others to be able to execute and read the
file, but not change it, you can set the read and execute
permissions and turn off the write permission with the
digit 5 (101). In this case, you would use the octal digits 755,
having the binary equivalent of 111 101 101.

```
$ chmod 755 myprog
```

Setting Permissions: Permission Symbols

The symbolic method of setting permissions uses the
characters r, w, and x for read, write, and execute,
respectively. Any of these permissions can be added
or removed. The symbol to add a permission is the plus
sign, +. The symbol to remove a permission is the minus
sign, –. In the next example, the `chmod` command adds
the execute permission and removes the write permission
for the `mydata` file for all categories. The read permission
is not changed.

```
$ chmod +x-w mydata
```

Permission symbols also specify each user category. The
owner, group, and others categories are represented by
the u, g, and o characters, respectively. Notice the owner
category is represented by a u, and can be thought of as
the user. The symbol for a category is placed before plus

and minus signs preceding the read, write, and execute permissions. If no category symbol is used, all categories are assumed, and the permissions specified are set for the user, group, and others. In the next example, the first chmod command sets the permissions for the group to read and write. The second chmod command sets permissions for other users to read. Notice no spaces are between the permission specifications and the category. The permissions list is simply one long phrase, with no spaces.

```
$ chmod g+rw mydata
$ chmod o+r mydata
```

A user may remove permissions as well as add them. In the next example, the read permission is set for other users, but the write and execute permissions are removed:

```
$ chmod o+r-wx mydata
```

Another permission character exists, a, which represents all the categories. The a character is the default. In the next example, the two commands are equivalent. The read permission is explicitly set with the a character denoting all types of users: other, group, and user.

```
$ chmod a+r mydata
$ chmod +r mydata
```

One of the most common permission operations is setting a file's executable permission. This is often done in the case of shell program files. The executable permission indicates a file contains executable instructions and can be directly run by the system. In the next example, the file lsc has its executable permission set and then executed:

```
$ chmod u+x lsc
$ lsc
main.c lib.c
$
```

Directory Permissions

You can also set permissions on directories. The read permission set on a directory allows the list of files in a directory to be displayed. The execute permission enables a user to change to that directory. The write permission enables a user to create and remove his or her files in that directory. If you allow other users to have write permission on a directory, they can add their own files to it. When you create a directory, it is automatically given read, write, and execute permission for the owner. You may list the files in that directory, change to it, and create files in it.

Like files, directories have sets of permissions for the owner, the group, and all other users. Often, you may want to allow other users to change to and list the files in one of your directories, but not let them add their own files to it. In this case, you would set read and execute permissions on the directory, but not write permission. This would allow other users to change to the directory and list the files in it, but not to create new files or to copy any of their files into it. The next example sets read and execute permission for the group for the thankyou directory, but removes the write permission. Members of the group may enter the thankyou directory and list the files there, but they may not create new ones.

```
$ chmod g+rx-w letters/thankyou
```

Just as with files, you can also use octal digits to set a directory permission. To set the same permissions as in the previous example, you would use the octal digits 750, which have the binary equivalents of 111 101 000.

```
$ chmod 750 letters/thankyou
```

Displaying Directory Permissions

The ls command with the −l option lists all files in a directory. To list only the information about the directory itself, add a d modifier. In the next example, ls −ld displays information about the thankyou directory. Notice the first character in the permissions list is d, indicating it is a directory.

```
$ ls -ld thankyou
drwxr-x--- 2 chris 512 Feb 10 04:30 thankyou
```

Parent Directory Permissions

If you have files you want other users to have access to, you not only need to set permissions for that file, you also must make sure the permissions are set for the directory in which the file is located. To access your file, a user must first access the file's directory. The same applies to parents of directories. Although a directory may give permission to others to access it, if its parent directory denies access, the directory cannot be reached. Therefore, you must pay close attention to your directory tree. To provide access to a directory, all other directories above it in the directory tree must also be accessible to other users.

Ownership Permissions

In addition to the read/write/execute permissions, you can also set ownership permissions for executable programs. Normally, the user who runs a program owns it while it is running, even though the program file itself may be owned by another user. The Set User ID permission allows the original owner of the program to own it always, even while another user is running the program. For example, most software on the system is owned by the root user, but is run by ordinary users. Some such software may have to modify files owned by the root. In this case, the ordinary user would need to run that program with the root retaining ownership so the program could have the permissions to change those root-owned files. The Group ID permission works the same way, except for groups. Programs owned by a group retain ownership, even when run by users from another group. The program can then change the owner group's files. There is a potential security risk involved in that you are essentially giving a user some limited root-level access.

Ownership Permissions Using the Binary Method

For the ownership permissions, you add another octal number to the beginning of the octal digits. The octal digit for User ID permission is 4 (100) and for Group ID, it is 2 (010), or use 6 to set both (110). The following example

sets the User ID permission to the `pppd` program, along
with read and execute permissions for the owner,
group,
and others:

`chmod 4555 /usr/sbin/pppd`

Ownership Permissions Using Symbols

To add both the User ID and Group ID permissions to a
file, you use the `s` option. The following example adds the
User ID permission to the `pppd` program, which is owned
by the root user. When an ordinary user runs `pppd`, the
root user retains ownership, allowing the `pppd` program
to change root-owned files.

`chmod +s /usr/sbin/pppd`

The Set User ID and Set Group ID permissions show
up as an `s` in the execute position of the owner and
group segments. Set User ID and Group ID are essentially
variations of the execute permission, `x`. Read, write, and
User ID permission would be `rws` instead of just `rwx`.

`ls -l /usr/sbin/pppd`
`-rwsr-sr-x 1 root root 184412 Jan 24 22:48 /usr/sbin/pppd`

Sticky Bit Permissions

One other special permission provides for greater security
on directories, the *sticky bit*. Originally, the sticky bit
was used to keep a program in memory after it finished
execution to increase efficiency. Current Linux systems
ignore this feature. Instead, it is used for directories to
protect files within them. Files in a directory with the
sticky bit set can only be deleted or renamed by the root
user or the owner of the directory.

Sticky Bit Permission
Using the Binary Method

As with ownership, for sticky bit permissions, you add
another octal number to the beginning of the octal digits.
The octal digit for the sticky bit is 1 (001). The following
example sets the sticky bit for the **myreports** directory. :

`chmod 1755 /home/dylan/myreports`

The next example would set both the sticky bit and the User ID permission on the `newprogs` directory. The permission 5755 has the binary equivalent of 101 111 101 101.

```
# chmod 5755 /usr/bin/newprogs
# ls -l /usr/bin/newprogs
drwsr-xr-t 1 root root 4096  /usr/bin/newprogs
```

Sticky Bit Permission Using Symbols

The sticky bit permission symbol is `t`. The sticky bit shows up as a `t` in the execute position of the other permissions. A program with read and execute permission with the sticky bit would have its permissions displayed as `r-t`.

```
# chmod +t /home/dylan/myreports
# ls -l /home/dylan/myreports
-rwxr-xr-t 1 root root 4096 /home/dylan/myreports
```

Permission Defaults: umask

Whenever you create a file, it is given default permissions. You can display the current defaults or change them with the `umask` command. The permissions are displayed in binary or symbolic format as described in the following sections. The default permissions include any execute permissions that would be applied to executable files like programs or scripts. Standard data files do not use the executable permissions. To display the current default permissions, use the `umask` command with no arguments. The -S option uses the symbolic format.

```
$ umask -S
u=rwx,g=rx,o=rx
```

This default umask provides rw-r--r-- permission for standard files, and adds execute permission for executable files, rwxr-xr-x.

You can set a new default by specifying permissions in either symbolic or binary format. To specify the new permissions, use the `-S` option. The following example denies others read permission, while allowing user and group read access, which results in permissions of rwxr-x---.

```
$ umask -S  u=rwx,g=rx,o=
```

When you use the binary format, the mask is the inverse of the permissions you want to set. So, to set both the read and execute permission on and the write permission off, you would use the octal number 2, a binary 010. To set all permissions on, you would use an octal 0, a binary 000. The following example shows the mask for the permission defaults rwx, rx, and rx.

```
$ umask
0022
```

To set the default to only deny read permission for others, you would use 0027, using the binary mask 0111 for the other permissions.

```
$ umask 0027
```

Disk Quotas

You can use disk quotas to control how much disk space a particular user makes use of on your system. On your Linux system, unused disk space is held as a common resource that each user can access as they need it. As a user creates more files, they take the space they need from the pool of available disk space. In this sense, all the users are sharing a single resource of unused disk space. However, if one user were to use up all the remaining disk space, none of the other users would be able to create files or even run programs. To counter this problem, you can create disk quotas on particular users, limiting the amount of available disk space they can use.

Quota Tools

Quota checks can be implemented on the file system of a hard disk partition mounted on your system. The quotas are enabled using the quotacheck and quotaon programs. On Red Hat, they are executed in the /etc/rc.d/rc .sysinit script, which is run whenever you start up your system. Each partition needs to be mounted with the quota options, usrquota or grpquota. usrquota enables quota controls for users, and grpquota works for groups. These options are usually placed in the mount entry in the /etc/fstab file for a particular partition (see Chapter 5). For example, to mount the /dev/hda6 hard disk partition mounted to the /home directory with support for user and group quotas, you would require a mount entry like the following:

```
/dev/hda6 /home ext2 defaults,usrquota,grpquota 1 1
```

You also need to create quota.user and quota.group files for each partition for which you enable quotas. These are the quota databases used to hold the quota information for each user and group. You can create these files by running the quotacheck command with the -a option or the device name of the file system where you want to enable quotas. The following example creates the quota database on the hda1 hard disk partition.

```
quotacheck -a  /dev/hda1
```

edquota

You can set disk quotas using the edquota command. With it, you can access the quota record for a particular user and group, which is maintained in the disk quota database. You can also set default quotas that will be applied to any user or group on the file system for which quotas have not been set. edquota will open the record in your default editor, and you can use your editor to make any changes. To open the record for a particular user, use the -u option and the username as an argument for edquota (see Table 2-6). The following example opens the disk quota record for the user larisa:

```
edquota -u larisa
```

edquota option	Description
-u	Edits the user quota. This is the default.
-g	Edits the group quota.
-p	Duplicates the quotas of the typical user specified. This is the normal mechanism used to initialize quotas for groups of users.
-t	Edits the soft time limits for each file system.

Table 2-5. edquota options

The limit you set for a quota can be hard or soft. A hard limit will deny a user the ability to exceed their quota, whereas a soft limit will just issue a warning. For the soft limit, you can designate a grace period during which time the user has the chance to reduce their disk space below the limit. If the disk space still exceeds the limit after the grace period expires, the user can be denied access to their account. For example, a soft limit is typically 75 megabytes, whereas the hard limit could be 100 megabytes. Users who exceed their soft limit could have a 48-hour grace period.

The quota record begins with the hard disk device name and the blocks of memory and inodes in use. The Limits segments have parameters for soft and hard limits. If these entries are 0, there are no limits in place. You can set both hard and soft limits, using the hard limit as a firm restriction. Blocks in Linux are currently about 1,000 bytes. The inodes are used by files to hold information about the memory blocks making up a file. To set the time limit for a soft limit, use the edquota command with the -t option. The following example displays the quota record for larisa:

```
Quotas for user larisa:
/dev/hda3: blocks in use: 9000, limits
 (soft = 40000, hard = 60000)
 inodes in use: 321, limits (soft = 0, hard = 0)
```

quotacheck, quotaon, and quotaoff

Thee quotoa records are maintained in the quota database for that partition. Each partition that has quotas enabled has its own quota database. You can check the validity of your quota database with the `quotacheck` command. You can turn quotas on and off using the `quotaon` and `quotaoff` commands. When you start up your system, `quotacheck` is run to check the quota databases, and then `quotaon` is run to turn on quotas.

repquota and quota

As the system administrator, you can use the `repquota` command to generate a summary of disk usage for a specified file system, checking to see what users are approaching or exceeding quota limits. `repquota` takes as its argument the file system to check; the `-a` option checks all file systems.

```
repquota /dev/hda1
```

Individual users can use the `quota` command to check their memory use and how much disk space they have left in their quota (see Table 2-6).

`quota` option	Description
`-g`	Prints group quotas for the group of which the user is a member.
`-u`	Prints the user's quota.
`-v`	Displays quotas on file systems where no storage is allocated.
`-q`	Prints information on file systems where usage is over quota.

Table 2-6.   Options for `edquota` **and** `quota`

Lightweight Directory Access Protocol

2

The Lightweight Directory Access Protocol (LDAP) is designed to implement network-accessible directories of users, providing information about them such as their e-mail address or phone number. Such directories can also be used for authentication purposes, identifying that a certain user belongs to a specified network. You can find out more information on LDAP at www.ldpaman.org. You can think of an LDAP directory as an Internet-accessible phone book, where anyone can look you up to find your e-mail address or other information. In fact, it may be more accurate to refer to such directories as databases. They are databases of user information, accessible over networks like the Internet. Normally, the users on a local network are spread across several different systems, and to obtain information about a user, you would have to know what system the user is on, and then query that system. With LDAP, user information for all users on a network is kept in the LDAP server. You only have to query the network's LDAP server to obtain information about a user. For example, Sendmail can use LDAP to look up user addresses. You can also use Mozilla or Netscape to query LDAP. In Mozilla, open the address book, then select File | New, and choose the LDAPD directory. Here you can enter the LDAP server. In the Preferences dialog, select addressing under the Mail & Newsgroup category. This displays a panel where you can enter the LDAP directory server.

LDAP Clients and Servers

LDAP directories are implemented as clients and servers, where you use an LDAP client to access an LDAP server that manages the LDAP database. Most Linux distributions, including Red Hat, use OpenLDAP, an open-source

version of LDAP (you can find out more about OpenLDAP
at www.openldap.org). This package includes an LDAP
server (`slapd`), an LDAP replication server (`slurpd`), an
LDAP client, and tools. `slurpd` is used to update other LDAP
servers on your network, should you have more than one.
Once the LDAP server is installed, you can start, stop,
and restart the LDAP server (`slapd`) with the `ldap`
startup script:

```
service ldap restart
```

 *Red Hat clients can enable LDAP
services and select an LDAP server
using the Red Hat Authentication tool (authconfig-gtk)
accessible as the Authentication entry in the System
Settings menu and window.*

LDAP Configuration Files

All LDAP configuration files are kept in the `/etc/openldap`
directory. These include `slapd.conf`, the LDAP server
configuration file, and `ldap.conf`, the LDAP clients and
tools configuration file. To enable the LDAP server, you
have to manually edit the `slapd.conf` file, and change
the domain value (dc) for the suffix and rootdn entries to
your own network's domain address. This is the network
that will be serviced by the LDAP server. To enable LDAP
clients and their tools, you have to specify the correct
domain address in the `ldap.conf` file in the BASE option,
along with the server's address in the HOST option (domain
name or IP address). For clients, you can either edit
the `ldap.conf` file directly or use the System Settings
Authentication tool, clicking the Configure LDAP button
on either the User Information or Authentication panel.
Here, you can enter your domain name and the LDAP
server's address.

LDAP Tools

An entry in an LDAP database consists of a name (known
as a *distinguished name*) followed by a set of attributes
and their values. For example, a name could be a username

and the attribute would be the user's e-mail address, the address being the attribute's value. Allowable attributes are determined by object class sets defined in the `/etc/openldap/schema` directory. To actually make or change entries in the LDAP database, you use the `ldapadd` and `ldapmodify` utilities. With `ldapdelete`, you can remove entries. Once you have created an LDAP database, you can then query it, through the LDAP server, with `ldapsearch`. For the LDAP server, you can create a text file of LDAP entries using an LDAP Data Interchange Format (LDIF) format. Such text files can then be read all at once to the LDAP database using the `slapadd` tool. The `slapcat` tool extracts entries from the LDAP database and saves them in an LDIF file. To reindex additions and changes, you use the `slapindex` utility.

 **SECURITY SCAN** *You can enable and designate LDAP servers with the authconfig-gtk tool (Authentication in the System Settings window and menu). You can also use the LDAP Browser/ Editor or the Gnome Directory Administrator to manage and edit LDAP directories.*

LDAP and PAM

With LDAP, you can also more carefully control the kind of information given out and to whom. Using a PAM module (pam_ldap), LDAP can perform user authentication tasks, providing centralized authentication for users. Login operations that users perform for different services such as mail POP server, system login, and Samba logins can all be carried out through LDAP using a single PAM-secured user ID and password. To configure PAM to use LDAP, use the System Settings Authentication tool (`authconfig-gtk`) and select Enable LDAP Support on the Authentication panel. You should also make sure that LDAP server is correctly specified. To use LDAP for authentication, you need to configure PAM to use it, as well as migrate authentication files to the LDAP format. The `/usr/share/openldap/migration` directory holds scripts you can use to translate the old files into LDAP versions.

LDAP and the Name Service Switch Service

With the `libnss_ldap` module, LDAP can also be used in the Name Service Switch (NSS) service along with NIS and system files for system database services like passwords and groups. Clients can easily enable LDAP for NSS by using the System Settings Authentication tool and selecting Enable LDAP Support in the User Information panel. You also need to make sure that the LDAP server is specified. You could also manually add `ldap` for entries in the `/etc/nsswitch.conf` file.

SECURITY SCAN *To better secure access to the LDAP server, you should encrypt your LDAP administrator's password. The LDAP administrator is specified in the rootdn entry, and its password in the rootpw entry. To create an encrypted password, use the `slappasswd` command. This prompts you for a password and displays its encrypted version. Copy that encrypted version in the rootpw entry.*

Pluggable Authentication Modules

Pluggable Authentication Modules (PAM) is an authentication service that lets a system determine the method of authentication to be performed for users. In a Linux system, authentication has traditionally been performed by looking up passwords. When a user logs in, the login process looks up their password in the password file. With PAM, users' requests for authentication are directed to PAM, which in turn uses a specified method to authenticate the user. This could be a simple password lookup or a request to an LDAP server, but it is PAM that provides authentication, not a direct password lookup by the user or application. In this respect, authentication becomes centralized and controlled by a specific service, PAM. The actual authentication procedures can be dynamically configured by the system administrator. Authentication is carried out by modules that can vary according to the kind of authentication needed. An administrator can add or replace modules by simply changing the PAM configuration files. See the PAM Web site at www.kernel.org/pub/linux/libs/pam for more information and a listing of PAM modules. PAM modules are located in the `/lib/security` directory.

PAM Configuration Files

On Red Hat, PAM uses different configuration files for different services that request authentication. Such configuration files are kept in the `/etc/pam.d` directory. For example, you have a configuration file for logging in to your system (`/etc/pam.d/login`), one for the graphical login (`/etc/pam.d/gdm`) and one for accessing your Samba server (`/etc/pam.d/samba`). A default PAM configuration file, called `/etc/pam.d/other`, is invoked if no services file is present. On Red Hat, the `system-auth` file contains standard authentication modules for system services generated by authconfig-gtk and is invoked in many of the other configuration files. In addition, Red Hat sets up an authentication for its configuration tools, such as redhat-config-services and redhat-config-network.

PAM Modules

A PAM configuration file contains a list of modules to be used for authentication. They have the following format:

```
module-type control-flag module-path args
```

The *module-path* is the module to be run, and *module-arguments* are the parameters you want passed to that module. Though there are a few generic arguments, most modules have their own. The *module-type* refers to different groups of authentication management: account, authentication, session, and password. The account management performs account verification, checking such account aspects as to whether the user has access, or whether the password has expired. Authentication (`auth`) verifies who the user is, usually through a password confirmation. Password management performs authentication updates such as password changes. Session management refers to tasks performed before a service is accessed and before it is shut down. These include tasks like initiating a log of a user's activity or mounting and unmounting home directories.

TIP   As an alternative to the `/etc/pam.d` directory, you could create one configuration file called the `/etc/pam .conf` file. Entries in this file have a service field, which refers to the application that the module is used for. If the `/etc/pam.d` directory exists, `/etc/pam.conf` is automatically ignored.

The *control-flag* field indicates how PAM is to respond if the module fails. The control can be a simple directive or a more complicated response that can specify return codes like `open_err` with actions to take. The simple directives are `requisite`, `required`, `sufficient`, and `optional`. The `requisite` directive ends the authentication process immediately if the module fails to authenticate. The `required` directive only ends the authentication after the remaining modules are run. The `sufficient` directive indicates that success of this module is enough to provide authentication unless a previous required module has failed. The `optional` directive indicates the module's success is not needed unless it is the only authentication module for its service. If you specify return codes, you can refine the conditions for authentication failure or success. Return codes can be given values such as `die` or `ok`. The `open_err` return code could be given the action `die`, which would stop all authentication and return failure. The `/etc/pam.d/vsftpd` configuration file for the FTP server is shown here.

```
#%PAM-1.0
auth required pam_listfile.so item=user sense=deny
          file=/etc/vsftpd.ftpusers onerr=succeed
auth     required  pam_stack.so service=system-auth
auth     required  pam_shells.so
account  required  pam_stack.so service=system-auth
session  required  pam_stack.so service=system-auth
```

Chapter 3

Software Management

Installing, uninstalling, or updating software packages
has always been a simple process in Red Hat Linux due
to the widespread use of the Red Hat Package Manager.
Instead of using a standard TAR archive, software is
packaged in a special archive for use with the Red Hat
Package Manager (RPM). An RPM archive contains all
the program files, configuration files, data files, and even
documentation that constitute a software application.
With one simple operation, the Red Hat Package Manager
installs all these for you. It also checks for any other
software packages that the program may need to run
correctly. You can even create your own RPM packages.
Red Hat provides an RPM window-based tool called
redhat-config-packages to manage your RPM packages,
installing new ones, updating or uninstalling ones you
already have. The redhat-config-packages tool provide
an easy-to-use interface for managing your packages,
enabling you to obtain detailed information on a package
easily, including a complete listing of the files it installs.

TIP   *The Red Hat Update Agent, through the Red Hat
Network, will automatically download and update any
Red Hat RPM packages for you that are installed on your
system and are part of the Red Hat distribution. The service
is provided on a subscription basis.*

You can also download source code versions of applications,
and then compile and install them on your system. Where
this process once was complex, it has been significantly
streamlined with the addition of *configure scripts*. Most
current source code, including GNU software, is distributed
with a configure script. The configure script automatically
detects your system configuration and generates a *Makefile*,
which is used to compile the application and create a binary
file that is compatible with your system. In most cases,

with a few Makefile operations, you can compile and install a complex source code on any system.

Software Repositories

You can download Linux software from many online sources. You can find sites for particular kinds of applications, such as Gnome and KDE, as well as for particular distributions, such as Red Hat. The Red Hat Network can automatically download and update software installed from RPM packages that make up the Red Hat distribution. Some sites are repositories for RPM packages, such as rpmfind.net, and others like freshmeat.net refer you to original development sites where you can download software packages. The freshmeat.net and www.linuxapps.com sites are useful for finding out about new available software. Many of the open-source Linux projects can be found at sourceforge.net. Here you will find detailed documentation and recent versions of software packages. For applications designed for the Gnome desktop, you can check www.gnome.org, and you can find KDE applications at apps.kde.com. For particular database and office applications, you can download software packages directly from the company's web site, such as www.oracle.com for the Oracle database. Table 3-1 lists several popular Linux software sites.

FTP and Web Sites	Applications
ftp.redhat.com	Software packaged in RPM packages for Red Hat
freshmeat.net	Linux software, including RPMs
linuxapps.com	Linux software, including RPMs
rpmfind.net	RPM package repository
freshrpms.net	Customized RPM packages
sourceforge.net	Linux open source software projects
www.gnome.org	Gnome software
apps.kde.com	KDE software
rmpseek.com	Linux software search site
www.filewatcher.org	Linux FTP site watcher

Table 3-1. Linux Software Sites

FTP and Web Sites	Applications
www.gnu.org	GNU archive
www.ximian.com	Ximian Gnome, office applications for Gnome

Table 3-1. Linux Software Sites *(continued)*

3

Software Package Types

The software packages on RPM sites like Red Hat and rpmfind.net will have the file extension .rpm. RPM packages that contain source codes have an extension .src.rpm. Other packages, such as those in the form of source code that you need to compile, come in a variety of compressed archives. These commonly have the extensions `.tar.gz`, `.tgz`, or `.tar.bz2`. They are explained in detail later in the chapter. Table 3-2 lists several common file extensions that you will find for the great variety of Linux software packages available to you.

Extension	File
`.rpm`	Software package created with the Red Hat Software Package Manager, used on Red Hat, Caldera, Mandrake, and SuSE distributions.
`.src.rpm`	Software packages that are source code versions of applications, created with the Red Hat Software Package Manager.
`.gz`	`gzip` compressed file (use `gunzip` to decompress).
`.bz2`	bzip2 compressed file (use `bunzip2` to decompress, also use the `j` option with `tar`, as in `xvjf`).
`.tar`	A tar archive file, use `tar` with `xvf` to extract.
`.tar.gz`	`gzip` compressed `tar` archive file. Use `gunzip` to decompress and `tar` to extract. Use the `z` option with `tar`, as in `xvzf` to both decompress and extract in one step.
`.tar.bz2`	bzip2 compressed `tar` archive file. Extract with `tar -xvzf`.

Table 3-2. Linux Software Package File Extensions

Extension	File
.tz	`tar` archive file compressed with the `compress` command.
.z	File compressed with the `compress` command (use the `decompress` command to decompress).
.deb	Debian Linux package.

Table 3-2. Linux Software Package File Extensions *(continued)*

Red Hat Package Manager (RPM)

Several Linux distributions, including Red Hat, Mandrake, Caldera, and SuSE, use RPM to organize Linux software into packages you can automatically install or remove. RPM is a command-line-driven package management system that is capable of installing, uninstalling, querying, verifying, and updating software packages installed on Linux systems. An RPM software package operates as its own installation program for a software application. A Linux software application often consists of several files that need to be installed in different directories. The program itself is most likely placed in a directory called `/usr/bin`, online manual files like man pages go in other directories, and library files in yet another directory. In addition, the installation may require modification of certain configuration files on your system. The RPM software package performs all these tasks for you. Also, if you later decide you don't want a specific application, you can uninstall packages to remove all the files and configuration information from your system. RPM works similarly to the Windows Install Wizard, automatically installing software, including configuration, documentation, image, sample, and program files, along with any other files an application may use. All are installed in their appropriate directories on your system. RPM maintains a database of installed software, keeping track of all the files installed. This enables you to use RPM also to uninstall software, automatically removing all files that are part of the application.

RPM Tools

To install and uninstall RPM packages, you can use the
`rpm` command directly from a shell prompt, or the Red Hat
distribution software management tool, redhat-config-
packages. The redhat-config-packages tool is a GUI
front end for the `rpm` command. Although you should
download RPM packages for your particular distribution,
numerous RPM software packages are designed to run
on any Linux system. You can learn more about RPM
at its web site at www.rpm.org. The site contains
up-to-date versions for RPM, documentation, and RPM
support programs, such as `rpm2html` and `rpm2cpio`.
`rpm2html` takes a directory containing RPM packages
and generates web pages listing those packages as
links that can be used to download them. `rpm2cpio`
is a Perl script to extract RPMs. Also, the Red Hat Linux
Customization Guide provides an excellent tutorial for
both RPM and redhat-config-packages.

RPM Packages

The naming conventions for RPM packages vary from
one distribution to another. On Red Hat, the package
name includes the package version along with its
platform (`i386` for Intel PCs) and the `.rpm` extension.
An example of the emacs editor's RPM package for
Intel systems is shown here:

```
emacs-21.2-18.i386.rpm
```

The RPM packages on your DVD-ROM or distribution
CD-ROM only represent a small portion of the software
packages available for Linux. An extensive repository for
RPM packages is also located at rpmfind.net. Packages here
are indexed according to distribution, group, and name.
It includes packages for every distribution, including
Red Hat.

TIP *RPM packages with the term `noarch` are used for
architecture-independent packages. This means that they
are designed to install on any Linux system. Packages
without `noarch` may be distribution- or architecture-
dependent, designed to install on a particular type of
machine.*

You could place these packages in a directory on your system, and then use either `rpm` or a GUI RPM utility such as the redhat-config-packages tool to install it. Normally, you should always try to use the version of the RPM package set up for your Red Hat distribution; for instance, if you run Red Hat 7.2, it is best to download the software package designated for Red Hat 7.2 instead of downloading the same package for Red Hat 6.2. Packages for specific releases will be kept in the release directories. In many cases, attempting to install an RPM package meant for a different distribution may fail.

Installing from the Desktop: redhat-config-packages

The redhat-config-packages tool provides an effective and easy-to-use interface for managing the Red Hat RPM packages provided by your Red Hat distribution, whether you installed from CD-ROMs, DVD-ROM, hard disk, or network. It runs on any window manager, including Gnome and KDE. You can access redhat-config-packages using the Packages icon in the System Settings window. This opens a Package Management window that initially displays a listing of package categories (see Figure 3-1). Most entries are preceded by a check box and have a Details link at the end. For example, to install web server software, you click to check the entry for Web Server. Critical package groups like the X Window System or basic printer support will have no check box, though you can click on the Detail button to add or remove extra packages for that group .

Selecting Packages

A package group is organized into standard (default) and extra packages. The standard packages will always be installed, whereas you can select which extra packages you want to install. You can remove standard packages later by uninstalling the entire package group, whereas extra packages can be removed individually. To choose which extra packages to install, click on the Details link at the end of the entry. This opens a new window with listings for both standard and extra packages. Uninstalled packages have empty check boxes, and installed packages have the check boxes already checked. Several extra packages will

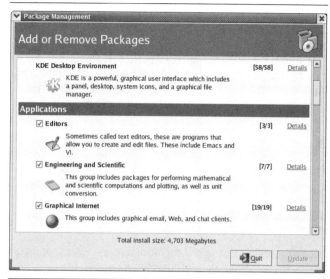

Figure 3-1. redhat-config-packages

already be installed depending on the type of installation you choose, such as Personal Desktop or Server.

Installing and Uninstalling Packages

Use the check boxes to install and uninstall packages. To install an uninstalled package or remove an installed package, click its check box. When you have finished making your selections, close the window and return to the Package Management window, where you can select other software to install or uninstall. Once you have made all your selections, click the Update button. redhat-config-packages then prepares a list of packages to install. If you are using CD-ROMs instead of the DVD-ROM, you will be prompted to enter the appropriate CD-ROM.

TIP *You can also install a particular RPM package directly. First, display it with the file manager, and then double-click it. This invokes the redhat-config-packages tool, which installs the package. It also checks for dependent packages and installs those as well. If you are using CD-ROMs instead of the DVD-ROM, you will be prompted to insert any other CD-ROMs as needed.*

Updating Software

You can update your Linux system automatically using a distribution update agent like the Red Hat Network. You can also manually download packages using an FTP client, web browser, or the Gnome or KDE file managers, and then use the `rpm` command or the redhat-config-packages tool to install the software.

For redhat-config-packages, you can use your file manager to locate the RPM file and double click the RPM package file. You can also, on Gnome, right-click it, and select Open With | Install Packages, or on KDE, select Install Package. redhat-config-packages starts up and checks for any dependent packages you may need. It then installs the RPM package for you.

If you are using the `rpm` command, use the `-U` option to upgrade packages. In the following example, the `rpm` command with the `-Uvh` option installs an upgrade for emacs:

```
# rpm -Uvh emacs-21.2-18.i386.rpm
```

Command-Line Installation: rpm

If you do not have access to the desktop, or you prefer to work from the command-line interface, you can use the `rpm` command to manage and install software packages. `rpm` is the command that actually performs installation, removal, and queries of software packages. In fact, redhat-config-packages uses the `rpm` command to install and remove packages. An RPM package is an archive of software files that includes information about how to install those files. The filenames for RPM packages end with `.rpm`, indicating software packages that can be installed by the Red Hat Package Manager.

The rpm Command

With the `rpm` command, you can maintain packages, query them, build your own, and verify the ones you have. Maintaining packages involves installing new ones, upgrading to new versions, and uninstalling packages.

The `rpm` command uses a set of options to determine what action to take. In addition, certain tasks, such as installing or querying packages, have their own options that further qualify the kind of action they take. For example, the `-q` option queries a package, but when combined with the `-l` option it lists all the files in that package. Table 3-3 lists the set of `rpm` options. The syntax for the `rpm` command is as follows (*rpm-package-name* is the name of the software package you want to install):

`rpm options rpm-package-name`

Mode of Operation	Effect
`rpm -ioptions package-file`	Installs a package; the complete name of the package file is required.
`rpm -eoptions package-name`	Uninstalls (erases) a package; you only need the name of the package, often one word.
`rpm -qoptions package-name`	Queries a package. An option can be a package name, a further option and package name, or an option applied to all packages.
`rpm -Uoptions package-name`	Upgrades; same as install, but any previous version is removed.
`rpm -Foptions package-name`	Upgrades, but only if package is currently installed.
`rpm -verifyoptions`	Verifies a package is correctly installed; uses same options as query. You can use `-V` or `-y` in place of `-verify`.
`--percent`	Displays percentage of package during installation.
`--replacepks`	Installs an already installed package.
`--replacefiles`	Replaces files installed by other packages.
`--redhatprovides dependent-files`	Searches for dependent packages.
`--oldfiles`	Installs an older version of a package already installed.
`--test`	Tests installation; does not install, only checks for conflicts.
`-h`	Displays # symbols as package is installed.
`--excludedocs`	Excludes documentation files.

Table 3-3.   Red Hat Package Manager (RPM) Options

Mode of Operation	Effect
`--nodeps`	Installs without doing any dependency checks (dangerous).
`--force`	Forces installation despite conflicts (dangerous).
Uninstall Options (to be used with `-e`)	
`--test`	Tests uninstall. Does not remove, only checks for what is to be removed.
`--nodeps`	Uninstalls without checking for dependencies.
`--allmatches`	Removes all versions of package.
Query Options (to be used with `-q`)	
`package-name`	Queries package.
`-qa`	Queries all packages.
`-qf filename`	Queries package that owns `filename`.
`-qR`	List packages on which this package depends.
`-qp package-name`	Queries an uninstalled package.
`-qi`	Displays all package information.
`-ql`	Lists files in package.
`-qd`	Lists only documentation files in package.
`-qc`	Lists only configuration files in package.
`-q --dump`	Lists only files with complete details.
General Options (to be used with any option)	
`-vv`	Debugs; displays descriptions of all actions taken.
`--quit`	Displays only error messages.
`--version`	Displays rpm version number.
`--help`	Displays detailed use message.
`--rootdirectory`	Uses directory as top-level directory for all operations (instead of root).
`--dbpathdirectory`	Uses RPM database in the specified directory.
`--dbpath cmd`	Pipes output of RPM to the command `cmd`.
`--rebuilddb`	Rebuilds the RPM database; can be used with the -root and -dbpath options.

Table 3-3. Red Hat Package Manager (RPM) Options *(continued)*

Mode of Operation	Effect
`--initdb`	Builds a new RPM database; can be used with the -root and -dbpath options.
Other Sources of Information	
www.rpm.org	The RPM web site with detailed documentation.
RPM Man page **(man rpm)**	Detailed list of options.

Table 3-3. Red Hat Package Manager (RPM) Options *(continued)*

A complete description of `rpm` and its capabilities is provided in the online manual:

```
# man rpm
```

NOTE *The software package filename is usually lengthy, including information about version and release in its name. All end with . rpm.*

Querying Information from RPM Packages and Installed Software

The -q option tells you if a package is already installed, and the `-qa` option displays a list of all installed packages. Piping this output to a pager utility, such as `more`, is best.

```
# rpm -qa | more
```

In the next example, the user checks to see if Mozilla is already installed on the system. Notice the full filename of the RPM archive is unnecessary. If the package is installed, your system has already registered its name and where it is located.

```
# rpm -q mozilla
mozilla-1.0.1-24
```

You can combine the `q` options with the `i` or `l` option to display information about the package. The option `-qi` displays information about the software, such as the version number or author (`-qpi` queries an uninstalled package file). The option `-ql` displays a listing of all the files in the software package. The `--h` option provides a complete list of `rpm` options. Common query options are shown in Table 3-4.

Option	Meaning
`-q application`	Checks to see if an application is installed.
`-qa application`	Lists all installed RPM applications.
`-qf filename`	Queries applications that own *filename*.
`-qR application`	Lists applications on which this application depends.
`-qi application`	Displays all application information.
`-ql application`	Lists files in the application.
`-qd application`	Lists only documentation files in the application.
`-qc application`	Lists only configuration files in the application.

Table 3-4. Query Options for Installed Software

TIP *Keep in mind the distinction between the installed software package name and the package filename. The filename ends in a* `.rpm` *extension and can only be queried with a* `p` *option.*

To display information taken directly from an RPM package, you add the `p` qualifier to the `q` options, as shown in Table 3-5. The `-qpi` combination displays information about a specific package, and `-qpl` displays a listing of the files a given RPM package contains. In this case, you must specify the entire filename of the RPM package. You can avoid having to enter the entire name

Option	Meaning
`-qpi RPM-file`	Displays all package information in the RPM package.
`-qpl RPM-file`	Lists files in the RPM package.
`-qpd RPM-file`	Lists only documentation files in the RPM package.
`-qpc RPM-file`	Lists only configuration files in the RPM package.
`-qpR RPM-file`	Lists packages on which this RPM package depends.

Table 3-5. Query Options for RPM Packages

simply by entering a unique part of the name and using the * filename-matching character to generate the rest.

If your RPM query outputs a long list of data, like an extensive list of files, you can pipe the output to the `more` command to look at it screen by screen, or even redirect the output to a file.

```
# rpm -ql mozilla | more
# rpm -qpl openmotif-2.2.2-5.386.rpm  > mytemp
```

Installing and Updating Packages with rpm

You use the `-i` option to install new packages and the `-U` option to update currently installed packages with new versions. With an `-e` option, `rpm` uninstalls the package. If you try to use the `-i` option to install a newer version of an installed package, you will receive an error saying the package is already installed. When a package is installed, RPM checks its signature, using imported public keys from the software vendor. If the signature check fails, an error message is displayed, specifying NOKEY if you do not have the appropriate public key. If you want to install over an already installed package, you can force installation with the `--replacepks` option. Sometimes a package will include a file, like a library, that is also installed by another package. To allow a package to overwrite the file installed by another package, you use the `--replacefiles` option. Many packages depend on the libraries installed by other packages. If these dependent packages are not already installed, you will first have to install them. RPM informs you of the missing dependent files and suggests packages to install. If no packages are suggested, you can use the `--redhatprovides` option with the missing files to search for needed packages.

The `-U` option also installs a package if it is not already installed, whereas the `-F` option will only update installed packages. If the package includes configuration files which will overwrite currently installed configuration file, it will save a copy of the current configuration file in a file ending with `.rpmsave`, such as `/etc/mtools.conf.rpmsave`. This preserves any customized configuration changes you may have made to the file. Be sure to also check for configuration compatibilities between the previous and updated versions. If you are trying to install a package that is older than the one already installed, then you need to use the `--oldpackages` option.

```
# rpm -Uvh mozilla-1.0.1-24.i386.rpm
```

If you are installing from a CD-ROM, you can change to the CD-ROM's RPMS directory, which holds the RPM packages (the RPMS directory may be located within a directory like RedHat on the Red Hat CD-ROM). An `ls` command lists all the software packages. If you know how the name of a package begins, you should include that with the `ls` command and an attached *. The list of packages is extensive and does not all fit on one screen. This is helpful for displaying the detailed name of the package. The following example lists most X Window System packages:

```
# ls x*
```

Installation Example

In the next example, the user first installs a new package with the `-i` option, and then updates a package with the `-U` option. Including the `-v` and `-h` options is customary. Here, `-v` is the verbose option that displays all files as they are installed, and `-h` displays a crosshatch symbol periodically to show RPM is still working. In the following example, the user installs the software package for the Balsa mail client. Notice the full filename is entered. To list the full name, you can use the `ls` command with the first few characters and an asterisk, `ls balsa*`. The rpm command with the `-q` option is then used to check that the software was installed. For installed packages only, the software name needs to be used—in this case, balsa-1.2.4-7.

```
 [root@turtle mypackages]# ls balsa*
balsa-1.2.4-7.i386.rpm
[root@turtle mypackages]# rpm -ivh
balsa-1.2.4-7.i386.rpm
balsa-1.2.4-7
#######################################
[root@turtle mypackages]# rpm -q balsa
balsa-1.2.4-7
```

To display information about the installed package,
use -qi; -ql displays a listing of the files a given
RPM package contains.

```
# rpm -qi balsa
# rpm -ql balsa
```

If you are worried that a software package will install
on your system incorrectly, you can use the test option
(--test) in the debug mode (vv) to see exactly what
actions RPM will take.

```
# rpm -ivv --test balsa-1.2.4-7.i386.rpm
```

Removing RPM Software Packages

To remove a software package from your system, first use
rpm -q to make sure it is actually installed. Then use the
-e option to uninstall it. You needn't use the full name of
the installed file. You only need the name of the application.
For example, if you decide you do not need Balsa, you can
remove it using the -e option and the software name, as
shown here:

```
# rpm  -e  balsa
```

Verifying an RPM Installation

You can use the verify option (-V) to check to see if any
problems occurred with the installation. RPM compares
the current attributes of installed files with information
about them placed in the RPM database when the
package was installed. If no discrepancies exist, RPM
outputs nothing. Otherwise, RPM outputs a sequence
of eight characters, one for each attribute, for each file
in the package that fails. Those that do not differ have
a period. Those that do differ have a corresponding
character code, as shown in Table 3-6:

The following example verifies the ProFTPD package:

```
[root@turtle mypackages]# rpm -V proftpd
```

To compare the installed files directly with the files in an
RPM package file, you use the -Vp option, much like the

Attribute	Explanation
5	MD5 checksum
S	File size
L	Symbolic link
T	File modification time
D	Device
U	User
G	Group
M	Mode (includes permissions and file types)

Table 3-6.   RPM Discrepancy Codes

-qp option. To check all packages, use the -Va option, as shown here:

```
# rpm -Va
```

If you want to verify a package, but you only know the name of a file in it, you can combine verify with the -f option. The following example verifies the RPM package containing the ftp command:

```
# rpm -Vf /bin/ftp
```

Rebuilding the RPM Database

RPM maintains a record of the packages it has installed in its RPM database. You may, at times, have to rebuild this database to ensure RPM has current information on what is installed and what is not. Use the --rebuilddb option to rebuild your database file:

```
# rpm --rebuilddb
```

To create a new RPM database, use the --initdb option. This option can be combined with --dbpath to specify a location for the new database.

Installing Software from RPM Source Code Files: SRPMs

Red Hat and several other distributors also make available source code versions of their binary RPM

packaged software. The source code is packaged into
RPM packages that will be automatically installed
into designated directories where you can easily compile
and install the software. Source code packages are called
SRPMs. The names for these packages end in the extension
.src.rpm. Source code versions for packages in the Red Hat
distribution are located on Red Hat releases in the SRPMS
directory. Many online sites like rpmfind.net also list
SRPM packages. Source code versions have the advantage
of letting you make your own modifications to the source
code, allowing you to generate your own customized
versions of RPM packaged software. You still use the
rpm command with the -i option to install source code
packages. In the following example, you install the source
code for Freeciv:

```
# rpm -i freeciv-1.13.0-2.src.rpm
```

Source Code RPM Directories

On Red Hat, SRPM files are installed in various
subdirectories in the /usr/src/redhat directory.
When SRPMs are installed, a spec file is placed in
the /usr/src/redhat/SPECS directory, and the
compressed archive of the source code files is placed
in the /usr/src/redhat/SOURCES directory. For
Freeciv, a spec file called freeciv.spec is placed in
/usr/src/redhat/SPECS, and a compressed archive
called freeciv-1.13.0.tar.gz is placed in the
/usr/src/redhat/SOURCES directory.

Building the Source Code

To build the source code files, you need to extract
them and run any patches on them that may be included
with the package. You do this by changing to the /usr/
src/redhat/SPECS directory and using the rpm command,
this time with the -bp option, to generate the source
code files:

```
# cd /usr/src/redhat/SPECS
# rpm -bp freeciv.spec
```

The resulting source code files are placed in their
own subdirectory with the package's name in the

/usr/src/redhat/BUILD directory. For Freeciv, the
Freeciv source code is placed in /usr/src/redhat/
BUILD/freeciv-1.13.0 directory. In this subdirectory,
you can then modify the source code, as well as compile
and install the application. Check the software's README and
INSTALL files for details.

Installing Software from Compressed Archives: .tar.gz

Linux software applications in the form of source code
are available at different sites on the Internet. You can
download any of this software and install it on your
system. Recent releases are often available in the form
of compressed archive files. Applications will always be
downloadable as compressed archives, if they don't have
an RPM version. This is particularly true for the recent
versions of Gnome or KDE packages. RPM packages are
only intermittently generated.

Decompressing Software

Many software packages under development or designed
for cross-platform implementation may not be in an RPM
format. Instead, they may be archived and compressed.
The filenames for these files end with the extensions
.tar.gz, .tar.bz2, or .tar.Z. The different extensions
indicate different decompression methods using different
commands: gunzip for .gz, bunzip2 for .bz2, and
decompress for .Z. In fact, most software with an RPM
format also has a corresponding .tar.gz format. After
you download such a package, you must first decompress
it, and then unpack it with the tar command. The
compressed archives could hold either source code that
you then need to compile or, as is the case with Java
packages, binaries that are ready to run.

A *compressed archive* is an archive file created with tar,
and then compressed with a compression tool like gzip.
To install such a file, you must first decompress it with
a decompression utility like gunzip utility, and then use

`tar` to extract the files and directories making up the software package. Instead of the `gunzip` utility, you could also use `gzip -d`. The next example decompresses the `htdig-3.1.6.tar.gz` file, replacing it with a decompressed version called `htdig-3.1.6.tar`:

```
# ls
 htdig-3.1.6.tar.gz
# gunzip htdig-3.1.6.tar.gz
# ls
 htdig-3.1.6.tar
```

You can download compressed archives from many different sites, including those mentioned previously. Downloads can be accomplished with FTP clients such as ncftp and Gftp, or with any web browser, such as Mozilla. Once downloaded, any file that ends with `.z`, `.bz2`, `.zip`, or `.gz` is a compressed file that must be decompressed.

For files ending with `.bz2`, you would use the `bunzip2` command. The following example decompresses the Java 2 SDK downloaded from www.blackdown.org:

```
# bunzip2 j2sdk-1.3.0-FCS-linux-i386.tar.bz2
# ls
j2sdk-1.3.0-FCS-linux-i386.tar
# tar -xvf j2sdk-1.3.0-FCS-linux-i386.tar
```

Selecting an Install Directory

Before you unpack the archive, move it to the directory where you want it. Source code packages should be placed in the `/usr/local/src` directory, and binary packages go in designated directories. Source code files are unpacked in the `/usr/local/src` directory, generating their own subdirectories from which you can compile and install the software. Once installed, you can delete this directory, keeping the original source code package file (`.tar.gz`).

Packages that hold binary programs ready to run, like Java, are meant to be extracted in certain directories. Usually, this is the `/usr/local` directory. Most archives, when they unpack, create a subdirectory named with the application name and its release, placing all those files or directories making up the software package into that subdirectory. For example, the file cdrchive-1.2.2.tar unpacks to a subdirectory called cdrchive-1.2.2. In certain cases, the software package that contains precompiled binaries is designed to unpack directly into the system subdirectory where it will be used. For example, it is recommended that j2sdk-1.3.0-FCS-linux-i386.tar be unpacked in the /usr/local directory where it will create a subdirectory called j2sdk-1.3.0. The /usr/local/j2sdk-1.3.0/bin directory will holds the Java binary programs.

Extracting Software

First, use tar with the t option to check the contents of the archive. If the first entry is a directory, then, when you extract the archive, that directory is created and the extracted files are placed in it. If the first entry is not a directory, you should first create one and then copy the archive file to it. Then, extract the archive within that directory. If no directory exists as the first entry, files are extracted to the current directory. You must create a directory yourself to hold these files.

```
# tar tvf htdig-3.1.6.tar
```

Now you are ready to extract the files from the tar archive. You use tar with the x option to extract files, the v option to display the pathnames of files as they are extracted, and the f option, followed by the name of the archive file:

```
# tar xvf htdig-3.1.6.tar
```

The tar utility provides decompression options you can use to have tar first decompress a file for you, invoking the specified decompression utility. The z option automatically invokes gunzip to unpack a .gz file, and the j option unpacks a .bz2 file. Use the Z option for .Z files. For example, to combine the decompressing and unpacking operation for a tar.gz file into one tar command, insert a z option to the option list, xzvf. The next example shows how you can combine decompression and extraction in one step:

```
# tar xzvf htdig-3.1.6.tar.gz
```

The extraction process creates a subdirectory consisting of the name and release of the software. In the previous example, the extraction created a subdirectory called `htdig-3.1.6`. You can change to this subdirectory and examine its files, such as the README and INSTALL files.

```
# cd htdig-3.1.6
```

Installation of your software may differ for each package. Instructions are usually provided along with an installation program. Be sure to consult the README and INSTALL files, if included. See the following section on compiling software for information on how to create and install the application on your system.

Compiling Software

Some software may be in the form of source code that you need to compile before you can install it. This is particularly true of programs designed for cross-platform implementations. Programs designed to run on various Unix systems, such as Sun, as well as on Linux, may be distributed as source code that is downloaded and compiled in those different systems. Compiling such software has been greatly simplified in recent years by the use of configuration scripts that automatically detect a given system's hardware and software configuration which then allows you to compile the program accordingly. For example, the name of the C compiler on a system could be gcc or cc. Configuration scripts detect which is present and select it for use in the program compilation.

A configure script works by generating a customized Makefile, designed for that particular system. A Makefile contains detailed commands to compile a program, including any preprocessing, links to required libraries, and the compilation of program components in their proper order. Many Makefiles for complex applications may have to access several software subdirectories, each with separate components to compile. The use of configure and Makefile scripts vastly automates the compile process, reducing the procedure to a few simple steps.

First, change to the directory where the software's source code has been extracted:

```
# cd /usr/local/src/cdrchive-1.2.2
```

Before you compile software, read the README or INSTALL files included with it. These give you detailed instructions on how to compile and install this particular program.

Most software can be compiled and installed in three simple steps. The first step is the ./configure command that generates your customized Makefile. The second step is the make command, which uses the Makefile in your working directory—in this case, the Makefile you just generated with the ./configure command—and uses it to compile your software. The final step also uses the make command, but this time with the install option. The Makefile generated by the ./configure command also contains instructions for installing the software on your system. Using the install option runs just those installation commands. To perform the installation, you have to be logged in as the root user, giving you the ability to add software files to system directories, as needed. If the software uses configuration scripts, compiling and installing usually involves only the following three simple commands:

```
# ./configure
# make
# make install
```

In the previous example, the ./configure command performs configuration detection. The make command performs the actual compiling, using a makefile script generated by the ./configure operation. The make install command installs the program on your system, placing the executable program in a directory, such as /usr/local/bin, and any configuration files in /etc. Any shared libraries it created may go into /usr/local/lib.

Once you have compiled and installed your application, and you have checked that it is working properly, you can remove the source code directory that was created when you extracted the software. You can keep the archive file (`tar`) in case you need to extract the software again. Use `rm` with the `-rf` options so all subdirectories will be deleted and you do not have to confirm each deletion:

```
# rm -rf cdrchive.1.2.2
```

TIP *Be sure to remember to place the period and slash before the* `configure` *command.* ./ *references a command in the current working directory, rather than another Linux command.*

configure Command Options

Certain software may have specific options set up for the `./configure` operation. To find out what these are, you use the `./configure` command with the `--help` option.

```
#  ./configure --help
```

A useful common option is the `-prefix` option, which lets you specify the install directory:

```
#  ./configure -prefix=/usr/bin
```

TIP *Some older X applications use* xmkmf *directly instead of a configure script to generate the needed Makefile. In this case, enter the command* xmkmf *in place of* ./configure. *Be sure to consult the* INSTALL *and* README *files for the software.*

Development Libraries

If you are compiling an X, Gnome, or KDE-based program, be sure their development libraries have been installed. For X applications, be sure the `xmkmf` program is also installed. If you chose a standard install when you installed your distribution system, these most likely were not installed. For distributions using RPM packages, these come in the form of a set of development RPM packages, usually with the word "development" or "develop" in their names. You need to install them using either `rpm` or redhat-config-packages. Gnome, in particular, has an extensive set of RPM packages for development libraries. Many X applications need special shared libraries. For example, some applications may need the `xforms` library or the `qt` library. Some of these you may need to obtain from online sites.

Shared and Static Libraries

Libraries can be either static, shared, or dynamic. A *static* library is one whose code is incorporated into the program when it is compiled. A *shared* library, however, has its code loaded for access whenever the program is run. When compiled, such a program simply notes the libraries it needs. Then, when the program is run, that library is loaded and the program can access its functions. A *dynamic* library is a variation on a shared library. Like a shared library, it can be loaded when the program is run. However, it does not actually load until instructions in the program tell it to. It can also be unloaded as the program runs, and another library could be loaded in its place. Shared and dynamic libraries make for much smaller code. Instead of a program including the library as part of its executable file, it only needs a reference to it.

Libraries made available on your system reside in the `/usr/lib` and `/lib` directories. The names of these libraries always begin with the prefix `lib` followed by the library name and a suffix. The suffix differs, depending on whether it is a static or shared library. A shared library has the extension `.so` followed by major and minor version numbers. A static library simply has a `.a` extension. A further distinction is made for shared libraries in the old `a.out` format. These have the extension `.sa`. The syntax for the library name is the following:

```
libname.so.major.minor
```

```
libname.a
```

The *name* can be any string, and it uniquely identifies a library. It can be a word, a few characters, or even a single letter. The name of the shared math library is `libm.so.5`, where the math library is uniquely identified by the letter `m` and the major version is 5. `libm.a` is the static math library. The name of the X Window library is `libX11.so.6`, where the X Window library is uniquely identified with the letters X11 and its major version is 6.

Most shared libraries are found in the /usr/lib and /lib directories. These directories are always searched first. Some shared libraries are located in special directories of their own. A listing of these is placed in the /etc/ld.conf configuration file. These directories will also be searched for a given library. By default, Linux first looks for shared libraries, then static ones. Whenever a shared library is updated or a new one installed, you need to run the ldconfig command to update its entries in the /etc/ld.conf file as well as links to it (if you install from an RPM package, this is usually done for you).

Makefile File

If no configure script exists and the program does not use xmkmf, you may have to enter the software's Makefile file directly. Be sure to check the documentation for such software to see if any changes must be made to the Makefile. Only a few changes may be necessary, but more detailed changes require an understanding of C programming and how make works with it. If you successfully configure the Makefile, you may only have to enter the make and make install commands. One possible problem is locating the development libraries for C and the X Window System. X libraries are in the /usr/X11R6/lib directory. Standard C libraries are located in the /usr/lib directory.

Command and Program Directories: PATH

Programs and commands are usually installed in several standard system directories, such as /bin, /usr/bin, /usr/X11R6/bin, or /usr/local/bin. Some packages place their commands in subdirectories, however, which they create within one of these standard directories or in an entirely separate directory. In such cases, you may be unable to run those commands because your system may be unable to locate them in the new subdirectory. Your system maintains a set of directories that search for commands each time you execute one. This set of directories is kept in a system variable called `PATH` that is created when you start your system. If a command is in a directory that is not in this list, your system will be unable to locate and run it. To use such commands, you first need to add the new directory to the set of directories in the `PATH` variable. Installation tools like RPM will automatically update the `PATH` with the appropriate directories for you.

On Red Hat systems, the PATH variable is originally assigned in the `/etc/rc.d/rc.sysinit` file, and further added to by different services that start up when the system boots. You could edit the `/etc/rc.d/rc.sysinit` file directly, but you should be very careful not to change anything else. A safer approach is to add a `PATH` definition in the `/etc/profile` file.

/etc/profile

To make an application available to all users, you can add the software's directory to the path entry in the `/etc/profile` script. The `/etc/profile` script is a system script executed for each user when the user logs in. Carefully edit the `/etc/profile` file using a text editor, such as kedit, gedit, emacs, or vi (you may want to make a backup copy first with the `cp` command). You add a line that begins with `PATH`, followed by an = sign, and the term `$PATH`, followed by a colon, and then the directory to be added. The $ before `PATH` extracts the path name from the `PATH` variable. If you add more than one directory, be sure a colon separates them. You should also have a colon at the end. For example, if you install the Java 2 SDK, the Java commands are installed in a subdirectory called `j2sdk-1.3.0/bin` in the `/usr/local` directory. The full pathname for this directory is `/usr/local/j2sdk-1.3.0/bin`. You need to add this directory to the list of directories assigned to `PATH` in the `/etc/profile` file. The following example shows the `PATH` variable with its list of directories and the `/usr/local/j2sdk-1.3.0/bin` directory added. Notice the $ before `PATH` after the = sign, PATH=$PATH

```
PATH=$PATH:/usr/local/j2sdk-1.3.0/bin
```

.bash_profile

Individual users can customize their PATH variables by placing a PATH assignment in either their .bashrc or .bash_profile files. In this way, users can access commands and programs they create or install for their own use in their own user directories (see Chapter 2 for more details). On Red Hat, user .bash_profile files already contain the following PATH definition. Notice the use of $PATH, which keeps all the directories already added to the PATH in previous startup scripts like /etc/profile and /etc/rc.d/rc.sysinit.

```
PATH=$PATH:$HOME/bin
```

The following entry in the .bash_profile file adds a user's newbin directory to the PATH variable. Notice both the colon placed before the new directory and the use of the $HOME variable to specify the pathname for the user's home directory.

```
PATH=$PATH:$HOME/bin/:$HOME/newbin
```

In the .bash_profile file for the root user, the PATH definition also includes sbin directories. The sbin directories hold system administration programs that the root user would need to have access to. The root user PATH is shown here:

```
PATH=/usr/local/sbin:/usr/sbin:/sbin:$PATH:$HOME/bin
```

The Concurrent Versions System: CVS

The Concurrent Versions System (CVS) is a software development method that allows developers from remote locations to work on software stored on a central server. CVS allows several developers to work on a file at the same time. This means that CVS supports parallel development, so programmers around the world can work on the same task at the same time through a simple Internet connection. It has become popular among Linux developers as a means of creating software using the Internet. CVS is also the source for the most up-to-date versions for different software. Ongoing projects like KDE and Gnome use CVS servers to post the most recent versions of their desktop applications, primarily because it is easy to use for program development over the Internet. The sourceforge.net site provides a CVS repository for many ongoing Linux Projects. Many CVS sites now support ViewsCVS (an enhanced version of WebCVS), a web browser front end to a CVS repository that lets you browse and select software versions easily. You can find out more about CVS from www.cvshome.org.

TIP *You can also use CVS GUI clients on Gnome and KDE, along with ViewCVS, to manage your CVS repositories or access those on the Internet. For Gnome, you can use Pharmacy, and for KDE, you can use Cervisia or LinCVS.*

Using a CVS repository for software development involves procedures for accessing a software version, making your changes locally on your system, and then uploading your changed version back to the CVS repository. In effect, you check out software, make your changes in such a way that they are carefully recorded, and then check your version back into the repository. CVS was originally developed as a front end to the older Revision Control System (RCS), and shares many of the same commands.

Checking in and Checking out

CVS uses check-in and check-out procedures for projects. To use CVS, you first create a directory to hold your project files, and then use the import option to install your project files there. In the following example, the /home/projects directory is designated as the CVS repository directory. You use the command cvs with the -d option, and the name of the directory along with the init option.

```
$ cvs -d /home/projects init
```

You can set the CVSROOT shell variable to the path of the repository directory, and then export the variable. The cvs command, whenever it is executed, will automatically check this variable for the location of the repository.

```
CVSROOT=/home/projects
export CVSROOT
```

Importing

To install files for an already existing project in the repository directory, you use the `import` option. You can install the files to a subdirectory in the repository. A CVS repository can support multiple projects, each in its own subdirectory. You also need to provide arguments specifying the supplier and the release. First, you change to the directory that holds your project files, then you issue the `cvs` command with the `import` option. The following example imports all the files in the current working directory—in this case, `myproject-so-far`—to the `myproject` directory in the CVS repository (`/home/projects/myproject`). The supplier is `richp`, and the release is the first release, as indicated by the `start` argument. If the current directory holds the file `main.c`, the `main.c` file will be installed in the `/home/projects/myproject` directory along with any other files in the current directory.

```
$ cd myproject-so-far
$ cvs import myproject richp start
```

Logging Messages

Whenever you install projects, or add, change, or remove files in a CVS repository, you need to supply a log message describing the action. CVS automatically opens your standard editor to let you enter the description. Alternatively, you can use the `-m` option to include the log message in the command. Be sure to quote the message string. You would use the editor for multiline detailed messages, and the `-m` option for short one-line messages. The following example includes a log message with the `import` command:

```
$ cvs import -m "Install myproject into CVS" myproject richp start
```

Committing Changes

To work on a file, you must first retrieve it from the repository using the check-out option, `co`. You then work on it in a project directory that will be created as a subdirectory in your local directory. When you are ready to check the file back into the repository, you use the `commit` option (ci). The following example extracts the `main.c` file from the CVS repository for `myproject`:

```
$ cvs co myproject/main.c
$ cd myproject
```

You then change to the subdirectory called `myproject` that has been created in the current working directory. There, you will find the extracted version of `main.c`. You can then edit and change `main.c`. To check it back into the CVS repository, use the `commit` option.

```
$ cvs commit -m "Modified main.c" main.c
```

To see the changes, use the `diff` option. The `rdiff` option lets you see any changes to the entire release.

```
$ cvs diff
```

To check out the entire project, you use the project name. All the files for the project will be extracted to a subdirectory with that project name.

```
$ cvs co myproject
$ cd myproject
```

You can then work on any of the files and then check in the entire project when you are finished.

```
$ cvs commit -m "Major changes to myproject" myproject
```

Updating, Adding, and Removing CVS Files

As you work on a project with numerous files, you can use the update option, `up`, to check out just the ones you need, selecting the ones that have been changed since your last access.

```
$ cvs up myproject
```

To add a new file, you use the `add` option, and to delete
a file, you use the `remove` option The file must be deleted
from its working directory before you can use remove option.
You effect the changes with the `commit` option.

```
$ cvs add mynewfile
$ cvs commit -m "Added mynefile" myproject
```

To create and extract new releases, you use the `-r` options
and specify the release number, such as 1.2 or 3.5. You
create a new version with the `commit` command. The
following example creates a new version, 1.2:

```
$ cvs commit -m "Created release 1.2" -r 1.2 myproject
```

You can then check out that release with the `co` option:

```
$ cvs co -r 1.2 myproject
```

Internet CVS Repositories

To access a repository on the Internet, you simply specify
as the repository root the Internet site and the remote
directory for that repository. If you are dealing with only
one CVS repository at a time, you can do this by assigning
the repository to the `CVSROOT` shell variable. The format
for specifying the remote repository is as follows:

`:method:user@hostname:/path/to/repository`

The following example assigns the repository for KDE to
the CVSROOT variable:

```
export CVSROOT=:pserver:anonymous@anoncvs.kde.org:/home/kde
```

If you want to operate several sessions at once to different
CVS repositories, use the cvs command with the `-d` option.

```
$ cvs -d :pserver:anonymous@anoncvs.kde.org:/home/kde
```

To access the remote repository, you first log in with the
`login` option:

```
$ cvs login
```

Then, use the standard `co` (check-out) and `commit`
options to check out and check in projects. When doing

Commands	Description
`commit,ci`	Updates a CVS file, creating new versions. `-r`*version* Allows you to specify the release and version number you want to begin with when creating a new version.
`checkout,co`	The `checkout` command retrieves a version of a CVS file. `-D` *date* Check out revisions for a specific date. `-d` *dir* Check out to a specified directory. `-r` *version* Check out a specified version.
`import`	Import files to CVS repository.
`login`	Log into a remote CVS repository.
`logout`	Log out from a remote CVS repository.
`rdiff`	Show the differences between releases.
`remove`	Remove an entry from a repository.
`update, up`	Update from a repository.
`init`	Create a CVS repository.
`admin`	Administer files in the repository. `-l`*release* Lock a revision. `-u`*release* Unlock a revision. `-o`*release* Delete revision from the repository.

Table 3-7.   CVS Commands and Options

so, you may want to use the compression options such as `-z4` to speed transmission time.

TIP *If you want to set up a repository on your own system that is accessible over the Internet, you need to install and configure the CVS server.*

Packaging Your Software with RPM

Many research and corporate environments develop their own customized software for distribution within their organization. Sometimes software packages are downloaded and then customized for use in a particular organization. To more easily install such customized software, administrators pack the programs into their own

RPM packages. In such packages, you can include your own versions of configuration files, documentation, and modified source and binaries. RPM automatically installs software on a system in the designated directories, along with any documentation, libraries, or support programs.

The package creation process is designed to take the program through several stages, starting with unpacking it from an archive, and then compiling its source code, and, finally, generating the RPM package. You can skip any of these stages, up to the last one. If your software is already unpacked, you can start with compiling it. If your software is compiled, you can start with installation. If it is already installed, you can go directly to creating the RPM package.

The build processes for RPM used to be included with the `rpm` command. They are now incorporated into a separate tool called `rpmb`. This tool, along with supporting libraries and documentation, is located in the *rpm-build* package. Be sure this package is installed before you try to build RPM packages. You can still run the `rpm` command with the build options, but these are simply aliases for corresponding `rpmb` commands.

The Build Components

RPM makes use of three components to build packages: the build tree, the `rpmrc` configuration files, and an `rpm` spec script. The build tree is a set of special instructions used to carry out the different stages of the packaging process. The `rpm` spec script contains instructions for creating the package, as well as the list of files to be placed in it. The `rpmrc` files are used to set configuration features for RPM. The `/usr/lib/rpm/rpmrc` file holds the default options for your system and is always read. You can also set up a `/etc/rpmrc` file for global options you want to set for your system. Entries here override those in the `/usr/lib/rpm/rpmrc` file. You can also set up a local `.rpmrc` file in your home directory, which overrides both of these. To obtain a listing of the `/usr/lib/rpm/rpmrc` file, enter

```
# rpm --showrc
```

Build Tree Directories

The build tree directories, listed in Table 3-8, are used to hold the different files generated at each stage of the packaging process. The SOURCES directory holds the compressed archive. The BUILD directory holds the source code unpacked from that archive. The RPMS directory is where the RPM package containing the executable binary program is placed, and SRPMS is where the RPM package containing the source code is placed. If you are creating a package from software stored in a compressed archive, such as a tar.gz file, you first must copy that file to the build tree's SOURCES directory.

The following example copies the compressed archive for the bookrec software to the SOURCES directory:

```
# cp bookrec-1.0.tar.gz  /usr/src/redhat/SOURCES
```

The topdir: entry in an rpmrc file, like /usr/lib/rpm/rpmrc, specifies the location of the build tree directories. In this file, you can find an entry for topdir:. Currently, the Red Hat system has already set this directory to /usr/src/redhat. You can find the SOURCES, BUILD, RPMS, and SRPMS directories here. You can specify a different directory for these subdirectories by placing the entry for topdir: in the /etc/rpmrc file.

```
topdir: /usr/src/redhat
```

Directory Name	Description
BUILD	The directory where RPM does all its building.
SOURCES	The directory where you should put your original source archive files and your patches.
SPECS	The directory where all spec files should go.
RPMS	The directory where RPM puts all binary RPMs when built.
SRPMS	The directory where all source RPMs are put.

Table 3-8. Build Tree Directories

A sample of the default values set by `/usr/lib/rpm/rpmrc`
is shown here:

```
# Default values, often overridden in /etc/rpmrc
dbpath:        /var/lib/rpm
topdir:        /usr/src/redhat
tmppath:       /var/tmp
cpiobin:       cpio
defaultdocdir:    /usr/doc
```

By default, RPM is designed to work with source code
placed in a directory consisting of its name and a release
number, separated by a hyphen. For example, a program
with the name `bookrec` and release 1.0 should have its
source-code files in a directory called `bookrec-1.0`. If
RPM needs to compile the software, it expects to find the
source code in that directory within the `BUILD` directory,
`BUILD/bookrec-1.0`. The same name and release number
also must be specified in the spec file.

RPM Spec File

To create a package, first create an `rpm` spec file for it.
The `rpm` spec file specifies the files to be included, any
actions to build the software, and information about the
package. The spec file is designed to take the program
through several stages, starting with unpacking it from
an archive, compiling its source code, and generating the
RPM package. In the spec file are segments for the different
stages, and special RPM macros that perform actions at
these stages. These are listed in Table 3-9.

File Segment or Macro	Description
%description	A detailed description of the software.
%prep	The prep stage for archives and patches.
%setup	The prep macro for unpacking archives. A -n *name* option resets the name of the build directory.
%patch	The prep macro for updating patches.
%build	The build stage for compiling software.
%install	The install stage for installing software.

Table 3-9. RPM File Segments and Macros

File Segment or Macro	Description
`%files`	The files stage that lists the files to be included in the package. A `-f` `filename` option specifies a file that contains a list of files to be included in the package.
`%config file-list`	A file macro that lists configuration files to be placed in the `/etc` directory.
`%doc file-list`	A file macro that lists documentation files to be placed in the `/usr/doc` directory with the subdirectory of the name-version-release.
`%dir directory-list`	The specification of a directory to be included as being owned by a package. (A directory in a file list refers to all files in it, not only the directory.)
`%pre`	A macro to do preinstall scripts.
`%preun`	A macro to do preuninstall scripts.
`%post`	A macro to do postinstall scripts.
`%postun`	A macro to do postuninstall scripts.

Table 3-9. RPM File Segments and Macros *(continued)*

A spec file is divided into five basic segments: header, prep, build, install, and files. These segments are separated in the file by empty lines. The header segment contains several lines of information, each preceded by a tag and a semicolon. For example, the following tag is used for a short description of the software:

```
Summary: bookrec program to manage book records
```

The name, version, and release tags are used to build the name of the RPM package. The name, version, and release are separated with hyphens. For example, the name `bookrec` with the `version 1.0` and `release 2` has the following name:

```
bookrec-1.0-2
```

The Group entry is a list of categories for the software and is used by the RPM package management utilities like redhat-config-packages to place the software in the correct category folder. The Source entry is the compressed archive where the software is stored on your system. Description is a detailed description of the software.

Following the header are the three stages for creating and installing the software on your system, indicated by the `%prep`, `%build`, and `%install` rpm macros. You can skip any of these stages, say, if the software is already installed. You can also leave any of them out of the spec file or comment them out with a preceding #. The spec file is capable of taking a compressed archive, unpacking it, compiling the source code files, and then installing the program on your system. Then, the installed files can be used to create the RPM package.

%prep Macro

The `%prep` macro begins the prep segment of the spec file. The prep segment's task is to generate the software's source code. This usually means unpacking archives, but it may also have to update the software with patches. The tasks themselves can be performed by shell scripts you write. Special macros can also automatically perform these tasks. The `%setup` macro can decompress and unpack an archive in the SOURCES directory, placing the source code files in the BUILD directory. The `%patch` macro applies any patches.

%build and %install Macros

The `%build` segment contains the instructions for compiling the software. Usually, this is a simple `make` command, depending on the complexity of your program. The `%install` segment contains the instructions for installing the program. You can use simple shell commands to copy the files or, as in the `bookspec` example that follows, the `install` command that installs files on systems. This could also be the `make install` command, if your makefile has the commands to install your program.

```
%build
make RPM_OPT_FLAGS="$RPM_OPT_FLAGS"

%install
install -s -m 755 -o 0 -g 0 bookrec /usr/bin/bookrec
install -m 644 -o 0 -g 0 bookrec.1 /usr/man/man1
```

%files, %config, and %doc Macros

The %files segment contains the list of files you want placed in the RPM package. Following the %files macro, you list the different files, including their full pathnames. The macro %config can be used to list configuration files. Any files listed here are placed in the /etc directory. The %doc macro is used for documentation, such as README files. These are placed in the /usr/doc directory under a subdirectory consisting of the software's name, version, and release number. In the bookspec example shown here, the readme file is placed in the /usr/doc/bookrec-1·.0-2 directory:

```
 Summary: bookrec program to manage book records
Name: bookrec
Version: 1.0
Release: 2
Copyright: GPL
Group: Applications/Database
Source: /root/rpmc/bookrec-1.0.tar.gz
%description
This program manages book records by title, providing
price information

%prep
%setup

%build
make RPM_OPT_FLAGS="$RPM_OPT_FLAGS"

%install
install -s -m 755 -o 0 -g 0 bookrec /usr/bin/bookrec
install -m 644 -o 0 -g 0 bookrec.1 /usr/man/man1

%files
%doc README

/usr/bin/bookrec
/usr/man/man1/bookrec.1
```

RPM Build Operation

To create an RPM software package, you use the rpm build options (listed in Table 3-10) with the rmpb command, followed by the name of a spec file. The -bl option checks

Option	Description
-ba	Create both the executable binary and source code packages. Perform all stages in the spec file: prep, build, install, and create the packages.
-bb	Create only the executable binary package. Perform all stages in the spec file: prep, build, install, and create the package.
-bp	Run only the prep stage from the spec file (%prep).
-bl	Do a "list check." The %files section from the spec file is macro-expanded, and checks are made to ensure the files exist.
-bc	Do both the prep and build stages, unpacking and compiling the software (%prep and %build).
-bi	Do the prep, build, and install stages, unpacking, compiling, and installing the software (%prep, %build, and %install).
--short-circuit	Skip to specified stage, not executing any previous stages. Only valid with -bc and -bi.
--clean	Remove the build tree after the packages are made.
--test	Do not execute any build stages. Used to test spec files.
--recompile source_package_file	RPM installs the source code package and performs a prep, compile, and install.
--rebuild source_package_file	RPM first installs the named source package and does a prep, compile, and install, and then rebuilds a new binary package.
--showrc	List the configuration variables for the /usr/lib/rpm/rpmrc file.

Table 3-10. The RPM rmpd Build Options

to see if all the files used for the software are present. The -bb option builds only the binary package, whereas -ba builds both binary and source packages. These options expect to find the compressed archive for the software in the build tree's SOURCES directory. The -ba and -bb options execute every stage specified in the rpm spec script, starting from the prep stage, to unpacking an archive, and then compiling the program, followed by installation on the system, and then creation of the package. The completed RPM package for executable binaries is placed in a subdirectory of the build tree's RPMS directory. This subdirectory has a name representing the current platform. For a PC, this is i386, and the package is placed in the RPMS/i386 subdirectory. The source code package is placed directly in the SRPMS directory.

The following program generates both a binary and a software package, placing them in the build tree's RPMS/i386 and SRPMS directories. The name of the spec file in this example is bookspec.

```
# rpmb -ba bookspec
```

An executable binary package has a name consisting of the software name, the version number, the release number, the platform name (i386), and the term "rpm." The name, version, and release are separated by hyphens, whereas the release, platform name, and the rpm term are separated by periods. The name of the binary package generated by the previous example, using the bookspec spec script, generates the following name:

```
bookrec-1.0-2.i386.rpm
```

The source code package has the same name, but with the term "src" in place of the platform name:

```
bookrec-1.0-2.src.rpm
```

TIP *You can also use the* autoconf *tool along with the* automake *tool to build your own source packages, installable with the* configure *command.*

Chapter 4

Filesystem Hierarchy Standard

Linux organizes its files and directories into one overall interconnected tree, beginning from the root directory and extending down to system and user directories. The organization and layout for the system directories is determined by the Filesystem Hierarchy Standard (FHS). The FHS provides a standardized layout that all Linux distributions should follow in setting up their system directories. For example, there must be an /etc directory to hold configuration files and a /dev directory for device files. You can find out more about FHS, including the official documentation, at www.pathname.com/fhs. Linux distributions, developers, and administrators all follow the FHS to provide a consistent organization to the Linux file system.

Linux uses a number of specifically named directories for specialized administration tasks. All these directories are at the very top level of your main Linux file system, the file system root directory represented by a single slash, /. For example, the /dev directory holds device files, and the /home directory holds the user home directories and all their user files. You only have access to these directories and files as the system administrator (though users normally have read-only access). You need to log in as the root user, placing you in a special root user administrative directory called /root. From here, you can access any directory on the Linux file system, both administrative and user.

Root Directory: /

The subdirectories held in the root directory, /, are listed in Table 4-1, along with other useful subdirectories. Directories that you may commonly access as an administrator are the /etc directory that holds configuration files, the /dev directory that holds device files, and the /var directory that holds server data files for DNS, Web, mail, and FTP servers, along with system logs and

Directory	Function
/	Begins the file system structure—called the root.
/boot	Holds the kernel image files and associated boot information and files.
/home	Contains users' home directories.
/sbin	Holds administration-level commands and any commands used by the root user.
/dev	Holds file interfaces for devices such as the terminal and printer.
/etc	Holds system configuration files and any other system files.
/etc/opt	Holds system configuration files for applications in /opt.
/etc/X11	Holds system configuration files for the X Window System and its applications.
/bin	Holds the essential user commands and utility programs.
/lib	Holds essential shared libraries and kernel modules.
/lib/modules	Holds the kernel modules.
/mnt	Used to hold directories for mounting file systems like CD-ROMs or floppy disks that are mounted only temporarily.
/opt	Holds added software applications (for example, KDE on some distributions).

Table 4-1. Linux File System Directories

Directory	Function
/proc	Process directory, a memory-resident directory containing files used to provide information about the system.
/tmp	Holds temporary files.
/usr	Holds those files and commands used by the system; this directory breaks down into several subdirectories.
/var	Holds files that vary, such as mailbox, Web, and FTP files.

Table 4-1. Linux File System Directories *(continued)*

scheduled tasks. For managing different versions of the kernel, you may need to access the /boot and /lib/modules directories as well as /usr/src/linux. The /boot directory holds the kernel image files for any new kernels you install, and the /lib/modules directory hold modules for your different kernels. Table 4-1 lists the root subdirectories.

System Directories

Your Linux directory tree contains certain directories whose files are used for different system functions (see Table 1-6). For basic system administration, you should be familiar with the system program directories where applications are kept, the system configuration directory (/etc) where most configuration files are placed, and the system log directory (/var/log) that holds the system logs, recording activity on your system. Both are covered in detail in Chapter 1. Table 4-2 lists the system directories.

Directories	Description
/bin	System-related programs
/sbin	System programs for specialized tasks
/lib	System libraries

Table 4-2. System Directories

Directories	Description
/etc	Configuration files for system and network services and applications
/home	The location of user home directories and server data directories, such as Web and FTP site files
/mnt	The location where CD-ROM and floppy disk files systems are mounted (Chapter 5)
/var	The location of system directories whose files continually change, such as logs, printer spool files, and lock files (Chapter 5)
/usr	User-related programs and files. Includes several key subdirectories, such as /usr/bin, /usr/X11, and /usr/share/doc
/usr/bin	Programs for users
/dev	Device files (Chapter 7)
/usr/X11	X Window System configuration files
/usr/share	Shared files
/usr/share/doc	Documentation for applications
/tmp	Directory for system temporary files

Table 4-2. System Directories *(continued)*

Program Directories

Directories with bin in the name are used to hold programs. The /bin directory holds basic user programs, such as login, shells (bash, tcsh, and zsh), and file commands (cp, mv, rm, ln, and so on). The /sbin directory holds specialized system programs for such tasks as file system management (fsck, fdisk, mkfs) and system operations like shutdown and startup (init). The /usr/bin directory holds program files designed for user tasks. The /usr/sbin directory holds user-related system operations, such as useradd for adding new users. The /lib directory holds all the libraries your system makes use of, including the main Linux library, libc, and subdirectories such as modules, which holds all the current kernel modules.

Configuration Directories and Files

When you configure different elements of your system, like user accounts, applications, servers, or network connections, you make use of configurations files kept in certain system directories. On Red Hat, configuration files are placed in the `/etc` directory, with more specific device and service configuration located in the `/etc/sysconfig` directory (see Chapter 1 for more details).

4

/usr Directory

The `/usr` directory contains a multitude of important subdirectories used to support users, providing applications, libraries, and documentation. `/usr/bin` holds numerous user-accessible applications and utilities. `/usr/sbin` hold user-accessible administrative utilities. The `/usr/share` directory holds architecture-independent data that includes an extensive number of subdirectories, including those for documentation, such as `man`, `info`, and `doc` files. Table 4-3 lists the subdirectories of the `/usr` directory.

Directory	Description
`/usr/bin`	Holds most user commands and utility programs.
`/usr/sbin`	Holds administrative applications.
`/usr/lib`	Holds libraries for applications, programming languages, desktops, and so on.
`/usr/games`	Holds games and educational programs.
`/usr/include`	Holds C programming language header files (`.h`).
`/usr/doc`	Holds Linux documentation.
`/usr/local`	Holds locally installed software.
`/usr/share`	Holds architecture independent-data such as documentation.

Table 4-3. /usr Directories

Directory	Description
/usr/src	Holds source code, including the kernel source codes.
/usr/X11R6	Holds X Window System–based applications and libraries.

Table 4-3. /usr Directories *(continued)*

/mnt Directory

The /mnt directory is usually used for mount points for your CD-ROM, DVD, floppy, Zip drives, or other mounted file systems such as Windows partitions. These are file systems you may be changing frequently, unlike partitions on fixed disks. Red Hat Linux installs by default a floppy and CD-ROMs subdirectory for mounting floppies and CD-ROMs, /mnt/floppy and /mnt/cdrom. Additional drives have a number attached to their name, as in /mnt/cdrom1 for a second CD-ROM drive. You can also create directories for any partitions you want to mount, such as /mnt/windows for a Windows partition.

/home Directory

The /home directory holds user home directories. When a user account is set up, a home directory is set up here for that account, usually with the same name as the user. As the system administrator, you can access any user's home directory, giving you control over their files.

/var Directory

The /var directory holds subdirectories for tasks whose files change frequently, such as lock files, log files, Web server files, or printer spool files. For example, the /var directory holds server data directories, such as /var/www for the Apache Web server Web site files or /var/ftp for your FTP site files, as well as `/var/named` for the DNS server. The `/tmp` directory is simply a directory to hold any temporary files programs may need to perform a particular task.

The `/var` directories are designed to hold data that changes with the normal operation of the Linux system. For example, spool files for documents that you are printing are kept here. A spool file is created as a temporary printing file and is removed after printing. Other files, like system log files, are changed constantly. Table 4-4 lists the subdirectories of the `/var` directory.

Directory	Description
/var/account	Processes accounting logs.
/var/cache	Holds application cache data for `man` pages, Web proxy data, fonts, or application-specific data.
/var/crash	Holds system crash dumps.
/var/games	Holds varying games data.
/var/lib	Holds state information for particular applications.
/var/local	Used for data that changes for programs installed in `/usr/local`.
/var/lock	Holds lock files that indicate when a particular program or file is in use.
/var/log	Holds log files such as `/var/log/messages` that contain all kernel and system program messages.
/var/mail	Holds user mailbox files.
/var/opt	Holds variable data for applications installed in `/opt`.
/var/run	Holds information about system's running processes.
/var/spool	Holds application's spool data such as that for mail, news, and printer queues, as well as `cron` and `at` jobs.
/var/tmp	Holds temporary files that should be preserved between system reboots.

Table 4-4. /var Subdirectories

Directory	Description
/var/yp	Holds Network Information Service (NIS) data files.
/var/www	Holds Web server Web site files.
/var/ftp	Holds FTP server FTP files.
/var/named	Holds DNS server domain configuration files.

Table 4-4. /var Subdirectories *(continued)*

/proc File System

The /proc file system is a special file system that is generated in system memory. It does not exist on any disk. /proc contains files that provide important information about the state of your system. For example, /proc/cpuinfo holds information about your computer's CPU processor. /proc/devices lists those devices currently configured to run with your kernel. /proc/filesystems lists the file systems. /proc files are really interfaces to the kernel, obtaining information from the kernel about your system (see Chapter 8 for more details). Table 4-5 lists the /proc subdirectories and files.

Files	Description
/proc/num	There is a directory for each process labeled by its number. /proc/1 is the directory for process 1.
/proc/cpuinfo	Contains information about the CPU, such as its type, make, model, and performance.
/proc/devices	Lists the device drivers configured for the currently running kernel.
/proc/dma	Displays the DMA channels currently used.
/proc/filesystems	Lists file systems configured into the kernel.
/proc/interrupts	Displays the interrupts in use.

Table 4-5. /proc Subdirectories and Files

Files	Description
/proc/ioports	Shows the I/O ports in use.
/proc/kcore	Holds an image of the physical memory of the system.
/proc/kmsg	Contains messages generated by the kernel.
/proc/ksyms	Holds the symbol table for the kernel.
/proc/loadavg	Lists the system load average.
/proc/meminfo	Displays memory usage.
/proc/modules	Lists the kernel modules currently loaded.
/proc/net	Lists status information about network protocols.
/proc/stat	Contains system operating statistics, such as page fault occurrences.
/proc/uptime	Displays the time the system has been up.
/proc/version	Displays the kernel version.

Table 4-5. /proc Subdirectories and Files *(continued)*

4

TIP You can use redhat-config-proc, the Kernel Tuning tool (Extras System Tools menu), to set proc file values you are allowed to change, like the maximum number of files, or to turn on IP forwarding.

Device Files: /dev

To mount a file system, you have to specify its device name. The interfaces to devices that may be attached to your system are provided by special files known as *device files*. The names of these device files are the device names. Device files are located in the /dev directories and usually have abbreviated names ending with the number of the device. For example, fd0 may reference the first floppy drive attached to your system. The prefix sd references SCSI hard drives, so sda2 would reference the second partition on the first SCSI hard drive. In most cases, you can use the `man` command with a prefix to obtain more detailed information about this kind of device. For example, `man sd` displays the Man pages for SCSI devices. A complete listing of all device names can be found in the `devices` file located in the `linux/doc/device-list` directory at the www.kernel.org Web site, and in the `devices.txt` file in the `/etc/usr/linux-2.4/ Documentation` directory on your Red Hat system. Table 4-6 lists several of the commonly used device names.

Device Name	Description
hd	IDE hard drives; 1–4 are primary partitions; 5 and up are logical partitions
sd	SCSI hard drives
scd	SCSI CD-ROM drives
fd	Floppy disks
st	SCSI tape drives
nst	SCSI tape drives, no rewind
ht	IDE tape drives
tty	Terminals
lp	Printer ports
pty	Pseudoterminals (used for remote logins)
js	Analog joysticks
midi	Midi ports
ttyS	Serial ports
md	RAID devices
rd/c*n*d*n*	The directory that holds RAID devices is rd; c*n* is the RAID controller and d*n* is the RAID disk for that controller
cdrom	Link to your CD-ROM device file
cdwriter	Link to your CD-R or CD-RW device file
modem	Link to your modem device file
floppy	Link to your floppy device file
tape	Link to your tape device file
scanner	Link to your scanner device file

Table 4-6. Device Name Prefixes

Floppy Devices

The device name for your floppy drive is `fd0`, and it is located in the directory `/dev`. `/dev/fd0` references your floppy drive. Notice the numeral `0` after `fd`. If you have more than one floppy drive, they are represented by `fd1`, `fd2`, and so on.

Hard Disk Devices

IDE hard drives use the prefix `hd`, whereas SCSI hard drives use the prefix `sd`. RAID devices, on the other hand, use the prefix `md`. The prefix for a hard disk is followed by a letter that labels the hard drive and a number for the partition. For example, `hda2` references the second partition on the first IDE hard drive, where the first hard drive is referenced with the letter `a`, as in `hda`. The device `sdb3` refers to the third partition on the second SCSI hard drive (`sdb`). RAID devices, however, are numbered from 0, like floppy drives. Device `md0` references the first RAID device, and `md1` references the second. On an IDE hard disk device, Linux supports up to four primary IDE hard disk partitions, numbered 1 through 4. You are allowed any number of logical partitions. To find the device name, you can use `df` to display your hard partitions or examine the `/etc/fstab` file.

CD-ROM Devices

The device name for your CD-ROM drive varies depending on the type of CD-ROM you have. The device name for an IDE CD-ROM has the same prefix as an IDE hard disk partition, `hd`, and is identified by a following letter that distinguishes it from other IDE devices. For example, an IDE CD-ROM connected to your secondary IDE port may have the name `hdc`. An IDE CD-ROM connected as a slave to the secondary port may have the name `hdd`. The actual name is determined when the CD-ROM is installed, as happened when you installed your Linux system. SCSI CD-ROM drives use a different nomenclature for their device names. They begin with `scd` for SCSI drive, and are followed by a distinguishing number. For example, the name of a SCSI CD-ROM could be `scd0` or `scd1`. The name of your CD-ROM was determined when you installed your system. You can find out what it is by examining the `/etc/fstab` file.

Chapter 5

File System Administration

Files reside on physical storage devices such as hard drives, CD-ROMs, or floppy disks. The files on each storage device are organized into a file system. The storage devices on your Linux system are presented as a collection of file systems that you can manage. When you want to add a new storage device, you will need to format it as a file system, and then attach it to your Linux file structure. Hard drives can be divided into separate storage devices called *partitions*, each of which would have its own file system. You can perform administrative tasks on your file systems, such as backing them up, attaching or detaching them from your file structure, formatting new devices or erasing old ones, and checking a file system for problems.

To access files on a device, you attach its file system to a specified directory. This is called *mounting* the file system. For example, to access files on a floppy disk, you first mount its file system to a particular directory. With Linux, you can mount a number of different types of file systems. You can even access a Windows hard drive partition or tape drive, as well as file systems on a remote server. Red Hat also configures CD-ROM and floppy media to be mounted automatically from Gnome or KDE.

Recently developed file systems for Linux now support *journaling*, which allows your system to recover from a crash or interruption easily. The ext3, ReiserFS, and JFS (IBM) file systems maintain a record of file and directory changes, called a *journal*, which can be used to recover files and directories in use when a system suddenly crashes due to unforeseen events such as power interruptions. Most distributions currently use the ext3 file system as their default, though you also have the option of using ReiserFS or JFS, an independently developed journaling system.

Your Linux system is capable of handling any number of storage devices that may be connected to it. You can configure your system to access multiple hard drives, partitions on a hard drive, CD-ROM disks, floppy disks, and even tapes. You can elect to attach these storage components manually or have them automatically mount when you boot. Automatic mounts are handled by configuring the /etc/fstab file. For example, the main partitions holding your Linux system programs are automatically mounted whenever you boot, whereas a floppy disk can be manually mounted when you put one in your floppy drive, though even these can also be automatically mounted.

File Systems

Although all the files in your Linux system are connected into one overall directory tree, parts of that tree may reside on different storage devices such as hard drives or CD-ROMs. Files on a particular storage device are organized into what is referred to as a *file system*. A file system is a formatted device, with its own tree of directories and files. Your Linux directory tree may encompass several file systems, each on different storage devices. On a hard drive with several partitions, you would have a file system for each partition. The files themselves are organized into one seamless tree of directories, beginning with the root directory. For example, if you attach a CD-ROM to your system, a pathname will lead directly from the root directory on your hard disk partition's file system to the files in the CD-ROM file system.

A file system has its files organized into its own directory tree. You can think of this as a *subtree* that must be attached to the main directory tree. The tree will remain separate from your system's directory tree until you specifically connect it. For example, a floppy disk with Linux files has its own tree of directories. You need to attach this subtree to the main tree on your hard drive partition. Until

they are attached, you cannot access the files on your
floppy disk.

Mounting File Systems

Attaching a file system on a storage device to your main
directory tree is called *mounting* the device. The file system
is mounted to an empty directory on the main directory
tree. You can then change to that directory and access
those files. If the directory does not yet exist, you will have
to create it. The directory in the file structure to which the
new file system is attached is referred to as the *mountpoint*.
For example, to access files on a CD-ROM, first you have
to mount the CD-ROM.

5

Mounting file systems can only be done as the root user.
This is a system administration task and cannot be
performed by a regular user. As the root user, you can,
however, make a particular device, like a CD-ROM,
user-mountable. In this way, any user could mount a
CD-ROM. You could do the same for a floppy drive.

TIP   *On Gnome, you can use the Disk Management
tool on the System Settings window and menu to mount
and unmount file systems, including floppy disks and
CD-ROMs. On KDE, you can use the KDiskFree utility
(Extra System Tools menu), which also lists your mountable
file as well as their disk usage.*

Even the file systems on your hard disk partition must be
explicitly mounted. When you install your Linux system
and create the Linux partition on your hard drive, however,
your system is automatically configured to mount your
main file system whenever it starts. When your system
shuts down, they are automatically unmounted. You have
the option of unmounting any file system, removing it
from the directory tree, and possibly replacing it with
another, as is the case when you replace a CD-ROM.

Once a file system is actually mounted, an entry for it is
made by the operating system in the **/etc/mstab** file. Here,
you will find listed all file systems currently mounted.

File System Information

The file systems on each storage device are formatted to take up a specified amount of space. For example, you may have formatted your hard drive partition to take up 3GB. Files installed or created on that file system take up part of the space, while the remainder is available for new files and directories. To find out how much space you have free on a file system, you can use the df command or, on Gnome, you can use either the Procman System Monitor or the KDE DiskFree utility (Extra System Tools menu). For the Procman System Monitor (System Tools menu), click the System Monitor tab to display a bar graph of the free space on your file system. KDE DiskFree displays a list of devices showing how much space is free on each partition, and the percentage used.

df

The df command reports file system disk space usage. It lists all your file systems by their device names, how much disk space they take up, and the percentage of the disk space used, as well as where they are mounted. With the -h option, it displays information in a more readable format, such as measuring disk space in megabytes instead of memory blocks. The df command is also a safe way to obtain a listing of all your partitions, instead of using fdisk (with fdisk, you could erase partitions). df only shows mounted partitions, however, whereas fdisk shows all partitions.

```
$ df
Filesystem blocks Used Available Capacity Mounted
/dev/hda3 297635 169499  112764  60%      /
/dev/hda1 205380 182320  23060   89%      /mnt/win
/dev/hdc  637986 637986  0       100%     / mnt/cdrom
```

You can also use df to tell you to what file system a given directory belongs. Enter df with the directory name or df . for the current directory.

```
$ df .
Filesystem blocks Used Available Capacity  Mounted
/dev/hda3 297635 169499  112764    60%         /
```

e2fsck and fsck

To check the consistency of the file system and repair it
if it was is damaged, you can use file system checking
tools. fsck checks and repairs a Linux file system. e2fsck
is designed to support ext2 and ext3 file systems,
whereas the more generic fsck also works on any other
file system. The ext2 and ext3 file systems are the file
systems normally used for Linux hard disk partitions and
floppy disks. Linux file systems beginning with Red Hat 7.3
are normally ext3, which you would use e2fsck to check.
fsck and e2fsck take as their argument the device name
of the hard disk partition that the file system uses.

```
fsck    device-name
```

Before you check a file system, be sure that the file system
is unmounted. e2fsck should not be used on a mounted
file system. To use e2fsck, enter e2fsck and the device
name that references the file system. The -p option
automatically repairs a file system without first requesting
approval from the user for each repair task. The following
examples check the disk in the floppy drive and the primary
hard drive:

```
# e2fsck /dev/fd0
# e2fsck /dev/hda1
```

With fsck, the -t option lets you specify the type of file
system to check, and the -a option automatically repairs
systems, whereas the -r option first asks for confirmation.
The -A option checks all systems in the /etc/fstab file.

TIP *In earlier distribution versions, fsck and e2fsck
were also used to recover file systems after disk crashes
or reset-button reboots. With recent releases, journaling
capabilities were introduced with file systems like ext3
and ReiserFS. Journaling provides for fast and effective
recovery in case of disk crashes, so recovering with fsck
or e2fsck is no longer necessary.*

Journaling

The ext3 and ReiserFS file systems introduced journaling capabilities to Linux systems. Journaling provides for fast and effective recovery in case of disk crashes, instead of using `e2fsck` or `fsck`. With journaling, a log is kept of all file system actions, which are placed in a journal file. In the event of a crash, Linux only needs to read the journal file and replay it to restore the system to its previous (stable) state. Files that were in the process of writing to the disk can be restored to their original state. Journaling also avoids lengthy `fsck` checks on reboots that occur when your system suddenly loses power or freezes and has to be restarted physically. Instead of using `fsck` to manually check each file and directory, your system just reads its journal files to restore the file system.

Keeping a journal entails more work for file system than a non-journal method. Though all journaling systems will maintain a file system's directory structure (what is known as the *meta-data*), they will offer various levels of file data recovery. Maintaining file data recovery information can be time-consuming, slowing down the file system's response time. At the same time, journaling systems make more efficient use of the file system, providing a faster response time than the non-journaled ext2 file system.

There are other kinds of journaling file systems you can use on Linux, including ReiserFS, JFS, and XFS. ReiserFS is named after Hans Reiser, and provides a completely reworked file system structure based on journaling (www.reiserfs.org). Most distributions also provide support for ReiserFS file systems. JFS is the IBM version of a journaling file system, designed for use on servers providing high throughput such as e-business enterprise servers (oss.software.ibm.com/developerworks/opensource/jfs/). It is freely distributed under the GNU public license. XFS is another high-performance journaling system developed by Silicon Graphics (oss.sgi.com/projects/xfs/). XFS is compatible with RAID and NFS file systems.

ext3 Journaling

Journaling is supported in the Linux kernel with ext3.
The ext3 file system is also fully compatible with the
earlier ext2 version it replaces. To create an ext3 file
system, you use the `mkfs.ext3` command. You can even
upgrade ext2 file systems to ext3 versions automatically,
with no loss of data or change in partitions. This upgrade
just adds a journal file to an ext2 file system and enables
journaling on it, using the `tune2fs` command. Be sure to
change the ext2 file type to ext3 in any corresponding
`/etc/fstab` entries. The following example converts the
ext2 file system on `/dev/hda3` to an ext3 file system by
adding a journal file (`-j`).

```
tune2fs -j /dev/hda3
```

Though the ext3 file system maintains full metadata
recovery support (directory tree recovery), it offers various
levels of file data recovery. In effect, you are trading off
less file data recovery for more speed. The ext3 file system
supports three options: `writeback`, `ordered`, and `journal`.
The default is `writeback`. The `writeback` option provides
only metadata recovery, no file data recovery. The `ordered`
option supports limited file data recovery, and the `journal`
option provides for full file data recovery. Any files in the
process of being changed during a crash will be recovered.
To specify a ext3 option, use the `data` option in the `mount`
command.

```
data=ordered
```

ReiserFS

Though journaling is often used to recover from disk
crashes, a journal-based file system can do much more.
The ext3, JFS, and XFS file systems only provide the
logging operations used in recovery, whereas ReiserFS
uses journaling techniques to completely rework file
system operations. In ReiserFS, journaling is used to read
and write data, abandoning the block structure used in
traditional Unix and Linux systems. This gives it the
capability to access a large number of small files very

quickly, as well as use only the amount of disk space they would need. However, efficiency is not that much better with larger files.

Mounting File Systems Automatically: /etc/fstab

File systems are mounted using the `mount` command described in the next section. Although you can mount a file system directly with only a `mount` command, you can simplify the process by placing mount information in the `/etc/fstab` configuration file. Using entries in this file, you can have certain file systems automatically mounted whenever your system boots. For others, you can specify configuration information, such as mountpoints and access permissions, which can be automatically used whenever you mount a file system. You needn't enter this information as arguments to a `mount` command as you otherwise must. This feature is what allows mount utilities on Gnome or KDE to enable you to mount a file system simply by clicking a window icon. All the mount information is already in the `/etc/fstab` file. For example, when you add a new hard disk partition to your Linux system, you most likely want to have it automatically mounted on startup, and then unmounted when you shut down. Otherwise, you must mount and unmount the partition explicitly each time you boot up and shut down your system. To have Linux automatically mount the file system on your new hard disk partition, you only need to add its name to the `fstab` file. You can do this by directly and carefully editing the `/etc/fstab` file to type in a new entry.

An entry in an `fstab` file contains several fields, each separated by a space or tab. These are described as the device, mountpoint, file system type, options, dump, and `fsck` fields, arranged in the sequence shown here:

```
<device> <mountpoint> <filesystemtype> <options>
<dump> <fsck>
```

The first field is the name of the file system to be mounted. This entry can be either a device name, or an ext2 or ext3

file system label. A device name usually begins with
/dev, such as /dev/hda3 for the third hard disk partition.
A label is specified by assigning the label name to the
tag LABEL, as in LABEL=/ for an ext2 root partition. The
next field is the directory in your file structure where you
want the file system on this device to be attached. These
are empty directories to be used for file systems, like **/dev/
floppy**. The third field is the type of file system being
mounted. Table 5-1 provides a list of all the different types
you can mount. The type for a standard Linux hard disk
partition is ext3. The next example shows an entry for
the main Linux hard disk partition. This entry is mounted
at the root directory, /, and has a file type of ext3.

5

```
/dev/hda3      /      ext3    defaults   0   1
```

The following example shows a LABEL entry for the hard
disk partition, where the label name is /.

```
LABEL=/      /      ext3    defaults   0   1
```

Auto Mounts

The file system type for a floppy may differ depending
on the disk you are trying to mount. For example, you
may want to read a Windows-formatted floppy disk at
one time and a Linux-formatted floppy disk at another
time. For this reason, the file system type specified for
the floppy device is auto. With this option, the type of
file system formatted on the floppy disk is detected
automatically, and the appropriate file system type is used.

```
/dev/fd0  /mnt/floppy  auto   defaults,noauto   0 0
```

mount Options

The field after the file system type lists the different
options for mounting the file system. You can specify a
default set of options by simply entering defaults, or
you can list specific options next to each other separated
by a comma (no spaces). The defaults option specifies

Types	Description
auto	Attempts to detect the file system type automatically.
minux	Minux file systems (filenames are limited to 30 characters).
ext	Earlier version of Linux file system, no longer in use.
ext3	Standard Linux file system supporting large filenames and file sizes. Includes journaling.
ext2	Older standard Linux file system supporting large filenames and file sizes. Does not have journaling.
xiaf	Xiaf file system.
msdos	File system for MS-DOS partitions (16-bit).
vfat	File system for Windows 95, 98, and Millennium partitions (32-bit).
ntfs	Windows NT, Windows XP, and Windows 2000 file systems (read-only access).
smbfs	Samba remote file systems, like NFS.
hpfs	File system for OS/2 high-performance partitions.
nfs	NFS file system for mounting partitions from remote systems.
umsdos	UMS-DOS file system.
swap	Linux swap partition or swap file.
sysv	Unix System V file systems.
iso9660	File system for mounting CD-ROM.
proc	Used by operating system for processes (Kernel support file system).
devpts	Unix 98 Pseudo Terminals·(ttys) (Kernel interface file system).
shmfs and tmpfs	Linux Virtual Memory, POSIX shared memory maintenance access (Kernel interface file system).

Table 5-1.　File System Types

that a device is read/write (`rw`), asynchronous (`async`), a block device (`dev`), cannot be mounted by ordinary users (`nouser`), and that programs can be executed on it (`exec`). By contrast, a CD-ROM only has two options listed for it: `ro` and `noauto`. `ro` specifies that the device is read-only, and `noauto` specifies it is not automatically mounted. The `noauto` option is used with both CD-ROMs and floppy drives so they won't automatically mount, because you don't know if you have anything in them when you start up. At the same time, the entries for both the CD-ROM and the floppy drive specify where they are to be mounted when you decide to mount them. On Red Hat, the `kudzu` option invokes the Red Hat Kudzu tool, which checks to see if the device has been installed on your system, and that the kernel is running the appropriate drivers for that CD-ROM or floppy disk. Table 5-2 lists the options for mounting a file system. An example of CD-ROM and floppy drive entries follows. Notice the type for a CD-ROM file system is different from a hard disk partition, `iso9660`.

```
/dev/hdc    /mnt/cdrom    iso9660  noauto,owner,kudzu,ro 0  0
/dev/fd0    /mnt/floppy   auto     noauto,owner,kudzu    0  0
```

Options	Description
async	Indicates that all I/O to the file system should be done asynchronously.
auto	Indicates that the file system can be mounted with the -a option. A `mount -a` command executed when the system boots, in effect, mounts file systems automatically.
defaults	Uses default options: `rw`, `suid`, `dev`, `exec`, `auto`, `nouser`, and `async`.
dev	Interprets character or block special devices on the file system.
kudzu	Checks that the device is installed and accessible.
noauto	Indicates that the file system can only be mounted explicitly. The -a option does not cause the file system to be mounted.
exec	Permits execution of binaries.
nouser	Forbids an ordinary (that is, nonroot) user to mount the file system.
remount	Attempts to remount an already mounted file system. This is commonly used to change the mount flags for a file system, especially to make a read-only file system writable.

Table 5-2.   `-o` and /etc/fstab

Options	Description
ro	Mounts the file system as read-only.
rw	Mounts the file system as read/write.
suid	Allows set-user-identifier or set-group-identifier bits to take effect.
sync	Indicates that all I/O to the file system should be done synchronously.
user	Enables an ordinary user to mount the file system. Ordinary users always have the following options activated: noexec, nosuid, and nodev.
nodev	Does not interpret character or block special devices on the file system.
noexec	Does not allow execution of binaries on the mounted file systems.
nosuid	Does not allow set-user-identifier or set-group-identifier bits to take effect.

Table 5-2. -o and /etc/fstab *(continued)*

Boot and Disk Check

The last two fields of an fstab entry consist of integer values. The first one is used by the dump command to determine if a file system needs to be dumped, backing up the file system. The second value is used by fsck to see if a file system should be checked at reboot, and in what order. If the field has a value of 1, it indicates a boot partition, and 2 indicates other partitions. The 0 value means fsck needn't check the file system.

A copy of an /etc/fstab file is shown here. Notice the first line is a comment. All comment lines begin with a #. The entry for the /proc file system is a special entry used by your Linux operating system for managing its processes, and is not an actual device. To make an entry in the /etc/fstab file, you can edit the /etc/fstab file directly. You can use the /etc/fstab example here as a guide to show how your entries should look. The /proc and swap partition entries are particularly critical. A sample /etc/fstab file is shown here:

```
<device>  <mountpt>  <filesys>    <opts>  <dump><fsck>
LABEL=/    /          ext3      defaults      0  1
none       /proc      proc      defaults      0  0
none       /dev/pts   devpts    gid=5,mode=620 0  0
none       /dev/shm   tmpfs     defaults      0  0
/dev/hda2  swap       swap      defaults      0  0
/dev/hdc   /mnt/cdrom iso9660   noauto,owner,
                                kudzu,ro      0  0
/dev/fd0   /mnt/floppy auto     noauto,owner,
                                kudzu         0  0
/dev/hda1  /mnt/windows vfat    defaults      0  0
```

CD-ROM and Floppy Defaults

5

Red Hat creates entries in the `fstab` file for any CD-ROM and floppy devices you may have. It also creates directories where these drives can be mounted. For Red Hat, these are `/mnt/cdrom` for your CD-ROM and `/mnt/floppy` for your floppy disk. If you have several CD-ROMs or floppy drives, directories are created for them with sequential numbers. So on Red Hat, a second CD-ROM drive will use a directory named `/mnt/cdrom1`.

Partition Labels: e2label

Red Hat uses file system labels for ext2 and ext3 file systems on hard disk partitions. So in the `/etc/fstab` file previously shown, the first entry would use a label for its device name, as shown here. In this case, the label is the slash, `/`, indicating the root partition. You could change this device's label with `e2label`, but be sure to also change the `/etc/fstab` entry for it.

```
LABEL=/    /     ext3    defaults    0    1
```

For ext2 and ext3 partitions, you can change or add a label with the `e2label` tool or `tune2fs` with the `-L` option. Specify the device and the label name. If you change a label, be sure to change corresponding entries in the `/etc/fstab` file. Just use `e2label` with the device name to find out what the current label is. In the next example, the user changes the label of the `/dev/hda3` device to TURTLE:

```
e2label /dev/hda3   TURTLE
```

Windows Partitions

You can mount either MS-DOS, Windows 95/98/ME, or Windows XP, NT, and 2000 partitions used by your Windows operating system onto your Linux file structure, just as you would mount any Linux file system. You only have to specify the file type of `vfat` for Windows 95/98/ME, and `msdos` for MS-DOS. Windows XP, NT, and 2000 use the `ntfs` file type. You may find it convenient to have your Windows partitions automatically mounted when you start up your Linux system. To do this, you need to put an entry for your Windows partitions in your `/etc/fstab` file and give it the `defaults` option, or be sure to include an `auto` option. You make an entry for each Windows partition you want to mount, and then specify the device name for that partition, followed by the directory in which you want to mount it. The `/mnt/windows` directory would be a logical choice (be sure the `windows` directory has already been created in `/mnt`). For a Windows 95/98/ME partition, use the `vfat` file system type. The next example shows a standard Windows partition entry for an `/etc/fstab` file. Notice the last entry in the `/etc/fstab` file example is an entry for mounting a Windows partition.

```
/dev/hda1 /mnt/windows vfat defaults 0 0
```

TIP *Linux kernel 2.4 systems currently can only reliably mount `ntfs` file systems (Windows NT, Windows 2000, and Windows XP) as read-only. They cannot write to these partitions, though experimental and unstable support is provided by the 2.5 development kernel and may be incorporated into the 2.6 kernel.*

Linux Kernel Interfaces

Your `/etc/fstab` file may also have entries for two special kernel interface file systems, `devpts` and `tmpfs`. Both provide kernel interfaces that are not supported by

standard devices. The /dev/pts entry mounts a devpts
file system for pseudo terminals. The /dev/shm entry
mounts the tmpfs file system (also known as shmfs) to
implement Linux Virtual Memory, POSIX shared memory
maintenance access. This is designed to overcome the
4GB memory limitation on current systems, extending
usable memory to 64GB.

If your /etc/fstab file ever becomes corrupt—say, if a
line gets deleted accidentally or changed—your system
will boot into a maintenance mode, giving you read-only
access to your partitions. To gain read/write access so you
can fix your /etc/fstab file, you have to remount your
main partition. The following command performs such an
operation:,

```
# mount -n -o remount,rw /
```

noauto

File systems listed in the /etc/fstab file are automatically
mounted whenever you boot, unless this feature is explicitly
turned off with the noauto option. Notice that the CD-ROM
and floppy disks in the sample fstab file earlier in this
chapter have a noauto option. Also, if you issue a mount
-a command, all the file systems without a noauto
option are mounted. If you want to make the CD-ROM
user-mountable, add the user option.

```
/dev/hdc /mnt/cdrom iso9660 ro,noauto,user 0 0
```

TIP *The "automatic" mounting of file systems from
/etc/fstab is actually implemented by executing a
mount -a command in the /etc/rc.d/rc.sysinit file
that is run whenever you boot. The mount -a command
mounts any file system listed in your /etc/fstab file that
does not have a noauto option. The umount -a option
unmounts the file systems in /etc/fstab (which is
executed when you shut down your system).*

Mounting File Systems Directly: mount and umount

You can also mount or unmount any file system using the `mount` and `umount` commands directly (notice that umount lacks an *n*). The mount operations discussed in the previous sections use the `mount` command to mount a file system. Normally, the mounting of file systems on hard disk partitions can only be done as the root user, whereas CD-ROMs and floppies can be mounted by any user. Table 5-3 lists the different options for the `mount` command.

Mount Options	Description
`-f`	Fakes the mounting of a file system. Use it to check if a file system can be mounted.
`-v`	Verbose mode. `Mmount` displays descriptions of the actions it is taking. Use with `-f` to check for any problems mounting a file system, `-fv`.
`-w`	Mounts the file system with read/write permission.
`-r`	Mounts the file system with read-only permission.
`-n`	Mounts the file system without placing an entry for it in the `mstab` file.
`-t` *type*	Specifies the type of file system to be mounted. See Table 5-1 for valid file system types.
`-a`	Mounts all file systems listed in `/etc/fstab`.
`-o` *option-list*	Mounts the file system using a list of options. This is a comma-separated list of options following `-o`. See Table 5-2 for a list of the options.

Table 5-3. The `mount` Command

mount Command

The mount command takes two arguments: the storage device through which Linux accesses the file system, and the directory in the file structure to which the new file system is attached. The *mountpoint* is the directory on your main directory tree where you want the files on the storage device attached. The *device* is a special device file that connects your system to the hardware device. The syntax for the mount command is as follows:

```
# mount device mountpoint
```

As noted in Chapter 4, device files are located in the /dev directories and usually have abbreviated names ending with the number of the device. For example, fd0 may refer to the first floppy drive attached to your system. The following example mounts a floppy disk in the first floppy drive device (fd0) to the /mydir mnt/floppy directory. The mountpoint directory needs to be empty. If you already have a file system mounted there, you will receive a message that another file system is already mounted there and that the directory is busy. If you mount a file system to a directory that already has files and subdirectories in it, those will be bypassed, giving you access only to the files in the mounted file system. Unmounting the file system, of course, restores access to the original directory files.

```
# mount /dev/fd0 /mnt/floppy
```

For any partition with an entry in the /etc/fstab file, you can mount the partition using only the mount directory specified in its fstab entry; you needn't enter the device filename. The mount command looks up the entry for the partition in the fstab file using the directory to identify the entry and, in that way, find the device name. For example, to unmount the /dev/hda1 Windows partition in the previous example, the mount command only needs to know the directory it is mounted to—in this case, /mnt/windows.

```
# mount /mnt/windows
```

If you are unsure as to the type of file system that the
floppy disk holds, you can mount it specifying the `auto` file
system type with the `-t` option. Given the `auto` file system
type, `mount` attempts to detect the type of file system on
the floppy disk automatically.

```
# mount -t auto /dev/fd0 /mnt/floppy
```

unmount Command

If you want to replace one mounted file system with
another, you must first explicitly unmount the one already
mounted. Say you have mounted a floppy disk, and now
you want to take it out and put in a new one. You must
unmount that floppy disk before you can put in and mount
the new one. You unmount a file system with the `umount`
command. The `umount` command can take as its argument
either a device name or the directory where it was
mounted. Here is the syntax:

```
# umount device-or-mountpoint
```

The following example unmounts the floppy disk wherever
it is mounted:

```
# umount /dev/fd0
```

Using the example where the device was mounted on the
`/mydir` directory, you could use that directory to unmount
the file system:

```
# umount /mydir
```

One important constraint applies to the `umount` command.
You can never unmount a file system in which you are
currently working. If you change to a directory within a
file system that you then try to unmount, you receive an
error message stating that the file system is busy. For
example, suppose you mount a CD-ROM on the `/mnt/`
`cdrom` directory and then change to the `/mnt/ cdrom`
directory. If you decide to change CD-ROMs, you first
have to unmount the current one with the `umount`
command. This will fail because you are currently in
the directory in which it is mounted. You have to leave
that directory before you can unmount the CD-ROM.

```
# mount /dev/hdc /mnt/cdrom
# cd /mnt/cdrom
# umount /mnt/cdrom
umount: /dev/hdd: device is busy
# cd /root
# umount /mnt/cdrom
```

TIP *If other users are using a file system you are trying to unmount, you can use the* `lsof` *or* `fuser` *commands to find out who they are.*

Mounting Floppy Disks

As noted previously, to access a file on a floppy disk, the disk first has to be mounted on your Linux system. The device name for your floppy drive is `fd0`, and it is located in the directory `/dev`. Entering `/dev/fd0` references your floppy drive. Notice the number `0` after `fd`. If you have more than one floppy drive, they are represented by `fd1`, `fd2`, and so on. You can mount to any directory you want. Red Hat creates a convenient directory to use for floppy disks, `/mnt/floppy`. The following example mounts the floppy disk in your floppy drive to the `/mnt/floppy` directory:

```
# mount /dev/fd0 /mnt/floppy
```

TIP *On Gnome, you can mount a floppy drive by right-clicking on the desktop background to display the desktop menu and then selecting Floppy in the Disk entry. To unmount, right-click on the Floppy icon and select Eject from the pop-up menu.*

Remember, you are mounting a particular floppy disk, not the floppy drive. You cannot simply remove the floppy disk and put in another one. The `mount` command has attached those files to your main directory tree, and your system expects to find those files on a floppy disk in your floppy drive. If you take out the disk and put another one in, you get an error message when you try to access it.

To change disks, you must first unmount the floppy disk already in your disk drive. Then, after putting in the new disk, you must explicitly mount that new disk. To do this, use the `umount` command.

```
# umount /dev/fd0
```

For the `umount` or `mount` operations, you can specify either the directory it is mounted on or the `/dev/fd0` device.

```
# umount /mnt/floppy
```

You can now remove the floppy disk, put in the new one, and then mount it:

```
# mount /mnt/floppy
```

When you shut down your system, any disk you have mounted is automatically unmounted. You do not have to unmount it explicitly.

Mounting CD-ROMs

Remember, when you mount a CD-ROM or floppy disk, you cannot then simply remove it to put another one in the drive. You first have to unmount it, detaching the file system from the overall directory tree. In fact, the CD-ROM drive remains locked until you unmount it. Once you unmount a CD-ROM, you can then take it out and put in another one, which you then must mount before you can access it. When changing several CD-ROMs or floppy disks, you are continually mounting and unmounting them. For a CD-ROM, instead of using the `umount` command, you can use the `eject` command with the device name or mount point, which will unmount and then eject the CD-ROM from the drive.

You can also mount CD-ROM disks to your Linux system using the `mount` command. On many distributions, the directory `/mnt/cdrom` has been reserved for CD-ROM file systems. You can see an entry for this in the `/etc/fstab` file presented earlier in the chapter. With such an entry, to mount a CD-ROM, all you have to do is enter the command `mount` and the directory `/mnt/cdrom`. You needn't specify the device name. Once mounted, you can access the CD-ROM through the `/mnt/cdrom` directory.

```
# mount /mnt/cdrom
```

TIP   *On Gnome, CD-ROMs are automatically mounted, though you can manually mount them by right-clicking the desktop background to display the desktop menu, and then selecting CD-ROM in the Disk entry. To unmount, right-click on the CD-ROM icon and select Eject from the pop-up menu.*

As with floppy disks, you have to unmount one CD-ROM before you can mount another. Use the `umount` command to unmount the CD-ROM. The CD-ROM will remain locked until you unmount it.

```
# umount /mnt/cdrom
```

5

If you want to mount a CD-ROM to another directory, you have to include the device name in the `mount` command. The following example mounts the disc in your CD-ROM drive to the `/mydir` directory. The particular device name for the CD-ROM in this example is `/dev/hdc`.

```
# mount /dev/hdc /mydir
```

When you burn a CD, you may need to create a CD image file. You could access such an image file from your hard drive, mounting it as if it were another file system (even ripped images could be mounted in this way). For this you use the `loop` option, specifying an open loop device such as `/dev/loop0`. If no loop device is indicated, `mount` will try to find an open one. The file system type is `iso9660`, a CD-ROM iso image file type.

```
# mount -t iso9660 -o loop=/dev/loop0 image mntdir
```

To mount the image file `mymusic.cdimage` to the `/mnt/mystuff` directory and make it read-only, you would use:

```
# mount -t iso9660 -o ro,loop=/dev/loop0 \
                mymusic.cdimage /mnt/mystuff
```

Once mounted, you can access files on the CD-ROM as you would in any directory.

TIP   *You use `mkisofs` to create a CD-ROM image made up from your files or another CD-ROM.*

Mounting Hard Drive Partitions: Linux and Windows

You can mount either Linux or Windows hard drive partitions with the `mount` command. However, it is much more practical to have them mounted automatically using the `/etc/fstab` file as described previously. The Linux hard disk partitions you created during installation are already automatically mounted for you. As noted previously, to mount a Linux hard disk partition, enter the `mount` command with the device name of the partition and the directory to which you want to mount it. IDE hard drives use the prefix `hd`, and SCSI hard drives use the prefix `sd`. The next example mounts the Linux hard disk partition on `/dev/hda4` to the directory `/mnt/mydata`:

```
# mount -t ext3 /dev/hda4 /mnt/mydata
```

You can also mount a Windows partition and directly access the files on it. As with a Linux partition, you use the `mount` command, but you also have to specify the file system type as Windows. For that, use the `-t` option, and then type `vfat` for Windows 95/98/ME (`msdos` for MS-DOS). For Windows XP, 2000, and NT, you would use `ntfs` (limited read-only access; write access is experimental and not recommended). In the next example, the user mounts the Windows hard disk partition `/dev/hda1` to the Linux file structure at directory `/mnt/windows`. The `/mnt/windows` directory is a common designation for Windows file systems, though you can mount it in any directory (such as `/mnt/dos` for MS-DOS). If you have several Windows partitions, you could create a Windows directory and then a subdirectory for each drive using the drive's label or letter, such as `/mnt/windows/a` or `/mnt/windows/mystuff`. Be sure you have already created the directory before mounting the file system.

```
# mount -t vfat /dev/hda1 /mnt/windows
```

Installing IDE CD-R/RW and DVD-R/RW Devices

Linux CD burning applications all treat CD-R/RW and DVD-R/RW drives as if they were SCSI drives. This means that IDE CD-R/RW drives have to emulate SCSI drives for them to be recognized and used by CD or DVD writing software. Even if you want to use an IDE CD-ROM or DVD-ROM in a CD writing applications—say, as just the reader to copy a CD disk—that IDE CD-ROM drive would still have to emulate a SCSI CD-ROM drive. Only SCSI drives (CD-R/RW/ROM or DVD-R/RW/ROM) are recognized by Linux CD or DVD writing software. For example, if you have a regular IDE CD-ROM and you want to use it with Linux CD-write software to copy CDs (ripping), you still have to have that IDE CD-ROM emulate a SCSI CD-ROM. Check the CD-Writing HOW-TO at www.linuxdoc.org for more details. A brief description is provided here.

5

TIP SCSI emulation for IDE devices is implemented in the kernel as SCSI Emulation Support in the IDE, ATA, and ATAPI Block Devices entry, located in the ATA/IDE/ MFM/RLL Support window opened from the main kernel configuration menu. Normally, it is compiled as a module.

IDE CD and DVD drives (CD-R/RW/ROM or DVD-R/RW/ ROM) are recognized as IDE devices during installation and installed as such. However, when you start up your system, you need to instruct the Linux kernel to have the IDE CD and DVD drives emulate SCSI CD or DVD drives. This means that a CD-R drive that would be normally recognized as a `/dev/hdc` drive has to be recognized as a `/dev/scd0` device, the first SCSI CD-ROM drive. You do this by loading the `ide-scsi` module, which allows an IDE CD drive to emulate a SCSI CD drive.

SCSI Emulation

You can implement SCSI emulation for IDE CD and DVD drives in one of two ways: either by loading the `ide-scsi` module as a kernel parameter, or by specifying the module in the `/etc/modules.conf` file (`/etc/modprob.conf` in 2.5 and 2.6 kernels). You will also have to indicate the IDE drives to emulate. If the `ide-scsi` module is compiled into the kernel (not as a separate module), then you have to load it as a kernel parameter. An `ide-scsi` module can be loaded either way.

TIP *During installation, Red Hat will recognize the IDE CD and DVD drives you have installed on your system, and will include the* ide-scsi *kernel parameter automatically as part of either your LILO or Grub GRUB boot loader configurations. You do not need to perform any of the specific configuration tasks described in this section.*

Kernel Parameters at Boot Time

As a kernel parameter, you can either manually enter the `ide-scsi` parameter at the boot prompt or place it in the `/etc/grub.conf` or `/etc/lilo.conf` files (depending on whether you are using the GRUB or LILO boot loader) to have it automatically entered. The parameter is read when the system starts up. List each IDE CD or DVD drive that needs to emulate a SCSI drive as using the `ide-scsi` module. You assign the `ide-scsi` module to the device name of the IDE CD drive to be emulated. The following example loads the `ide-scsi` module to have the master IDE drive on the secondary IDE connection (`hdc`) emulate a SCSI drive.

```
hdc=ide-scsi
```

Grub and CD Writers

If you installed Red Hat with your IDE CD-R/RW drive already attached, then GRUB would have automatically detected it and listed the `ide-scsi` module for that drive in its boot parameters. You can always manually enter the parameter by typing `a` at the GRUB boot entry for your Linux system, displayed when you start up your computer. The parameters for your Linux system will be listed. Just add the CD-R/RW `ide-scsi` module assignment.

The following example shows how two IDE CD drives are specified at the Linux boot prompt:

```
grub append> ro root=/dev/hda3 hdc=ide-scsi
```

For the `/etc/grub.conf` file, add these parameters to the Linux kernel line, just as you would to a boot entry:

```
kernel /boot/vmlinuz-2.4.18-3 ro
                    root=/dev/hda3 hdc=ide-scsi
```

TIP *If you are not using GRUB, or for some reason you do not want to modify the* `/etc/grub.conf` *file, you can configure the* `/etc/modules.conf` *file (*`/etc/modprob`*
.conf on 2.5 and 2.6 kernels) to load and implement the SCSI emulation for your IDE CD drives. This involves entering several module configuration commands in the* `/etc/modules.conf` *file. When your system starts up, it will load the modules as specified in that file.*

scanbus

To check that your IDE drives are being recognized as SCSI drives, run `cdrecord` with the `-scanbus` option (or `dvdrecord` for DVD writers). This example shows two IDE CD drives now emulating SCSI CD drives. One is a Plextor IDE CD-RW drive (`scd0`) and the other is a Toshiba DVD-ROM drive (`scd1`).

```
# cdrecord -scanbus
Cdrecord 1.9 (i686-pc-linux-gnu)
Linux sg driver version: 3.1.17
Using libscg version 'schily-0.1'
scsibus0:
0,0,0 0) 'PLEXTOR ' 'CD-R    PX-W1210A' Rem CD-ROM
0,1,0 1) 'TOSHIBA ' 'DVD-ROM SD-M1402' Rem CD-ROM
0,2,0 2) *
0,3,0 3) *
0,4,0 4) *
0,5,0 5) *
0,6,0 6) *
0,7,0 7) *
```

Creating File Systems: mkfs, mke2fs, mkswap, parted, and fdisk

Linux provides a variety of tools for creating and managing file systems, letting you add new hard disk partitions, create CD images, and format floppies. To use a new hard drive, you will first have to partition it and then create a file system on it. You can use either `parted` or `fdisk` to partition your hard drive. To create the file system on the partitions, use the `mkfs` command which is a front-end for various file system builders. For swap partitions, you use a special tool, `mkswap`, and to create file systems on a CD-ROM, you use the `mkisofs` tool. Linux partition and file system tools are listed in Table 5-4.

fdisk

To start `fdisk`, enter `fdisk` on the command line with the device name of the hard disk you are partitioning. This brings up an interactive program you can use to create your Linux partition. Be careful using Linux `fdisk`. It can literally erase your entire hard disk partitions and all the data on those partitions if you are not careful. The following command invokes `fdisk` for creating partitions on the `hdb` hard drive.

```
fdisk    /dev/hdb
```

The partitions have different types that you need to specify. Linux `fdisk` is a line-oriented program. It has a set of one-character commands that you simply press. Then you may be prompted to type in certain information and press enter. If you run into trouble during the `fdisk` procedure, you can press Q at any time, and you will return to the previous screen without any changes having been made. No changes are actually made to your hard disk until you press w. This should be your very last command; it makes the actual changes to your hard disk and then quits `fdisk`, returning you to the installation

Tool	Description
fdisk	Menu-driven program to create and delete partitions.
cfdisk	Screen-based interface for fdisk.
parted	GNU partition management tool.
mkfs	Creates a file system on a partition or floppy disk using the specified file system type. Front-end to formatting utilities.
mke2fs	Creates an ext2 file system on a Linux partition; use the -j option to create an ext3 file system.
mkfs.ext3	Creates an ext3 file system on a Linux partition.
mkfs.ext2	Creates an ext2 file system on a Linux partition.
mkfs.reiserfs	Creates a Reiser journaling file system on a Linux partition (links to mkreiserfs).
mkfs.jfs	Creates a JFS journaling file system on a Linux partition.
mkfs.dos	Creates a DOS file system on a given partition.
mkfs.vfat	Creates a Windows 16-bit file system on a given partition (Windows 95, 98, and ME).
mkswap	Tool to set up a Linux swap area on a device or in a file.
mkdosfs	Creates an MS-DOS file system under Linux.
mkisofs	Creates an ISO CD-ROM disk image.
Gfloppy	Gnome tool to format a floppy disk (Floppy Formatter entry on the System Tools menu).

Table 5-4. Linux Partition and File System Creation Tools

program. Table 5-5 lists the commonly used fdisk commands. Perform the following steps to create a Linux partition.

When you press n to define a new partition, you will be asked if it is a primary partition. Press P to indicate that

Command	Action
A	Toggle a bootable flag
L	List known partition types
M	List commands
N	Add a new partition
P	Print the partition table
Q	Quit without saving changes
T	Change a partition's system ID
W	Write table to disk and exit

Table 5-5.   A List of Commonly Used fdisk Commands

it is a primary partition. Linux supports up to four primary partitions. Enter the partition number for the partition you are creating. Enter the beginning cylinder for the partition. This is the first number in parentheses at the end of the prompt. You are then prompted to enter the last cylinder number. You can either enter the last cylinder you want for this partition or enter a size. You can enter the size as +1000M for 1GB, preceding the amount with a + sign. Bear in mind that the size cannot exceed your free space. You then specify the partition type. The default type for a Linux partition is 83. If you are creating a different type of partition, like a swap partition, press T to indicate the type you want. Enter the partition number, such as 82 for a swap partition. When you are finished, press w to write out the changes to the hard disk, and then press enter to continue.

parted

As an alternative to fdisk, you can use parted (www.gnu .org/software/parted). parted lets you manage hard disk partitions, create new ones and delete old ones. Unlike fdisk, it also lets you resize partitions. To use parted on the partitions in a given hard drive, none of the partitions on that drive can be in use. This means that if you wish to use parted on partitions located on that same hard drive as your kernel, you have to boot your system in the rescue mode and choose not to mount your system files. For any other hard drives, you only need to unmount their partitions and turn your swap space off with the `swapoff` command. You can then start `parted` with the `parted` command and the device name of the hard disk you want to work on. The following example starts `parted` for the hard disk `/dev/hda`.

```
parted  /dev/hda
```

You use the `print` command to list all your partitions. The partition number for each partition will be listed in the first column under the Minor heading. The Start and End columns list the beginning and end position that the partition uses on the hard drive. The numbers are in megabytes, starting from the first megabyte to the total available. To create a new partition, use the `mkpart` command with either `primary` or `extended`, the file system type, and the beginning and end positions. You can create up to three primary partitions and one extended partition (or four primary partitions if there is no extended partition). The extended partition can, in turn, have several logical partitions. Once you have created the partition, you can later use `mkfs` to format it with a file system. To remove a partition, use the `rm` command and the partition number. To `resize` a partition, use the resize command with the partition number and the beginning and end positions. You can even move a partition using the `move` command. The `help` command lists all commands.

mkfs

Once you create your partition, you have to create a file system on it. To do this, use the `mkfs` command to build the Linux file system and pass the name of the hard disk partition as a parameter. A hard disk partition is a device with its own device name in the `/dev` directory (see Chapter 4). You must specify its full pathname with the `mkfs` command. Table 5-6 lists the options for the `mkfs` command. For example, the second partition on the first hard drive has the device name `/dev/hdb1`. You can now mount your new hard disk partition, attaching it to your file structure. The next example formats that partition:

```
# mkfs -t ext3 /dev/hdb1
```

Options	Description
Blocks	Number of blocks for the file system. There are 1,440 blocks for a 1.44MB floppy disk.
-t *file-system-type*	Specifies the type of file system to format. The default is the standard Linux file system type, ext3.
file-system-options	Options for the type of file system specified. Listed before the device name, but after the file system type.
-V	Verbose mode. Displays description of each action mkfs takes.
-v	Instructs the file system builder program that mkfs invokes to show actions it takes.
-c	Checks a partition for bad blocks before formatting it (may take some time).
-l *file-name*	Reads a list of bad blocks.

Table 5-6.   The mkfs Options

mkfs is really just a front-end for several different file system builders. A file system builder performs the actual task of creating a file system. Red Hat supports various file system builders, including several journaling file systems and Windows file systems. The name of a file system builder has a prefix mkfs and a suffix for the name of the type of file system. For example, the file system builder for the ext3 file system is mkfs.ext3. For Reiser file systems, it is mkfs.reiserfs, and for Windows 16-bit file systems (95,98, ME), it is mkfs.vfat. Some of these file builders are just other names for traditional file system creation tools. For example, the mkfs.ext2 file builder is just another name for the mke2fs ext2 file system creation tool, and mkfs.msdos is the mkdosfs command. As ext3 is an extension of ext2, mkfs.ext3 simply invokes mke2fs, the tool for creating ext2 and ext3 file systems, and directs it to create an ext3 file system (using the -j option). Any of the file builders can be used directly to create a file system of that type. Options are listed before the device name. The next example is equivalent to the previous one, creating an ext3 file system on the hdb1 device.

```
mkfs.ext3 /dev/hdb1
```

The syntax for the mkfs command is as follows. You can add options for a particular file system after the type and before the device. The block size is used for file builders that do not detect the disk size.

```
mkfs options [-t type] file-sysoptions device size
```

TIP   *Once you have formatted your disk, you can label it with the e2label command as described earlier in the chapter.*

The same procedure works for floppy disks. In this case, the mkfs command takes as its argument the device name. It uses the ext2 file system (the default for mkfs), because a floppy is too small to support a journaling file system.

```
# mkfs /dev/fd0
```

TIP   *On the desktop, you can use the Floppy Formatter tool listed in the System Tools menu to format your floppy disks. The formatter enables you to choose an MS-DOS or Linux file system type.*

mkswap

If you want to create a swap partition, you first use fdisk or parted to create the partition, if it does not already exist, and then you use the mkswap command to format it as a swap partition. mkswap formats the entire partition unless otherwise instructed. It takes as its argument the device name for the swap partition.

```
mkswap /dev/hdb2
```

You then need to create an entry for it in the `/etc/fstab` file so that it will be automatically mounted when your system boots.

CD-ROM Recording

Recording data to CD-ROM disks on Linux involves creating a CD image file of the CD-ROM, and then writing that image file to a CD-R or CD-RW disk in your CD-R/RW drive. With the `mkisofs` command, you can create a CD image file, which you can then write to a CD-R/RW write device. Once you create your CD image file, you can write it to a CD-write device, using the `cdrecord` or `cdwrite` applications. The `cdrecord` application is a more powerful application with many options. You can also use Gnome and KDE CD recording applications such as KOnCD and Gnome Toaster to create your CDs easily. Most are front-ends to the `mkisofs` and `cdrecord` tools. To record DVD disks on DVD writers, you can use `dvdrecord` (the counterpart to `cdrecord`) for DVD-R/RW drives and the dvd+rw tools for DVD+RW/+R drives. If you want to record CD-ROMs on a DVD writer, you can just use cdrecord.

TIP *dvdrecord currently works only on DVD-R/RW drives, and is part of the dvdrtools package. If you want to use DVD+RW/+R drives, you would use the dvd+rw tools such as* `growisofs` *and* `dvd+rw-format`. *dvd+rw tools is currently included only in the Debian distribution. For Red Hat, you have to download and compile dvd+rw tools from the DVD+RW/+R for Linux page at http:// fy.chalmers.se/~appro/linux/DVD+RW.*

mkisofs

To create a CD image, you first select the files you want on your CD. Then you can use `mkisofs` to create an ISO CD image of them.

mkisofs Options

You may need to include several important options with
`mkisofs` to create a data CD properly. The `-o` option is
used to specify the name of the CD image file. This can
be any name you want to give it. The `-R` option specifies
RockRidge CD protocols, and the `-J` option provides for
long Windows 95/98/ME or XP names. The `-r` option, in
addition to the RockRidge protocols (`-R`), sets standard
global permissions for your files, like read access for all
users and no write access because the CD-ROM is read only.
The `-T` option creates translation tables for filenames for
use on systems that are not RockRidge- compliant. The `-U`
option provides for relaxed filenames that are not standard
ISO- compliant, such as long filenames, those with more
than one period in their name, those that begin with a
period such as shell configuration files, and ones that use
lowercase characters (there are also separate options for
each of these features if you just want to use a few of
them). Most RPM and source code package names fall in
this category. The `-iso-level` option lets you remove
ISO restrictions such as the length of a filename. The `-V`
option sets the volume label (name) for the CD. Finally,
the `-v` option displays the progress of the image creation.

Disk Image Creation

The last argument is the directory that contains the files
for which you want to make the CD image. For this, you
can specify a directory. For example, if you are creating a
CD-ROM to contain the data files in the `mydocs` directory,
you would specify that directory. This top directory will
not be included, just the files and subdirectories in it.
You can also change to that directory and then use . to
indicate the current directory.

If you were creating a simple CD to use on Linux, you
would use `mkisofs` to first create the CD image. Here,
the verbose option will show the creation progress, and
the `-V` option lets you specify the CD label. A CD image
called `songs.iso` is created using the file located in the
`newsong` directory.

```
mkisofs -v -V "mysongs" -o songs.iso newsong
```

If you also wanted to use the CD on a Windows system, you would add the -r (RockRidge with standard global file access) and -J (Joliet) options:

```
mkisofs -v -r -J -V "mysongs" -o songs.iso newsong
```

You need to include certain options if you are using filenames that are not ISO compliant, such as ones with more than 31 characters or ones that use lowercase characters. The -U option let you use completely unrestricted filenames, whereas certain options like -L for the unrestricted length will release specific restrictions only. The following example creates a CD image called mydoc.iso, using the files and subdirectories located in the mdoc directory, and labels the CD image with the name "doc":

```
mkisofs -v -r -T -J -U -V "doc" -o mydoc.iso mdoc
```

Mounting Disk Images

Once you have created your CD image, you can check to see if it is correct by mounting it as a file system on your Linux system. In effect, to test the CD image, you mount it to a directory, and then access it as if it were simply another file system. Mounting a CD image requires the use of a loop device. Specify the loop device with the loop option as shown in the next example. Here the mydoc.iso is mounted to the /mnt/cdrom directory as a file system of type iso9660. Be sure to unmount it when you finish.

```
mount -t iso9660 -o ro,loop=/dev/loop0
                            mydoc.iso /mnt/cdrom
```

Bootable CD-ROMs

If you are creating a bootable CD-ROM, you will need to indicate the boot image file to use and the boot catalogue. With the -c option, you specify the boot catalogue. With the -b option, you specify the boot image. The *boot image* is a boot disk image, like that used to start up an installation procedure. For example, on the Red Hat CD-ROM, the boot image is isolinux/isolinux.bin, and the boot catalogue is isolinux/boot.cat (you can also use images/boot.img. and boot.cat). Copy those files to your hard disk. The following example creates a bootable

CD-ROM image using Red Hat distribution files located on the CD-ROM drive.

```
mkisofs -o rd8-0.iso -b isolinux/isolinux.bin \
  -c isolinux/boot.cat -no-emul-boot \
  -boot-load-size 4 -boot-info-table \
  -v -r -R -T -J -V "Red8.0"  /mnt/cdrom
```

cdrecord

Once `mkisofs` has created the CD image file, you can use `cdrecord` or `cdwrite` to write it to a CD write disk. If you have more than one CD-writer device, you should specify the CD-R/RW drive to use by indicating its SCSI bus number (recall that even IDE CD-R/RW drives are treated as SCSI devices on Linux). You can use `cdrecord` with the `-scanbus` option to find out the SCSI numbers of your rewritable devices. In this example, as shown previously in the `-scanbus` example, the device number for the rewritable CD/RW drive is `0,0`. The `dev=` option is used to indicate this drive. The final argument for `cdrecord` is the name of the CD image file. `dvdrecord` works the same way as DVD-R/RW writers, and is, in fact, an extension of `cdrecord`.

```
cdrecord  dev=0,0  mydocuments.iso
```

If you are creating an audio CD, use the `-audio` option, as shown here. This option uses the CD-DA audio format.

```
cdrecord  dev=0,0 -audio moresongs.iso
```

TIP   *The* `dummy` *option for* `cdrecord` *lets you test the CD writing operation for a given image.*

Backups

You can back up and restore your system archive tools like `tar`, restoring the archives later. For backups, `tar` is usually used with a tape device. To automatically schedule backups, you can schedule appropriate `tar` commands with the `cron` utility.

Anacron

As an alternative to `cron`, you can use `anacron`, which activates only when scheduled tasks need to be executed. `anacron` jobs are entered in the `/etc/anacrontab` file. For each scheduled task, you specify the number of intervening days when it is executed (7 is weekly, 30 is monthly), the time of day it is run (numbered in minutes), a description of the task, and the command to be executed. For backups, the command would be `tar` operation. You can use `redhat-config-services` to turn on the `anacron` service or have it start up automatically at boot time.

Amanda

To back up hosts connected to a network, you can use the Advanced Maryland Automatic Network Disk Archiver (Amanda) to archive hosts. Amanda uses `tar` tools to back up all hosts to a single host operating as a backup server. Backup data is sent by each host to the host operating as the Amanda server, where they are written out to a backup media such as tape. With an Amanda server, the backup operations for all hosts becomes centralized in one server, instead of each host having to perform their own backup. Any host that needs to restore data simply requests it from the Amanda server, specifying the file system, date, and file names. Amanda has its own commands corresponding to the common backup tasks, beginning with "am," such as `amdump`, `amrestore`, and `amrecover`. Configuration files are placed in `/etc/amanda` and log, and database files in `/var/adm/amanda`.

TIP   *The Unix-based dump and restore utilities are also available on your Linux system. However, they are now deprecated and are no longer reliable on 2.4- kernel-based systems like Red Hat Linux 8.0.*

TIP   *You can use the `mt` command to control your tape device. `mt` has options to rewind, erase, and position the tape. The `rmt` command controls a remote tape device.*

Chapter 6

RAID and LVM

With the onset of cheap, efficient, and very large hard
drives, even the most professional systems employ
several hard drives. The use of multiple hard drives opens
up opportunities for ensuring storage reliability as well as
more easily organizing access to your hard disks. Linux
provides two methods for better managing your hard
disks: Redundant Arrays of Independent Disks (RAID)
and Logical Volume Management (LVM). RAID is a way
of storing the same data in different places on multiple
hard disks. These multiple hard drives are treated as a
single hard drive. They include recovery information
that allows you to restore your files should one of the
drives fail. LVM is a method for organizing all your hard
disks into logical volumes, letting you pool the storage
capabilities of several hard disks into a single logical
volume. Your system then sees one large storage device,
and you do not have to micromanage each underlying
hard disk and their partitions.

Enabling RAID and LVM in the Kernel

Red Hat provides methods for creating, installing, and
configuring RAID and LVM devices during the Linux
installation process. If, instead, you wish to add these
devices later, you need to first enable support for RAID
in the kernel. RAID is not enabled by default unless you
installed RAID devices during installation. As discussed
in Chapters 7 and 8, you need to configure kernel modules,
in this case, modules for RAID and LVM devices. During
kernel configuration, select multidevice support (RAID
and LVM) from the Linux Kernel Configuration window.
You can then choose to enable support for RAID and LVM,
either as modules or as a built-in kernel feature (If you

make them parts of the kernel, you will have to rebuild the entire kernel). For RAID devices, you can choose the type of Linux software RAID devices you want to install.

Configuring RAID Devices

RAID is a method of storing data across several disks to provide greater performance and redundancy. In effect, you can have several hard disks treated as just one hard disk by your operating system. RAID then efficiently stores and retrieves data across all these disks, instead of having the operating system access each one as a separate file system. Lower-level details of storage and retrieval are no longer a concern of the operating system. This allows greater flexibility in adding or removing hard disks, as well as implementing redundancy in the storage system to provide greater reliability. With RAID, you can have several hard disks that are treated as one virtual disk, where some of the disks are used as real-time mirrors, duplicating data. You can use RAID in several ways depending upon the degree of reliability you need. By placing data on multiple disks, I/O operations can overlap in a balanced way, improving performance. Because having multiple disks increases the mean time between failures (MTBF), storing data redundantly also increases fault-tolerance.

RAID can be implemented on a hardware or software level. On a hardware level, you can have hard disks connected to a RAID hardware controller, usually a special PC card. Your operating system then accesses storage through the RAID hardware controller. Alternatively, you can implement RAID as a software controller, letting a software RAID controller program manage access to hard disks treated as RAID devices. The software version lets you use IDE hard disks as RAID disks. Linux uses the MD driver, supported in the 2.4 kernel, to implement a software RAID controller. Linux software RAID supports five levels (linear, 0, 1, 4, and 5) whereas hardware RAID supports many more. Hardware RAID levels, such as

6 through 10, provide combinations of greater performance and reliability.

TIP   *Before you can use RAID on your system, make sure it is supported on your kernel, along with the RAID levels you want to use. If not, you will have to reconfigure and install a RAID module for the kernel. Check the Multi-Driver Support component in your kernel configuration. You can specify support of any or all of the RAID levels.*

Linux Software RAID Levels

Linux software RAID can be implemented at different levels, depending on whether you want organization, efficiency, redundancy, or reconstruction capability. Each capability corresponds to different RAID levels. For most levels, the size of the hard disk devices should be the same. For mirroring RAID 1, disks of the same size are required, and for RAID 5, they are recommended. Linux software RAID supports five levels, as shown in Table 6-1 (On Red Hat, level 4 is implemented as part of level 5).

RAID Levels	Capability	Description
linear	Appending	Simply treats RAID hard drives as one virtual drive with no striping, mirroring, or parity reconstruction.
0	Striping	Implements disk striping across drives with no redundancy.
1	Mirroring	Implements a high level of redundancy. Each drive is treated as mirror for all data.
5	Distributed Parity	Implements data reconstruction capability using parity information. Parity information is distributed across all drives, instead of using a separate drive as in RAID 4.

Table 6-1.   Linux Software RAID Levels

Linear

The Linear level lets you simply organize several hard disks
into one logical hard disk, providing a pool of continuous
storage. Instead of being forced to set up separate
partitions on each hard drive, in effect you have only one
hard drive. The storage is managed sequentially. When
one hard disk fills up, the next one is used. In effect, you
are *appending* one hard disk to the other. This level
provides no recovery capability. If you had a hard disk
RAID array containing two 80GB disks, after you used
up the storage on one, you would automatically start on
the next.

RAID 0: Striping

For efficiency, RAID stores data using disk *striping*, where
data is organized into standardized stripes that can be
stored across the RAID drives for faster access (level 0).
RAID 0 also organizes your hard disks into common RAID
devices, but treats them like single hard disks, storing
data randomly across all the disks. If you had a hard disk
RAID array containing two 80GB disks, you could access
them as one 160GB RAID device.

RAID 1: Mirroring

RAID level 1 implements redundancy through *mirroring*.
In mirroring, the same data is written to each RAID drive.
Each disk has a complete copy of all the data written so
that if one or more disks fail, the others still have your data.
Though extremely safe, redundancy can be very inefficient
and consumes a great deal of storage. For example, on a
RAID array of two 80GB disk drives, one disk is used for
standard storage and the other is a real-time backup. This
leaves you with only 80GB for use on your system. Write
operations also have to be duplicated across as many
mirrored hard disks used by the RAID array, slowing
down operations.

RAID 5: Distributed Parity

As an alternative to mirroring, data can be reconstructed
using *parity information* in case of a hard drive crash.
Parity information is saved instead of full duplication of

the data. Parity information takes up the space equivalent of one drive, leaving most of the space on the RAID drives free for storage. RAID 5 combines both striping and parity (see RAID 4), where parity information is distributed across the hard drives, rather than in one drive dedicated to that purpose. This allows the use of the more efficient access method, striping. With both striping and parity, RAID 5 provides both fast access and recovery capability, making it the most popular RAID level used. For example, a RAID array of four 80GB hard drives would be treated as one 320GB hard drive with part of that storage (80 GB) used to hold parity information, giving 240 GB free.

RAID 4: Parity

Though it is not supported in Red Hat due to overhead costs, RAID 4, like RAID 5, supports a more compressed form of recovery using parity information instead of mirrored data. With RAID 4, parity information is kept on a separate disk, while the others are used for data storage, much like a linear model.

TIP *Red Hat also allows you to create and format RAID drives during installation. At that time, you can create your RAID partitions and devices.*

RAID Devices: md

A RAID device is named an md, and uses the MD driver. These devices are already defined on your Linux system in the /etc/dev directory, starting with md0. /dev/md0 is the first RAID device, and /dev/md1 is the second, and so on. Each RAID device, in turn, uses hard disk partitions, where each partition contains an entire hard disk. These partitions are usually referred to as RAID disks, whereas a RAID device is an array of the RAID disks it uses.

Corresponding Hard Disk Partitions

The term *device* can be confusing, because it is also used to refer to the particular hard disk partitions that make up a RAID device. In fact, a software RAID device is an array of hard disk partitions, where each partition could, but not necessarily, take up an entire hard disk. In that case, you can think of a RAID device as consisting of a set (array) of hard disks (devices). In practice, the hard disks in your RAID configuration would normally contain several corresponding hard disk partitions, each set having the same size. Each set of corresponding partitions would make up a RAID device. So you could have several RAID devices using the same set of hard disks. This is particularly true for Linux partition configurations, where different system directories are placed in their own partitions. For example, /boot could be in one partition, /home in another, and / (the root) in yet another partition. To set up RAID devices so that you have separate partitions for /boot, /home, and /root, you need to create three different RAID devices, say md0 for /boot, md1 for /home, and md2 for the root. If you have two hard disks, for example hda and hdb, each would have three partitions, /boot, /home, and /. The first RAID device, md0, would consist of the two /boot partitions, the one on hda and the one on hdb. Similarly, the second raid device, md1, would be made up of the two root partitions, /, the one on hda and the other on hdb. md3 would consist of the /home partitions on hda and hdb (see Figure 6-1).

When you create the partitions for a particular RAID device, it is important to make sure that each partition has the same size. For example, the / partition used for the md0 device on the hda disk must have the same size as the corresponding md0 partition on the hdb disk. So if the md1 partition on hda is 20GB, then its corresponding partition on hdb must also be 20GB. If md2 is 100GB on one drive, its corresponding partitions on all other drives must also be 100GB.

TIP   *During installation, Red Hat Disk Druid supports the Clone tool that lets you automatically create the corresponding partitions on other hard disks based on one already set up. In effect, you set up the RAID partitions for each RAID device on one hard disk, and then use the Clone tool to create their corresponding partitions on your other hard disks.*

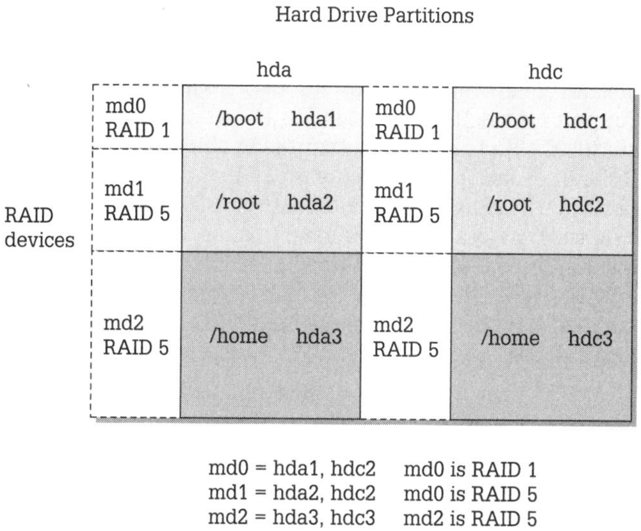

Hard Drive Partitions

md0 = hda1, hdc2   md0 is RAID 1
md1 = hda2, hdc2   md0 is RAID 5
md2 = hda3, hdc3   md2 is RAID 5

Figure 6-1.   RAID devices

Booting from a RAID Device

As part of the installation process, Red Hat lets you create
RAID devices from which you can also boot your system.
Your Linux system will be configured to load RAID kernel
support and automatically detect your RAID devices.
The boot loader will be installed on your RAID device,
meaning on all the hard disks making up that device.

Red Hat does not support booting from RAID 5, only RAID 1.
This means that if you want to use RAID 5 and still boot
from RAID disks, you will need to create at least two (or
more if you want) RAID devices using corresponding
partitions for each device across your hard disks. One
device would hold your /boot partition and be installed
as a RAID 1 device. This RAID 1 device would be the
first RAID device, md0, consisting of the first partition on
each hard disk. The second RAID device, md1, could then
be a RAID 5 device. It would consist of corresponding
partitions on the other hard disks. Your system could then
boot from the RAID 1 device, but use the RAID 5 device.

If you do not create RAID disks during installation, but create them later and want to boot from them, you will have to make sure your system is configured correctly. The RAID devices need to be created with persistent superblocks. Support for the RAID devices has to be enabled in the kernel. On Red Hat, this support is enabled as a module. Difficulties occur if you are using RAID 5 for your / (root) partition. This partition contains the RAID 5 module, but to access the partition, you have to already load the RAID 5 module. To work around this limitation, you can create a RAM disk in the /boot partition that contains the RAID 5 module. Use the `mkinitrd` command to create the RAM disk and the `-with` option to specify the module to include.

```
mkinitrd --preload raid5 --with=raid5 raid-ramdisk 2.4.20-8
```

Automatic Detection: Persistent Superblocks

Linux software RAID now supports automatic detection of RAID devices. This allows your RAID devices to be detected automatically whenever your system boots, just like standard partitions. You can then use any RAID device (`md`) as you would a hard disk partition (`hd` or `sd`), using them in `/etc/fstab` file (see Chapter 5). Automatic detection is implemented using persistent superblocks placed on each RAID disk to hold configuration information. A persistent superblock needs to be created when you create the RAID device using `mkraid`. To instruct mkraid to create a persistent superblock, you specify the `persistent-superblock` option in the `/etc/raidtab` file, the RAID configuration file. Without the persistent superblock option, you would have to manually start your RAID devices with the `raidstart` command. `raidstart` `-a` starts up all your devices.

RAID Tools

The RAID tools are useful for managing software RAID devices on Linux. `mkraid` creates a RAID device, `raidstop` stops the device, and `raidstart` turns it on (see Table 4-2). These are discussed in detail in the next section.

Tool	Description
mkraid	Creates (configures) RAID devices from a set of block devices, initializing them.
raidstart	Activates RAID devices.
raid0start	Activates older non-persistent linear and RAID 0 RAID devices.
raidstop	Turns off a RAID device.

Table 6-2.   RAID Tools

Creating and Installing RAID Devices

If you created your RAID devices and their partitions during the installation process, you should already have working RAID devices. Your RAID devices will be configured in the /etc/raidtab file, and the status of your RAID devices will be listed in the /proc/mdstat file. You can manually start or stop your RAID devices with the raidstart and raidstop commands. The -a option operates on all of them, though you can specify particular devices if you want.

To create a new RAID device manually for an already installed system, follow these steps:

1. Make sure that your kernel supports the RAID level you want for the device you are creating. To enable support for a RAID level in the kernel, use the kernel configuration tool to create a module for it, as discussed previously.

2. If you have not already done so, create the RAID disks (partitions) you will use for your RAID device.

3. Configure your RAID device (/dev/mdn) in the /etc/raidtab file, specifying the RAID disks to use. Be sure to specify the persistent superblock option to have your RAID devices automatically detected when you boot.

4. Create your RAID device with mkraid.

5. Activate the RAID device with `raidstart`.

6. Create a file system on the RAID device (`mkfs`) and then mount it.

Creating Hard Disk Partitions: fd

To add new RAID devices or to create them in the first place, you need to manually create the hard disk partitions they will use, and then configure RAID devices to use those partitions. To create a hard disk partition for use in a RAID array, use `fdisk` or `parted` and specify `fd` as the file system type. You invoke `fdisk` or `parted` with the device name of the hard disk you want to create the partition on. Be sure to specify `fd` as the partition type. The following example invokes `fdisk` for the hard disk `/dev/hdb` (the second hard disk on the primary IDE connection):

```
fdisk /dev/hdb
```

Though technically partitions, these hard disk devices are referred to as disks in RAID configuration documentation and files.

Configuring RAID: /etc/raidtab

Once you have your disks, you then need to configure them as RAID devices. RAID devices are configured in the `/etc/raidtab` file. This file will be used by the `mkraid` command to create the RAID device. In the `/etc/raidtab` file, you create a `raiddev` entry for each RAID device, and specify which disks they will use along with any RAID options. For a `raiddev` entry, you specify the name of the RAID device you are configuring, such as `/dev/md0` for the first RAID device.

```
raiddev   /dev/md0
```

You then specify the level for the RAID device, such as 0, 1, or 5 using the keyword `raid-level` followed by the rail level number. Then add any options you may need, along with the list of disks making up the RAID array. A disk is defined with the `device` entry, and its position

in the RAID array with the `raid-disk` option. The
configuration directives and options are listed in Table 6-3.
A sample entry for the `/etc/raidtab` file is shown here:

```
raiddev /dev/md0
    raid-level              5
    nr-raid-disks           3
    nr-spare-disks          1
    persistent-superblock   1
    chunk-size              4
    parity-algorithm        left-symmetric
    device                  /dev/hdb1
    raid-disk               0
    device                  /dev/hdc1
    raid-disk               1
    device                  /dev/hdd1
    raid-disk               0
```

The previous example configures the RAID device `/dev/md0`
as a RAID 5 (`raid-level` 5) device. There are three disks
(partitions) that make up this RAID array, `/dev/hdb1`,
`/dev/hdc1`, and `/dev/hdd1`, of which `/dev/hdb1` is the
first and `/dev/hdc1` is the second. There is one spare
disk, `/dev/hdd1`. There are three RAID disks altogether
(`nr-raid-disks`) and one spare partition (`nr-spare-
disks`). The RAID file system uses persistent superblocks
(`persistent-superblock`) to hold file system
configuration information, allowing your devices to be
automatically detected. The `parity-algorithm` option
is used for RAID 5 devices to specify the type of parity
algorithm to use for parity restoration, in this example,
left-symmetric.

Directives and Options	Description
`raiddev` *device*	Starts a configuration section for a particular RAID device.
`raid-level` *num*	The RAID level for the RAID device, such as 0, 1, 4, 5, and –1 (linear).

Table 6-3.   raidtab Options

Directives and Options	Description
`device` *disk-device*	The disk device (partition) to be added to the RAID array. The number of device entries specified for a RAID device must match that specified by `nr-raid-disks`.
`nr-raid-disks` *count*	Number of RAID devices in an array. Each RAID device section must have this directive. The maximum limit is 12.
`nr-spare-disks` *count*	The number of spare devices in the array. Used only for RAID 4 and RAID 5. The kernel must be configured to and allow the automatic addition of new RAID disks as needed. You can add and remove spare disks with `raidhotadd` and `raidhotremove`.
`persistent-superblock` *0/1*	Specifies whether a newly created RAID array should use a persistent superblock. Used to help the kernel automatically detect the RAID array. RAID array information is kept in a superblock on each RAID member.
`chunk-size` *size*	Sets the stripe size to *size* bytes, in powers of 2.
`device` *devpath*	Adds the most recently defined device to the list of devices which make up the RAID system.
`raid-disk` *index*	Inserts the most recently defined RAID device at the specified position in the RAID array.
`spare-disk` *index*	Inserts the most recently defined RAID device as a spare device at the specified position in the RAID array.

Table 6-3. raidtab Options *(continued)*

Directives and Options	Description
parity-disk *index*	The most recently defined device is used as the parity device, placing it at the end of the RAID array.
parity-algorithm *algorithm*	For RAID 5 devices, specifies the parity algorithm to use: left-asymmetric, right-asymmetric, left-symmetric, or right-symmetric.
failed-disk *index*	The most recently defined device is added to a RAID array as a failed device at the specified position.

Table 6-3. raidtab Options *(continued)*

6

The mkraid Command

Once you have configured your RAID devices in the /etc/ raidtab file, you then use the mkraid command to create your RAID devices. mkraid takes as its argument the name of the RAID device, such as /dev/md0 for the first RAID device. It then locates the entry for that device in the /etc/ raidtab file and uses that configuration information to create the RAID file system on that device. You can specify an alternative configuration file with the -c option, if you wish. mkraid operates as a kind of mkfs command for RAID devices, initializing the partitions and creating the RAID file systems. Any data on the partitions making up the RAID array will be erased.

mkraid /dev/md0

The raidstart Command

Once you have created your RAID devices, you can then activate them with the raidstart command. raidstart makes your RAID file system accessible. raidstart takes as its argument the name of the RAID device you want to start. The -a option activates all RAID devices.

raidstart /dev/md0

Creating a File System

Once the RAID devices are activated, you can then create file systems on the RAID devices and mount those file systems. The following example creates a standard Linux file system on the /dev/md0 device:

```
mkfs.ext3 /dev/md0
```

In the following example, the user then creates a directory called /myraid and mounts the RAID device there:

```
mkdir /myraid
mount /dev/md0 /myraid
```

If you plan to use your RAID device for maintaining your user directories and files, you would mount the RAID device as your /home partition. Such a mounting point might normally be used if you created your RAID devices when installing your system. To transfer your current home directories to a RAID device, first back them up on another partition, and then mount your RAID device, copying your home directories to it.

The raidstop Command

If you decide to change your RAID configuration or add new devices, you first have to deactivate your currently active RAID devices. To deactivate a RAID device, you use the raidstop command. Be sure to close any open files and unmount any file systems on the device first.

```
umount /dev/md0
raidstop /dev/md0
```

TIP *Hot swapping is the practice of replacing drives while the system is running. Its feasibility is limited. Never try to hot swap an IDE drive; you could destroy the drive. SCSI drives might successfully swap, though most likely not. IBM SCA drives can successfully swap. You can use the* raidhotadd and raidhotremove *commands to perform such a swap.*

RAID Example

Figure 6-1 shows a simple RAID configuration with three
RAID devices using corresponding partitions on two hard
disks for /boot, /root, and /home partitions. The boot
partition is configured as a RAID 1 device because systems
can only be booted from a RAID 1 device, not RAID 5. The
other partitions are RAID 5 devices, a more commonly
used RAID access method.

You could set up such a system during installation, selecting
and formatting your RAID devices and their partitions
using Disk Druid. The steps described here assume you
have your system installed already on a standard IDE
drive and are setting up RAID devices on two other IDE disk
drives. You can then copy your file from your standard drive
to your RAID devices.

First, you create the hard disk partitions using a partition
tool like parted or fdisk.

Then, configure the three raid devices in the /etc/raidtab
file.

```
raiddev /dev/md0
                raid-level              1
                nr-raid-disks           2
                nr-spare-disks          0
                persistent-superblock   1
                chunk-size              4
                device                  /dev/hda1
                raid-disk               0
                device                  /dev/hdc1
                raid-disk               1

raiddev /dev/md1
                raid-level              5
                nr-raid-disks           2
                persistent-superblock   1
                chunk-size              4
                parity-algorithm        left-symmetric
                device                  /dev/hda2
                raid-disk               0
                device                  /dev/hdc2
```

```
                raid-disk                 1

raiddev /dev/md2
                raid-level                5
                nr-raid-disks             2
                persistent-superblock     1
                chunk-size                4
                parity-algorithm          left-symmetric
                device                    /dev/hda3
                raid-disk                 0
                device                    /dev/hdc3
                raid-disk                 1
```

Then, create your RAID devices with mkraid.

```
mkraid md0 md1 md2
```

Activate the RAID devices with raidstart.

```
raidstart md0 md1 md2
```

Create your file systems on the raid devices.

```
mkfs.ext3 md0 md1 md2
```

You can then migrate the /boot, /, and /home files from your current hard disk to your RAID devices. Install your boot loader on the first RAID device, md0, and load the root file system from the second RAID device, md1.

Logical Volume Manager

For easier hard disk storage management, you can set up your system to use the Logical Volume Manager (LVM), creating LVM partitions that are organized into logical volumes to which free space is automatically allocated. Logical Volumes provide a more flexible and powerful way of dealing with disk storage, organizing physical partitions into logical volumes in which you can easily manage disk space. Disk storage for a logical volume is treated as one pool of memory, though the volume may in fact contain several hard disk partitions spread across different hard disks. Adding a new LVM partition merely increases the pool of storage accessible to the entire system.

LVM Structure

In an LVM structure, LVM physical partitions, also known as extents, are organized into logical groups, which are in turn used by logical volumes. In effect, you are dealing with three different levels of organization. At the lowest level, you have physical volumes. These are physical hard disk partitions that you create with partition creation tools like `parted` or `fdisk`. The partition type can be any standard Linux partition type, like `ext3` or `ext2`. These physical volumes are organized into logical groups, known as volume groups, that operate much like logical hard disks. You assign collections of physical volumes to different logical groups. For example, if you have physical volumes consisting of the hard disk partitions `hda2`, `hda3`, `hdb1`, `hdb2`, and `hdb3` on two hard disks, `hda` and `hdb`, you could assign some of them to one logical group and others to another logical group. The partitions making up the different logical groups can be from different physical hard drives. For example, `hda2` and `hdb3` could belong to the logical group turtle and `hda3`, `hdb2`, and `hdb3` could make up a different logical group, say rabbit. The logical group name could be any name you want to give it. It is much like naming a hard drive.

Once you have your logical groups, you can then create logical volumes. Logical volumes function much like hard disk partitions on a standard setup. For example, on the `turtle` group volume, you could create a `/var` logical volume, and on the rabbit logical group, you could create a `/home` and a `/projects` logical volume. You can have several logical volumes on one logical group, just as you can have several partitions on one hard disk.

You treat the logical volumes as you would any ordinary hard disk partition. You create a file system on it with the `mkfs` command, and then you can mount the file system to use it with the `mount` command.

6

Storage on logical volumes is managed using what are known as extents. A logical group defines a standard size for an extent, say 4MB, and then divides each physical volume in its group into extents of that size. Logical volumes are, in turn, divided into extents of the same size, which are then mapped to those on the physical volumes.

There is one restriction and recommendation for Logical Volumes. The boot partition cannot be part of a logical volume. You still have to create a separate hard disk partition as your boot partition with the /boot mount point in which your kernel and all needed boot files are installed. In addition, it is recommended that you do not place your root (/) partition on a logical volume. Doing so can complicate any needed data recovery.

Creating LVMs with Disk Druid

Creating logical volumes involves several steps. First, you create physical LVM partitions, then the volume groups you place these partitions in, and then from the volume groups, you create the logical volumes for which you then specify mount points and file system types. On Red Hat, you can create LVM partitions during the installation process using Disk Druid. In Disk Druid, click New and select "physical volume (LVM)" for the File System Type. Create an LVM physical partition for each partition you want on your hard disks. Once you have created LVM physical partitions, you click the LVM button to create your logical volumes. You first need to assign the LVM physical partitions to volume groups. Volume groups are essentially logical hard drives. You could assign LVM physical partitions from different hard disks to the same volume group, letting the volume group span different hard drives. Once the volume groups are created, you are ready to create your logical volumes. You can create several logical volumes within each group. The logical volumes function like partitions. You will have to specify a file system type and mount point for each logical volume you create.

LVM Tools

On Red Hat, you can create logical volumes either
during the installation process, or later use a collection
of LVM tools to manage your LVM volumes, adding
new LVM physical partitions and removing current
ones. LVM maintains configuration information in the
`/etc/lvmconf` directory.

Displaying LVM Information

You can use `pvdisplay`, `vgdisplay`, and `lvdisplay`
commands to show detailed information about a physical
partition, volume groups, and logical volumes. `pvscan`,
`vgscan`, and `lvscan` list your physical, group, and
logical volumes.

6

Managing LVM Physical Volumes

A physical volume can be any hard disk partition or RAID
device. A RAID device is seen as a single physical volume.
You can create physical volumes either from a single
hard disk or from partitions on a hard disk. On very large
systems with many hard disks, you would more likely
use an entire hard disk for each physical volume.

To create a new physical volume, you initialize it with
the `pvcreate` command with the partition's device name,
as shown here:

`pvcreate /dev/hda3`

To initialize a physical volume on an entire hard disk, you
use the hard disk device name, as shown here:

`pvcreate /dev/hdc`

Then, use the `vgextend` command to add the partition to
a logical group, in this case, `rabbit`. In effect, you are
extending the size of the logical group by adding a new
physical partition.

`vgextend  rabbit  /dev/hda3`

To remove a physical partition, first remove it from its
logical volume. You may have to use the `pmove` command

to move any data off the physical partition. Then, use the `vgreduce` command to remove it from its logical group.

Managing LVM Groups

You can manually create a volume group using the `vgcreate` command and the name of the group along with a list of physical partitions you want in the group. The following example creates a group called `rabbit` consisting of three physical partitions, `/dev/hda3`, `/dev/hdb4`, and `/dev/hdb4`.

```
vgcreate rabbit  /dev/hda3 /dev/hdb2 /dev/hdb4
```

You can remove a volume group by first deactivating it with `vgchange -a n` operation and then using the `vgremove` command.

Activating Volume Groups

Whereas in a standard file system structure, you mount and unmount hard disk partitions, with an LVM structure, you activate and deactivate entire volume groups. The group volumes are accessible until you activate them with the `vgchange` command with the `-a` option. To activate a group, first reboot your system, and then enter the `vgchange` command with the `-a` option and the `y` argument to activate the logical group (an `n` argument will deactivate the group).

```
vgchange -a  y  rabbit
```

Managing LVM Logical Volumes

To create logical volumes, you use the `lvcreate` command. With the `-n` option, you specify the volume's name, which functions like a hard disk partition's label. You use the `-L` option to specify the size of the volume. The following example creates a logical volume named `projects` on the `rabbit` logical group with a size of 20GB.

```
lvcreate -n projects  -L 20000M rabbit
```

You can remove a logical volume with the `lvremove` command. With `lvextend`, you can increase the size of the logical volume, and `lvreduce` will reduce its size.

LVM Example

Using the example in Figure 6-2, the steps involved in creating and accessing logical volumes are described in following commands. First, use a partition creation tool like `fdisk` or `parted` to create the physical partitions on the hard disks `hda` and `hdb`. In this example, you create the partitions `hda1`, `hda2`, `hda3`, `hdb1`, `hdb2`, `hdb3`, and `hdb4`.

Then, you initialize the physical volumes with the `pvcreate` command. The `hda1` and `hda2` partitions are reserved for the boot and root partitions and are not initialized.

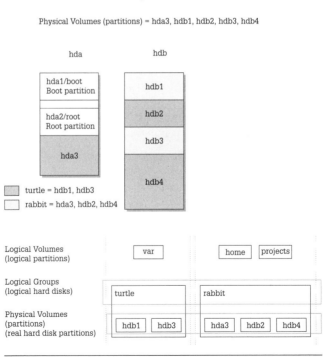

Logical Volumes

Physical Volumes (partitions) = hda3, hdb1, hdb2, hdb3, hdb4

hda   hdb

| hda1/boot Boot partition |
| hda2/root Root partition |
| hda3 |

hdb1
hdb2
hdb3
hdb4

turtle = hdb1, hdb3
rabbit = hda3, hdb2, hdb4

Logical Volumes (logical partitions)   var   home   projects

Logical Groups (logical hard disks)   turtle   rabbit

Physical Volumes (partitions) (real hard disk partitions)   hdb1   hdb3   hda3   hdb2   hdb4

Figure 6-2. Logical Volume Management

```
pvcreate  /dev/hda3  /dev/hdb1  /dev/hdb2
pvcreate  /dev/hdb3  /dev/hdb4
```

You then create the logical groups you want using the
`vgcreate` command. In this case, there are two logical
groups, `turtle` and `rabbit`. The `turtle` group uses
`hdb1` and `hdb3`, and `rabbit` uses `hda3`, `hdb2`, and `hdb4`.
If you create a physical volume later and want to add it
to a volume group, you would use the `vgextend` command.

```
vgcreate turtle  /dev/hdb1 /dev/hdb3
vgcreate rabbit  /dev/hda3  /dev/hdb2 /dev/hdb4
```

You can now create the logical volumes in each volume
group, using the `lvcreate` command.

```
lvcreate  -n var        -l 2000M     turtle
lvcreate  -n home       -l 50000M    rabbit
lvcreate  -n projects   -l 20000M    rabbit
```

Then, you can activate the logical volumes. Reboot and
use `vgchange` with the `-a y` option to activate the logical
volumes.

```
vgchange -a y turtle rabbit
```

You can now make file systems for each logical volume.

```
mkfs.ext3 var
mkfs.ext3 home
mkfs.ext3 projects
```

Then, you can mount the logical volumes.

```
mount var   /var
mount home  /home
mount projects /mnt/myprojects
```

Chapter 7

Devices and Modules

All devices, such as printers, terminals, and CD-ROMs, are connected to your Linux operating system through special files called *device files*. Such a file contains all the information your operating system needs to control the specified device. This design introduces great flexibility. The operating system is independent of the specific details for managing a particular device; the specifics are all handled by the device file. The operating system simply informs the device what task it is to perform, and the device file tells it how. If you change devices, you only have to change the device file, not the whole system.

7

To install a device on your Linux system, you need a device file for it, a software configuration such as that provided by a configuration tool, and kernel support—usually supplied by a module or support that is already compiled and built into the kernel. An extensive number of device files are already set up for different kinds of devices. Usually you only need one, which is specific to your device. When you add new hardware devices, Kudzu, the Red Hat hardware probing tool, checks for the new hardware when your system boots. The Kudzu tool automatically detects a new device and lets you configure it. A profile of your hardware configurations are saved by Kudzu in the `/etc/sysconfig/hwconf` file. For more specialized kernel support, you may have to load a kernel module or recompile the kernel, both simple procedures (see Chapter 9). In most cases, support is already built into the kernel.

Device Files

The name of a device file is designed to reflect the task of the device. Printer device files begin with `lp` for "line print." Because you could have more than one printer connected to your system, the particular printer device files are distinguished by two or more numbers or letters following the prefix lp, such as lp0, lp1, lp2. The same is true for terminal device files. They begin with the prefix tty, for "teletype," and are further distinguished by numbers or letters such as tty0, tty1, ttyS0, and so on. You can obtain a complete listing of the current device filenames and the devices for which they are used from the kernel.org web site at http://www.kernel.org/pub/linux/docs/device-list/devices.txt.

Device Symbolic Links

All of these filenames will be implemented as device files in your /dev directory. Here, you can find printer, CD-ROM, hard drive, SCSI, and sound device files, along with many others. Certain files are really symbolic links that bear common device names that are often linked to the actual device file used. A *symbolic link* is used as another name for a file, linking you to that file. For example, a /dev/cdrom symbolic link links to the actual device file used for your CD-ROM. If your CD-ROM is an IDE device, it may use the device file hdc. In this case, /dev/cdrom would be a link to /dev/hdc. In effect, /dev/cdrom is another name for /dev/hdc. A /dev/modem link file also exists for your modem. If your modem is connected to the second serial port, its device file would be /dev/ttyS1. In this case, /dev/modem would be a link to that device file. Applications can then use /dev/modem to access your modem, instead of having to know the actual device file used. A listing of commonly used device links is shown in Table 7-1.

TIP *You will notice that there are no entries for the Ethernet devices in the /dev file, such as eth0 or eth1. That is because these are really aliases for kernel modules defined in the /etc/modules.conf file, or devices handled by the kernel directly. They are not device files.*

Link	Description
/dev/mouse	Current mouse device
/dev/tape	Current tape device
/dev/cdrom	Current CD-ROM device
/dev/cdwriter	Current CD-writer device
/dev/scanner	Current scanner device
/dev/modem	Current dial-out device, modem port
/dev/root	Current root file system
/dev/swap	Current swap device

Table 7-1. Device Links

Hardware Device Installation: Kudzu

Hardware devices are automatically detected by the Red Hat hardware probing tool known as Kudzu. Kudzu is a tool that detects and configures new or changed hardware on a system. Kudzu is run when you boot to configure new hardware devices and detect removed ones. You can also run Kudzu manually. When you start Kudzu, it detects the current hardware, and checks it against a database stored in /etc/sysconfig/hwconf. It then determines if any hardware has been added to or removed from the system. When it detects new or added hardware, Kudzu will, if needed, invoke the appropriate configuration tool for the device, like redhat-config-xfree86 for video cards, or redhat-config-keyboard for keyboards. For simple hardware configurations like CD-ROMs, Kudzu just links the cdrom device symbolic link to the new device, /dev/cdrom.

Kudzu then updates its database in /etc/sysconfig/ hwconf. If a removed device is detected, the hwconf file is updated accordingly. If the device was installed simply with a device link like /dev/cdrom or /dev/mouse, that link is removed. In the case of network cards, alias entries like that for eth0 will be removed.

Creating Device Files Manually

Linux implements two types of devices: block and character. A *block device,* such as a hard disk, transmits data a block at a time. A *character device,* such as a printer or modem, transmits data one character at a time, or rather as a continuous stream of data, not as separate blocks. Device driver files for character devices have a *c* as the first character in the permissions segment displayed by the `ls` command. Device driver files for block devices have a *b.* In the next example, lp0 (the printer) is a character device and hda1 (the hard disk) is a block device:

```
# ls -l hda1 lp0
brw-rw---- 1 root disk 3, 1 Jan 30 02:04 hda1
crw-rw---- 1 root lp   6, 0 Jan 30 02:04 lp0
```

Device Types

The device type can be either *b, c, p,* or *u.* As already mentioned, the *b* indicates a block device, and *c* is for a character device. The *u* is for an unbuffered character device, and the *p* is for a FIFO (First In First Out) device. Devices of the same type often have the same name, for example, serial interfaces all have the name: ttyS. Devices of the same type are then uniquely identified by a number attached to the name. This number has two components: the major number and the minor number. Devices may have the same major number, but if so, the minor number is always different. This major and minor structure is designed to deal with situations in which several devices may be dependent on one larger device, such as several modems connected to the same I/O card. All the modems would have the same major number that references the card, but each modem would have a unique minor number. Both the minor and major numbers are required for block and character devices (*b, c,* and *u*). They are not used for FIFO devices, however.

Valid device names along with their major and minor numbers are listed in the devices.txt file located in the /Documentation directory for the kernel source code,

`/usr/src/linux-`*ver*`/Documentation`. When you create a device, you use the major and minor numbers as well as the device name prefix for the particular kind of device you are creating. Most of these devices are already created for you, and are listed in the `/etc/dev` directory.

mknod

Although most distributions include an extensive set of device files already set up for you, you can create your own. You use the `mknod` command to create a device file, either a character or block type. The `mknod` command has the following syntax:

```
mknod options device device-type major-num minor-num
```

For example, Linux systems usually provide device files for three parallel ports (`lp0-2`). If you need more, you can use the `mknod` command to create a new one. Printer devices are character devices, and must be owned by the root and daemon. The permissions for printer devices are read and write for the owner and the group, 660 (see Chapter 2 for a discussion of file permissions). The major device number is set to 6, while the minor device number is set to the port number of the printer, such as 0 for LPT1 and 1 for LPT2. Once the device is created, you use `chown` to change its ownership to the `root` user, since only the administrator should control it. Change the group to `lp` with the `chgrp` command.

Most devices belong to their own groups, such as `disks` for hard disk partitions, `lp` for printers, and `floppy` for floppy disks, and `tty` for terminals. In the next example, a parallel printer device is made on a fourth parallel port, `/dev/lp3`. The `-m` option specifies the permissions—in this case, 660. The device is a character device, as indicated by the `c` argument following the device name. The major number is 6, and the minor number is 3. If you were making a device at `/dev/lp4`, the major number would still be 6, but the minor number would be 4. Once the device is made, the `chown` command then changes the ownership of the parallel printer device to `root`. For printers, be sure that a spool directory has been created for your device. If not, you need to make one. Spool directories contain files for

7

data that varies according to the device output or input, like printers or scanners.

```
# mknod -m 660 /dev/lp3 c 6 3
# chown root /dev/lp3
# chgrp lp /dev/lp3
```

Device Information: /proc and /etc/sysconfig/hwconf

On Red Hat, Kudzu maintains a complete profile of all your installed hardware devices in the /etc/sysconfig/ hwconf file (/etc/sysconfig is discussed in Chapter 1). As noted previously, this file is updated by Kudzu (kudzu); your new hardware is added and old ones removed. Entries define configuration variables such as the device's class (video, CD-ROM, hard drive, and so on), the bus it uses (PCI, IDE, and so on), its device name (such as hdd or st0), the drivers it uses, and a description of the device. A mouse entry is shown here:

```
class: MOUSE
bus: PSAUX
detached: 0
device: psaux
driver: generic3ps/2
desc: "Generic 3 Button Mouse (PS/2)"
```

The /proc file system (see Chapter 4) maintains special information files for your devices. The /proc/devices file lists all your installed character and block devices along with their major numbers. IRQs, DMAs, and I/O ports currently used for devices are listed in the interrupts, dma, and ioports files, respectively. Certain files list information covering several devices, such as pci, which lists all your PCI devices, and sound, which lists all your sound devices. The sound file lists detailed information about your sound card. Several subdirectories, such as net, ide, and scsi, contain information files for different devices. Certain files hold configuration information that can be changed dynamically, like the IP packet forwarding

File	Description
/proc/devices	Lists the device drivers configured for the currently running kernel
/proc/dma	Displays the DMA channels currently used
/proc/interrupts	Displays the IRQs (interrupts) in use
/proc/ioports	Shows the I/O ports in use
/proc/pci	Lists PCI devices
/proc/sound	Lists sound devices
/proc/scsi	Directory for SCSI devices
/proc/ide	Directory for IDE devices
/proc/net	Directory for network devices

Table 7-2. Proc Device Information Files

capability and the maximum number of files. You can change these values with the redhat-config-proc tool (Kernel Tuning in the System Tools menu) or by manually editing certain files. Table 7-2 lists several device-related /proc files (see Chapter 4 for other entries).

Installing and Managing Terminals and Modems

In Linux, several users may be logged in at the same time. Each user needs his or her own terminal through which to access the Linux system, of course. The monitor on your PC acts as a special terminal, called the *console*, but you can add other terminals either through the serial ports on your PC or a special multiport card installed on your PC. The other terminals can be standalone terminals or PCs using terminal emulation programs. For a detailed explanation of terminal installation, see the Term-HOWTO file in /usr/share/doc/HOWTO (installed as part of Red Hat documentation CD-ROM) or at the Linux Documentation Project site (www.tldp.org). A brief explanation is provided here.

Serial Ports

The serial ports on your PC are referred to as COM1, COM2, COM3, and COM4. These serial ports correspond to the terminal devices `/dev/ttyS0` through `/dev/ttyS3`. Note that several of these serial devices may already be used for other input devices such as your mouse, and for communications devices such as your modem. If you have a serial printer, one of these serial devices is already used for that. If you installed a multiport card, you have many more ports from which to choose. For each terminal you add, you must create a character device on your Linux system. As with printers, you use the `mknod` command to create terminal devices. The permissions for a terminal device are 660. *Terminal devices* are character devices with a major number of 4 and minor numbers usually beginning at 64.

TIP   *The `/dev/pts` entry in the `/etc/fstab` file mount a `devpts` file system at `/dev/pts` for Unix98 Psuedo-TTYs. These pseudo terminals are identified by devices named by number.*

mingetty, mgetty, and agetty

Terminal devices are managed by your system using the `getty` program and a set of configuration files. When your system starts, it reads a list of connected terminals in the `inittab` file and then executes an appropriate `getty` program for each one, either `mingetty`, `mgetty`, or `agetty`. Such `getty` programs set up the communication between your Linux system and a specified terminal. `mingetty` provides minimal support for virtual consoles, whereas `agetty` provides enhanced support for terminal connections. `agetty` also includes parameters for the baud rate and timeout. `mgetty` is designed for fax/modem connections, letting you configure dialing, login, and fax parameters. `mgetty` configuration files are held in the `/etc/mgetty+sendfax` directory. Modem connection information is held in the `/etc/mgetty+sendfax/mgetty.config` file. All `getty` programs can read an initial message placed in the `/etc/issue` file, which can contain special codes to provide the system name and current date and time.

termcap and inittab Files

The `/etc/inittab` file holds instructions for your system on how to manage terminal devices. A line in the `/etc/inittab` file has four basic components: an ID, a runlevel, an action, and a process. Terminal devices are identified by ID numbers, beginning with 1 for the first device. The runlevel at which the terminal operates is usually 1. The action is usually *respawn,* which means to run the process continually. The process is a call to the `mingetty`, `mgetty`, or `agetty` with the terminal device name. The `/etc/termcap` file holds the specifications for different terminal types. These are the different types of terminals users could use to log in to your system. Your `/etc/termcap` file is already filled with specifications for most of the terminals currently produced. An entry in the `/etc/termcap` file consists of various names that can be used for a terminal separated by a pipe character (`|`) and then a series of parameter specifications, each ending in a colon. You find the name used for a specific terminal type here. You can use `more` to display your `/etc/termcap` file, and then use a search, `/`, to locate your terminal type. You can set many options for a terminal device. To change these options, use the `stty` command instead of changing configuration files directly. The `stty` command with no arguments lists the current setting of the terminal.

tset

When a user logs in, having the terminal device initialized using the `tset` command is helpful. Usually, the `tset` command is placed in the user's `.bash_profile` file and is automatically executed whenever the user logs in to the system. You use the `tset` command to set the terminal type and any other options the terminal device requires. A common entry of `tset` for a `.bash_profile` file follows. The `-m dialup:` option prompts the user to enter a terminal type. The type specified here is a default type that is displayed in parentheses. The user presses ENTER to choose the default. The prompt looks like this: `TERM=(vt100)?.`

```
eval 'tset -s -Q -m dialup:?vt00'
```

Input Devices

Input devices, such as mice and keyboards, are displayed on several levels. Initial configuration is performed during installation where you select the mouse and keyboard types. You can change that configuration with your administration configuration tools, such as redhat-config-mouse and redhat-config-keyboard (Mouse and Keyboard in the System Settings menu and window). Special configurations also exist for mice and keyboard for the X Window System, and for the KDE and Gnome desktops. You select the keyboard layout and language, as well as configure the speed and display of the mouse.

Installing Sound, Network, and Other Cards

To install a new card, your kernel must first be configured to support it. Support for most cards is provided in the form of modules that can be dynamically loaded into the kernel. Installing support for a card is usually a simple matter of loading a module that includes the drives for it. For example, drivers for the Sound Blaster sound card are in the module sb.o. Loading this module makes your sound card accessible to Linux. Most distributions automatically detect the cards installed on your system and load the needed modules. If you change sound cards, the new card is automatically detected by Kudzu, invoking redhat-config-soundcard to configure it. For network cards, Kudzu invokes redhat-config-network to perform the configuration. You could also load modules you need manually, removing an older conflicting one. The section "Modules" later in this chapter describes this process.

Device files for most cards are already set up for you in the /dev directory. For example, the device name for your sound card is /dev/audio. The device names for network cards are aliases for network modules instead of device files. For example, the device name for your Ethernet card begins with eth, with the numbering starting from 0, as in `eth0` for the first Ethernet card on your system. They alias the module used for that particular card, for example, a 3Com Etherlink XL card aliases the 3c59x network module, whose alias would be `eth0` if it is the first Ethernet card. The modules themselves are kept in the kernel's module directory, `/lib/modules`, as described in the last section.

Sound Devices

On Red Hat, you can use the redhat-config-soundcard utility to install most sound cards on Linux. A listing of the different sound devices is provided in Table 7-3. Some sound cards may require more specialized support. For sound cards, you can tell what your current sound configuration is by listing the contents of the `/dev/sndstat` file. You can test your card by simply redirecting a sound file to it, as shown here:

```
cat sample.au > /dev/audio.
```

For the 2.4 kernel, most Linux sound drivers are developed as part of the Open Sound System (OSS) and freely distributed as OSS/Free. These are installed as part of Linux distributions. The OSS device drivers are intended to provide a uniform API for all Unix platforms, including Linux. They support Sound Blaster and Windows Sound System compatible sound cards (ISA and PCI). OSS is also available for a nominal fee and features configuration interfaces for device setup.

Device	Description
/dev/sndstat	Sound driver status
/dev/audio	Audio output device
/dev/dsp	Sound sampling device
/dev/mixer	Control mixer on sound card
/dev/music	High-level sequencer
/dev/sequencer	Low-level sequencer
/dev/midi	Direct MIDI port

Table 7-3. Sound Devices

The Advanced Linux Sound Architecture (ALSA) replaces OSS in the 2.6 Linux kernel. ALSA provides a modular sound driver, API, and configuration manager that aims to be a better alternative to OSS, while maintaining compatibility with it. ALSA is a GNU project and is entirely free; its web site at www.alsa-project.org contains extensive documentation, applications, and drivers. Currently available are the ALSA sound driver, the ALSA Kernel API, the ALSA library to support application development, and the ALSA manager to provide a configuration interface for the driver. ALSA evolved from the Linux Ultra Sound Project.

The Linux Musical Instrument Digital Interface (MIDI) and Sound Pages, currently at www.xdt.com/ar/linux-snd, hold links to web and FTP sites for Linux sound drivers for various sound cards. They also include links to sites for Linux MIDI and sound software.

Video, TV, and DVD Devices

Device names used for TV, video, and DVD devices are listed in Table 7-4. Drivers for DVD and TV decoders have been developed. mga4linux (marvel.sourceforge.net) is developing video support for the Matrox Multimedia cards like the Marvel G200. The General ATI TV and Overlay Software (GATOS) (gatos.sourceforge.net) has developed drivers for the currently unsupported features of ATI video cards, specifically TV features. The BTTV Driver Project has developed drivers for the Booktree video chip.

Device Name	Type of Device
/dev/video	Video capture interface
/dev/vfx	Video effects interface
/dev/codec	Video codec interface
/dev/vout	Video output interface
/dev/radio	AM/FM radio devices
/dev/vtx	Teletext interface chips
/dev/vbi	Data services interface

Table 7-4. Video Devices

Creative Labs sponsors Linux drivers for the Creative line of DVD DXR2 decoders (opensource.creative.com).

Modules

The Linux kernel employs the use of modules to support different operating system features, including support for various devices such as sound and network cards. In many cases, you do have the option of implementing support for a device either as a module or by directly compiling it as a built-in kernel feature, which requires you to rebuild the kernel (see Chapter 9). A safer and more robust solution is to use modules. *Modules* are components of the Linux kernel that can be loaded as needed. To add support for a new device, you can now simply instruct a kernel to load its module. In some cases, you may have to recompile only that module to provide support for your device. The use of modules has the added advantage of reducing the size of the kernel program as well as making your system more stable. The kernel can load modules in memory only as they are needed. Should a module fail, only the module stops running, not the entire system. For example, the module for the PPP network interface used for a modem only needs to be used when you connect to an ISP.

Kernel Module Tools

The modules your system needs are usually determined during installation, based on the kind of configuration information you provided and the automatic detection performed by Kudzu. For example, if your system uses an Ethernet card whose type you specified during installation, the system loads the module for that card. You can, however, manually control what modules are to be loaded for your system. In effect, this enables you to customize your kernel whatever way you want. You can use several commands, configuration tools, and daemons to manage kernel modules. The 2.4 Linux kernel includes the Kernel Module Loader (Kmod), which has the capability to load modules automatically as they are needed. Kernel module loading support must also be enabled in the Kernel, though this is usually considered part of a standard configuration and is included with Red Hat distributions. In addition, several tools enable you to load and unload modules manually, if you must. The Kernel Module Loader uses certain kernel commands to perform the task of loading or unloading modules. The `modprobe` command is a general-purpose command that calls `insmod` to load modules and `rmmod` to unload them. These commands are listed in Table 7-5. Options for particular modules, general configuration, and even specific module loading can be specified in the `/etc/modules.conf` file. You can use this file to automatically load and configure modules. You can also specify modules to be loaded at the boot prompt or in `grub.conf` (see Chapter 1).

Module Files and Directories

The filename for a module has the extension `.o`. Kernel modules reside in the `/lib/modules/`*version* directory, where *version* is the version number for your current kernel. The directory for the 2.4.20-8 kernel is `/lib/modules/2.4.20-8`. As you install new kernels on your system, new module directories are generated

Command	Description
`lsmod`	Lists modules currently loaded.
`insmod`	Loads a module into the kernel. Does not check for dependencies.
`rmmod`	Unloads a module currently loaded. Does not check for dependencies.
`modinfo`	Displays information about a module: `-a` (author), `-d` (description), `-p` (module parameters), `-f` (module filename), `-v` (module version)
`depmod`	Creates a dependency file listing all other modules on which the specified module may rely.
`modprobe`	Loads a module with any dependent modules it may also need. Uses the file of dependency listings generated by `depmod`: `-r` (unload a module), `-l` (list modules)

Table 7-5. Kernel Module Commands

for them. One method to access the directory for the current kernel is to use the `uname -r` command to generate the kernel version number. This command needs to have backquotes.

```
cd /lib/modules/`uname -r`
```

In this directory, modules for the kernel reside in the `/kernel` directory. Within the `/kernel` directory are several subdirectories, including the `/drivers` directory that holds subdirectories for modules like the sound drivers or video drivers. These subdirectories serve to categorize your modules, making them easier to locate. For example, the `kernel/drivers/net` directory holds modules for your Ethernet cards, and the `kernel/drivers/sound` directory contains sound card modules.

Managing Modules with /etc/modules.conf

As noted previously, there are several commands you can use to manage modules. The `lsmod` command lists the modules currently loaded into your kernel, and `modinfo` provides information about particular modules. Though you can use the `insmod` and `rmmod` commands to load or unload modules directly, you should only use `modprobe` for these tasks. See Table 7-5 for kernel module commands. Often, however, a given module requires other modules to be loaded. For example, the module for the Sound Blaster sound card, `sb.o`, requires the `sound.o` module to be loaded also.

The depmod Command

Instead of manually trying to determine what modules a given module depends on, you use the `depmod` command to detect the dependencies for you. The `depmod` command generates a file that lists all the modules on which a given module depends. The `depmod` command generates a hierarchical listing, noting what modules should be loaded first and in what order. Then, to load the module, you use the `modprobe` command using that file. `modprobe` reads the file generated by `depmod` and loads any dependent modules in the correct order, along with the module you want. You

need to execute `depmod` with the `-a` option once, before
you ever use `modprobe`. Entering `depmod -a` creates a
complete listing of all module dependencies. This command
creates a file called `modules.dep` in the module directory
for your current kernel version, `/lib/modules/version`.

```
depmod -a
```

The modprobe Command

To install a module manually, you use the `modprobe`
command and the module name. You can add any
parameters the module may require. The following
command installs the Sound Blaster sound module
with the I/O, IRQ, and DMA values. `modprobe` also
supports the use of the `*` character to enable you to
use a pattern to select several modules. This example
uses several values commonly used for sound cards.
You would use the values recommended for your
sound card on your system.

```
modprobe sb io=0x220 irq=5 dma=1
```

To discover what parameters a module takes, you can use
the `modinfo` command with the `-p` option.

```
modinfo -p sb
```

You can use the `-l` option to list modules and the `-t`
option to look for modules in a specified subdirectory.
In the next example, the user lists all modules in the
`sound` directory:

```
# modprobe -l -t sound
/lib/modules/2.4.20-8/kernel/drivers/sound/sb.o
/lib/modules/2.4.20-8/kernel/drivers
                                /sound/sb_lib.o
/lib/modules/2.4.20-8/kernel/drivers
                                /sound/sound.o
/lib/modules/2.4.20-8/kernel/drivers
                                /sound/soundcore.o
```

Options for the `modprobe` command are placed in the
`/etc/modules.conf` file. Here, you can enter configuration
options, such as default directories and aliases. An alias
provides a simple name for a module. For example, the
following entry enables you to reference the `3c59x.o`
Ethernet card module as `eth0` (Kmod automatically

detects the 3Com Ethernet card and loads the 3c59x module):

```
alias eth0 3c59x
```

The insmod Command

The `insmod` command performs the actual loading of modules. Both modprobe and the Kernel Module Loader make use of this command to load modules. Though `modprobe` is preferred, because it checks for dependencies, you can load or unload particular modules individually with `insmod` and `rmmod` commands. The `insmod` command takes as its argument the name of the module, as does `rmmod`. The name can be the simple base name, like `sb` for the `sb.o` module. You can specify the complete module file name using the `-o` option. Other helpful options are the `-p` option, which lets you probe your system first to see if the module can be successfully loaded, and the `-n` option, which performs all tasks except actually loading the module (a dummy run). The `-v` option (verbose) lists all actions taken as they occur. In those rare cases where you may have to force a module to load, you can use the `-f` option. In the next example, `insmod` loads the `sb.o` module.

```
# insmod -v sb
```

The rmmod Command

The `rmmod` command performs the actual unloading of modules. It is the command used by `modprobe` and the Kernel Module Loader to unload modules. You can use the `rmmod` command to remove a particular module as long as it is not being used or required by other modules. You can remove a module and all its dependent modules by using the `-r` option. The `-a` option removes all unused modules. With the `-e` option, when `rmmod` unloads a module, it saves any persistent data (parameters) in the persistent data directory, usually `/var/lib/modules/persist`.

The /etc/modules.conf File

Notice that there is no device name for Ethernet devices in the `/dev` directory. This is because the device name is

really an alias for a Ethernet network module that has
been defined in the `modules.conf` file. If you were to
add another Ethernet card of the same type, you would
place an alias for it in the `modules.conf` file. For a
second Ethernet card, you would use the device name
`eth1` as the alias. This way, the second Ethernet device
can be referenced with the name `eth1`. A `modules.conf`
entry is shown here:

```
alias eth1 ne2k-pci
```

TIP   *After making changes to* `/etc/modules.conf`, *you
should run* `depmod` *again to record any changes in module
dependencies.*

The previous entry assumes that the Ethernet card was
of the same model. If you had added a different model
Ethernet card, you would have to specify the module used
for that kind of card. In the following example, the second
card is a standard PCI Realtek card. Kmod has already
automatically detected the new card and loaded the
`ne2k-pci` module for you. You only need to identify
this as the `eth1` card in the `/etc/modules.conf` file.

```
alias eth0 3c59x
alias eth1 ne2k-pci
```

A sample `modules.conf` file is shown here. Notice the
aliases for the USB controller and the sound card.

```
alias eth0 3c59x
alias eth1 ne2k-pci
alias parport_lowlevel parport_pc
alias usb-controller usb-uhci
alias sound-slot-0 i810_audio
```

TIP   *In some cases, Kmod may not detect a device
in the way you want, and thereby not load the kernel
module you would like. This was the case in Chapter 5,
where you needed to provide SCSI emulation for IDE
CD write devices. In this case, kernel parameters were
specified to the GRUB boot loader to load the correct
modules.*

Installing New Modules for the Kernel

The source code for your Linux kernel contains an extensive set of modules, of which only a few are actually used on your system. When you install a new device, you may have to install the kernel module that provides the drivers for it. This involves selecting the module you need from a list, and then regenerating your kernel modules with the new module included. Then the new module is copied into the module library, installing it on your system. You can then enter it in the `/etc/modules.conf` file with any options, or use `modprobe` to install it manually.

First, make sure you have installed the kernel source code in the `/usr/src/linux` directory (see Chapter 9). If not, simply use an installation utility such as rpm or an RPM utility like redhat-config-packages to install the kernel source RPM packages. If you are using the source code version of the kernel, unpack it and move its contents to the `/usr/src` directory.

Now change to the `/usr/src/linux`*version* directory, where *version* is the kernel version. Red Hat includes the version number in the directory name. Then use the `make` command with the `xconfig` or `menuconfig` argument to display the kernel configuration menus, invoking them with the following commands. The `make xconfig` command starts an X Window System interface that needs to be run on your desktop from a terminal window.

```
make xconfig
make menuconfig
```

Using the menus described in Chapter 9, select the modules you need. Make sure each is marked as a module, clicking the Module check box in `xconfig` or typing `M` for `menuconfig`. Once the kernel is configured, save it and exit from the configuration menus. Then you compile the modules, creating the module binary files with the following command:

```
make modules
```

This places the modules in the kernel source modules directory: `/usr/src/linux`*version*`/`. You can copy the one you want to the kernel modules directory, `/lib/modules/`*version*`/kernel`, where *version* is the version number of your Linux kernel. A simpler approach is to reinstall all your modules, using the following command. This copies all the compiled modules to the `/lib/modules/`*version*`/kernel` directory.

```
make modules_install
```

For example, if you want to provide AppleTalk support, and your distribution did not create an AppleTalk module or incorporate the support into the kernel directly, you can use this method to create and install the AppleTalk modules. First, check to see if your distribution has the module already included in it. The AppleTalk modules should be in the `/lib/modules/`*version*`/kernel/net/appletalk` directory. If not, you can move to the `/usr/src/linux`*version* directory, run `make xconfig`, and select AppleTalk as a module. Then, generate the modules with the `make modules` command. You could then use the `make modules_install` command to install the new module, along with your other modules. Or, you can copy the `appletalk` directory and the modules it holds to the module directory.

Chapter 8

Print Servers

Although printer installation is almost automatic on most Linux distributions, it helps to understand the underlying process. Once treated as devices attached to a system directly, printers are now treated as network resources managed by print servers. In the case of a single printer attached directly to a system, the networking features become transparent and the printer appears as just one more device. On the other hand, you could easily make use of a print server's networking capability to let several systems use the same printer. You can find out more information about printing in Linux at www.linuxprinting.org.

CUPS and LPRng

Currently, there are two printer servers available for use on Red Hat Linux, the Line Printer, Next Generation (LPRng) and the Common Unix Printing System (CUPS). LPRng was the traditional print server for Linux and Unix systems, but has since been deprecated by Red Hat and will be dropped from their distribution in later versions. It is described briefly here. With Red Hat 9, CUPS is now the primary print server for Red Hat Linux and is supported by redhat-config-printer. However, in Red Hat 8.0, LPRng is still used as the default and LPRng is the server supported by redhat-config-printer.

You can easily switch from one system to the other with the redhat-switch-printer tool. A dialog box displays entries for either LPRng or CUPS. You then have to use redhat-config-services (Services), accessible in the Server Settings window and menu, to start your selected print server. The print server for CUPS is `cups` and for LPRng it is `lpd`. Select the server, and then select Actions | Restart.

Once you have installed your printers and configured your print server, you can print and manage your print queue using print clients. There are a variety of printer clients available for the CUPS server, redhat-config-printer, Gnome print manager, the CUPS configuration tool, and various line printing tools like `lpq` and `lpc`. These are described in further detail later in this chapter. The CUPS configuration tool is a web-based configuration tool that can also manage printers and print jobs (open your browser and enter the URL `http://localhost:631`). A web page is displayed with entries for managing jobs, managing printers, and administrative tasks. Select the Manage Jobs entry to remove or reorder jobs you have submitted. There are a variety of printer clients available for the LPRng server, including Klpq and various line printing tools like `lpq` and `lpc` that work much like their CUPS counterparts.

Printer Devices and Configuration

Before you can use any printer, you first have to install it on a Linux system on your network. A local printer is installed directly on your own system. This involves creating an entry for the printer in a printer configuration file that defines the kind of printer it is, along with other features such as the device file and spool directory it uses. Installing a printer is fairly simple: determine which device file to use for the printer and the configuration entries for it. On Red Hat, you can use the redhat-config-printer configuration tool to enable you to set up and configure your printer easily. Depending on the interface you are using, redhat-config-printer will invoke either redhat-config-printer-gui, a GUI Gnome printer configuration tool, or redhat-config-printer-tui, the same tool with a screen-based cursor driven interface.

TIP *If you cannot find the drivers for your printer, you may be able to download them from www.linuxprinting .org. The site maintains an extensive listing of drivers.*

Printer Device Files

Linux creates three device names for parallel printers
automatically during installation: lp0, lp1, and lp2.
(Most systems currently use lp1.) The number used in
these names corresponds to a parallel port on your PC.
lp0 references the LPT1 parallel port, lp1 references
the LPT2 parallel port, and lp2 references LPT3. Serial
printers use the serial ports, referenced by the device
files ttyS0, ttyS1, ttyS2, and so on.

Spool Directories

When your system prints a file, it makes use of special
directories called *spool directories*. A *print job* is a file to
be printed. When you print a file to a printer, a copy of
it is made and placed in a spool directory set up for that
printer. The location of the spool directory is obtained
from the printer's entry in its configuration file. On Linux,
the spool directory is located at /var/spool/lpd under
a directory with the name of the printer. For example, the
spool directory for the myepson printer would be located
at /var/spool/lpd/myepson. The spool directory contains
several files for managing print jobs. Some files use the
name of the printer as their extension. For example, the
myepson printer has the files control.myepson, which
provides printer queue control, and active.myepson
for the active print job, as well as log.myepson, which
is the log file.

Printer Configuration with redhat-config-printer

The redhat-config-printer utility is an easy interface for
setting up and managing your printers. Using only
redhat-config-printer, you can easily install a printer on
your Linux system. You can start redhat-config-printer
by selecting the Printing entry in the System Settings
window or menu. The redhat-config-printer utility enables

you to select the appropriate driver for your printer, as well as set print options such as paper size and print resolutions. Once you have configured your printer with redhat-config-printer, it generates an entry for the print in CUPS. With Red Hat 9, redhat-config-printer now supports the CUPS printing server, instead of LPRng. Configurations are saved in CUPS printer configuration files, as described in the following CUPS section.

When you start up redhat-config-printer, you are presented with a window that lists your installed printers (see Figure 8-1). To add a new printer, click the New button. To edit an installed printer, double-click its entry or select it and click the Edit button. Once you have made your changes, click the Apply button to save your changes and restart the printer daemon. If you have more than one printer on your system, you can make one the default by selecting it and then clicking the Default button. The Delete button removes a printer configuration. You can test your printer with a PostScript, A4, or ASCII test sheet selected from the Test menu.

Configuring a New Printer

When you select New, a series of dialog boxes is displayed where you can enter the printer name, its type, and its driver. In the Queue Type dialog box, you can specify whether this is a remote or local printer. For local printers, select Locally-connected from the drop-down menu. For remote printers, you need to select the kind of network or

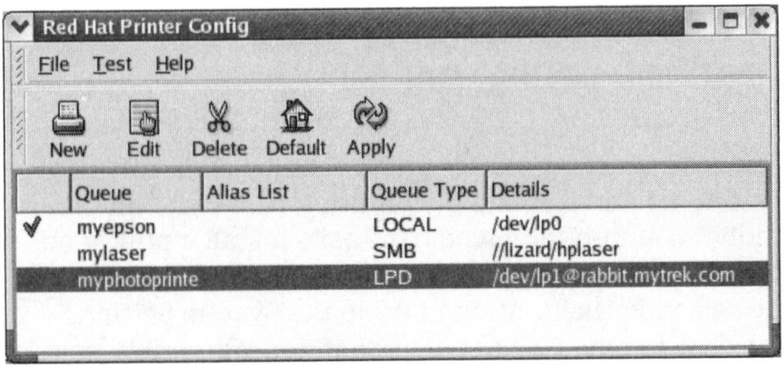

Figure 8-1.   redhat-config-printer

server the printer is attached to, such as CUPS server, Novell for Novell networks, or Windows for printers attached to a Windows computer. You then select the device the printer is connected to. The device is the port to which the printer is connected. For the first three parallel ports, these are lp0, lp1, and lp2. For serial ports, these are ttyS0, ttyS1, and ttyS2, and so on. In the Printer model dialog, you are presented with a drop-down menu of printer types. You first select the manufacturer, such as Canon or Apple, which then expands to a list of particular printer models. Choose the entry for your model. You will be notified that the printer configuration is about to be created. Click the Apply button. You then see your printer listed in the redhat-config-printer window. You are now ready to print.

Editing Printer Configurations

You can also edit a printer to change any settings. When you click the Edit button, a set of five tabbed panes are displayed for the printer name, queue type, queue options, driver, and driver options. For the queue selection, you can specify entries for the printer device and spool directory. You can also specify whether the printer is local or remotely connected through a Linux/Unix, Windows (SMB), Networked CUPS, or NetWare network, with a drop-down menu. For the queue options selection, you can specify printer features such as paper size and resolution. When you finish, click OK to close the window.

Configuring Network Printers

You can also use redhat-config-printer to set up a remote printer on Linux, Unix, Microsoft, Networked CUPS, or Novell networks. When you add a new printer, a pane is displayed with selections for whether this is a local, Networked CUPS, Unix (lpd share), Windows (SMB share), Novell (NCP queue), or JetDirect printer. (If you edit an existing printer, the queue panel displays a drop-down menu where you can select a remote entry.) A networked CUPS server panel displays entries for entering the server address and its queue directory. For a remote Linux or Unix printer, select Unix Printer (lpd share). This displays a dialog box for configuring the remote printer with entries for the server and the queue. For the server, enter the hostname for the system that controls the printer. For the queue, enter the device name on that host for the printer. A Novell (NCP queue) screen adds entries for the user and the password. The Windows (SMB share) screen has entries for the share name, host IP address, workgroup, user, and password.

A Windows (SMB share) printer is one located on a Windows network. To access an SMB share remote printer, you need to install Samba and have the Server Message Block services enabled using the smbd daemon. You must also enable printer sharing must on the Windows network. In the printer configuration utility, you need to enter the name of the share, its IP address, the name of the printer's workgroup, and the username and password. The share is the hostname and printer name in the format \\hostname\printername. The hostname is the computer where the printer is located, and printer name is the name of the printer as it is known to remote hosts. The username and password can be one for the printer resource itself, or for access by a particular user. You can then use a print client like lpr to print a file to the Windows printer. lpr invokes the Samba client smbclient to send the print job to the Windows printer.

Managing Printers with CUPS

The Common Unix Printing System (CUPS) is an alternative for LPRng that provides printing services. It is freely available under the GNU Public License. Though it is now included with most distributions, you can also download the most recent source-code version of CUPS from www.cups.org. The site also provides detailed documentation on installing and managing printers. Whereas LPRng is derived from the old Berkeley line printer daemon (LPD), CUPS is based on the newer Internet Printing Protocol (IPP). The Internet Printing Protocol is designed to establish a printing standard for the Internet (for more information, see www.pwg.org/ipp). Whereas

the older LPD-based printing systems focused primarily
on line printers, an IPP-based system provides networking,
PostScript, and web support. CUPS works like an Internet
server and employs a configuration setup much like that
of the Apache web server. Its network support lets clients
directly access printers on remote servers, without having
to configure the printers themselves. Configuration needs
only to be maintained on the print servers.

With the RPM version used by Red Hat, a `cups` startup
script is installed in the `/etc/rc.d/init.d` directory.
You can start, stop, and restart CUPS using the `service`
command and the `cups` script. When you make changes
or install printers, be sure to restart CUPS to have your
changes take effect. On Red Hat, you can use the following:

```
service cups restart
```

CUPS Configuration Tool

The easiest way to configure and install printers with
CUPS is to use redhat-config printer, as described in the
previous section. You can also use the CUPS configuration
tool, which is a web browser-based configuration tool.
To ensure browser access, be sure to first select CUP with
the Printer System Switcher, or, if you are using `xinetd`
for CUPS, turn on `cups` with the `chkconfig` command.

To start the web interface on Red Hat, enter the following
URL into your web browser.

```
http://localhost:631
```

This opens an administration screen where you can manage
and add printers. You will first be asked to enter the
administrator's username (usually `root`) and password
(usually the root user's password).

You install a printer on CUPS through a series of web
pages, each of which requests different information. To
install a printer, click the Add Printer button to display
a page where you enter the printer name and location
(see Figure 8-2). The location is the host to which the
printer is connected.

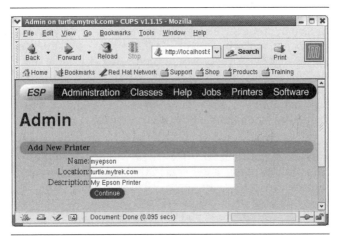

Figure 8-2. CUPS Add Printer Page

Subsequent pages will prompt you to enter the model of
the printer and driver, which you select from available
listings. Once you have added the printer, you can configure
it. Clicking the Manage Printers entry in the Administration
page lists your installed printers. You can then click a
printer to display a page that lets you control the printer.
You can stop the printer, configure its printing, modify
its installation, and even delete the printer. Clicking the
Configure Printer button displays a page where you can
configure how your printer prints, by specifying the
resolution or paper size.

NOTE *You can perform all administrative tasks from
the command line using the* `lpadmin` *command. See the
CUPS documentation for more details.*

Configuring Remote Printers on CUPS

To install a remote printer that is attached to a Windows
system or another Linux system running LPRng or LPD,
you specify its location using special URL protocols. For
a Windows printer, you first need to install, configure,
and run Samba. CUPS uses Samba to access Windows

printers. When you install the Windows printer on CUPS, you specify its location using the URL protocol `smb`. The user allowed to log in to the printer is entered before the hostname and separated by a `@` sign. On most configurations, this is the `guest` user. The location entry for a Windows printer called `myhp` attached to a Windows host named `lizard` is shown here. Its Samba share reference would be `//lizard/myhp`.

```
smb://guest@lizard/myhp
```

To enable CUPS on Samba, you also have to set the printing option in the `/etc/samba/smb.conf` file to `cups`, as shown here:

```
printing = cups
printcap name = cups
```

To enable CUPS to work with samba, you have to link the `smbspool` to the CUPS `smb` spool directory:

```
ln -s /usr/bin/smbspool    /usr/cups/backend/smb
```

8

To access a printer connected to a Linux or Unix system running LPRng, use the `lpd` protocol to specify its location. In the following example, the printer `mylaser` is connected to the Linux host `rabbit.mytrek.com`:

```
lpd://rabbit.mytrek.com/mylaser
```

CUPS Printer Classes

CUPS features a way to let you select a group of printers to print a job instead of selecting just one. That way, if one printer is busy or down, another printer can be automatically selected to perform the job. Such groupings of printers are called *classes*. Once you have installed your printers, you can then group them into different classes. For example, you may want to group all inkjet printers in one class and laser printers in another, or you might want to group printers connected to one specific printer server in their own class. To create a class, select Classes on the Administration page and enter the name of the class. You can then add printers to it.

CUPS Configuration

CUPS configuration files are placed in the /etc/cups directory. These files are listed in Table 8-1. The classes.conf, printers.conf, and client.conf files can be managed by the web interface. The printers.conf file contains the configuration information for the different printers you have installed. Any of these files can be edited manually, if you wish.

cupsd.conf

The CUPS server is configured with the cupsd.conf file. You must edit configuration options manually; the server is not configured with the web interface. Your installation of CUPS installs a commented version of the cupsd.conf file with each option listed, though most options will be commented out. Commented lines are preceded with a # symbol. Each option is documented in detail. The server configuration uses an Apache web server syntax consisting of a set of directives. As with Apache, several of these directives can group other directives into blocks.

CUPS Directives

Certain directives allow you to place access controls on specific locations. These can be printers or resources, such as the administrative tool or the spool directories. Location controls are implemented with the Location directive. Allow From and Deny From directives can permit or deny access from specific hosts. CUPS supports both Basic and Digest forms of authentication, specified

Filename	Description
classes.conf	Configurations for different printer classes
client.conf	Lists specific option for specified clients
cupsd.conf	Configures the CUPS server, cupsd
printers.conf	Printer configurations

Table 8-1. CUPS Configuration Files

in the `AuthType` directive. Basic authentication uses a user and password. For example, to use the web interface, you are prompted to enter the root user and the root user password. Digest authentication makes use of user and password information kept in the CUPS `/etc/cups/passwd.md5` file, using MD5 versions of a user and password for authentication. The `AuthClass` directive specifies the class allowed access. The `System` class includes the `root`, `sys`, and system users. The following example shows the `Location` directive for the `/admin` resource, the administrative tool:

```
<Location /admin>

AuthType Basic
AuthClass System

## Restrict access to local domain
Order Deny,Allow
Deny From All
Allow From 127.0.0.1

</Location>
```

CUPS Command-line Print Clients

Once a print job is placed on a print queue, you can use any of several print clients to manage the printing jobs on your printer or printers, such as Klpq for LPRng and the Gnome Print Manager and the CUPS Printer Configuration tool for CUPS. You can also use several command-line print CUPS clients (for which there are corresponding applications by the same name for LPRng). These include the `lpr`, `lpc`, `lpq`, and `lprm` commands. The Printer System Switcher moves you from one set to the other. With these clients, you can print documents, list a print queue, reorder it, and remove print jobs, effectively canceling them. For network connections, CUPS features an encryption option for its commands , `-E`, to encrypt print jobs and print information sent of a network. Table 8-2 shows various printer commands.

Printer Management	Description
Gnome Print Manager	Gnome print queue management tool (CUPS)
CUPS Configuration Tool	Manage and configure CUPS
lpr *options file-list*	Prints a file; copies the file to the printer's spool directory and places it on the print queue to be printed in turn. -P *printer* prints the file on the specified printer.
lpq *options*	Displays the print jobs in the print queue. -P *printer* prints the queue for the specified printer. -l prints a detailed listing.
lpstat *options*	Displays printer status.
lprm *options printjob-id* or *printer*	Removes a print job from the print queue. You identify a particular print job by its number as listed by lpq. -P *printer* removes all print jobs for the specified printer.
lpc	Manages your printers. At the lpc> prompt, you can enter commands to check the status of your printers and take other actions.

Table 8-2. CUPS Print Clients

lpr

The lpr client submits a job, and lpd then takes it in turn and places it on the appropriate print queue. lpr takes as its argument the name of a file. If no printer is specified, then the default printer is used. The -P option enables you to specify a particular printer. In the next example, the user first prints the file preface, then prints the file report to the printer with the name myepson:

```
$ lpr preface
$ lpr -P myepson report
```

lpc

You can use `lpc` to enable or disable printers, reorder their print queues, and re-execute configuration files. To use `lpc`, enter the command `lpc` at the shell prompt. You are then given an `lpc>` prompt at which you can enter `lpc` commands to manage your printers and reorder their jobs. The `status` command with the name of the printer displays whether the printer is ready, how many print jobs it has, and so on. The `stop` and `start` commands can stop a printer and start it back up. The printers shown depend on the printers configured for a particular print server. A printer configured on CUPS will only show if you have switched to CUPS. If you switch to the LPRng, those printers you configured for LPRng will show up.

```
# lpc
lpc> status myepson
myepson:
 printer is on device 'parallel'
 queuing is enabled
 printing is enabled
 1 entry in spool area
```

lpq and lpstat

You can manage the print queue using the `lpq` and `lprm` commands. The `lpq` command lists the printing jobs currently on the print queue. With the `-P` option and the printer name, you can list the jobs for a particular printer. If you specify a username, you can list the print jobs for that user. With the `-l` option, `lpq` displays detailed information about each job. If you want information on a specific job, simply use that job's ID number with `lpq`. To check the status of a printer, use `lpstat`.

```
# lpq
myepson is ready and printing
Rank     Owner  Jobs  File(s)        Total Size
active   chris    1    report         1024
```

lprm

The `lprm` command enables you to remove a print job from the queue, erasing the job before it can be printed.

The `lprm` command takes many of the same options as `lpq`. To remove a specific job, use `lprm` with the job number. To remove all printing jobs for a particular printer, use the `-P` option with the printer name. `lprm` with no options removes the job printing currently. The following command removes the first print job in the queue.

```
# lprm 1
```

CUPS Administrative Tools

CUPS provides command line administrative tools like `lpadmin`, `lpoptions`, `lpinfo`, `enable`, `disable`, `accept`, and `reject`. The `enable` and `disable` commands start and stop print queues directly, whereas the `accept` and `reject` commands start and stop particular jobs. `lpinfo` provides information about printers, and `lpoptions` lets you set printing options. The `lpadmin` command lets you perform administrative tasks like adding printers and changing configurations.

lpadmin

You can use the lpadmin command to either set the default printer or configure various options for a printer. You can use the `-d` option to specify a particular printer as the default destination (you can also do this in redhat-config-printer). Here `myepson` is made the default printer:

```
lpadmin -d myepson
```

The -p option lets you designate a printer for which to set various options. The following example sets printer description information:

```
lpadmin -p myepson  -D  Epson550
```

Certain options let you control per-user quotas for print jobs. The `job-k-limit` sets the size of a job allowed per user, `job-page-limit` sets the page limit for a job, and the `job-quota-period` limits the number of jobs with a specified timeframe. The following command sets a page limit of 100 for each user.

```
lpadmin -p myepson  -o job-page-limit=100
```

User access control is determined with the `-u` option with an `allow` or `deny` list. Users allowed access are listed following the `allow:` entry, and those denied access are listed with a `deny:` entry. Here, access is granted to `chris`, but denied to `aleina` and `larisa`.

```
lpadmin -p myepson -u allow:chris  deny:aleina,larisa
```

Use `all` or `none` to permit or deny access to all or no users. You can create exceptions by using `all` or `none` in combination with user specific access. The following example allows access to all users except `justin`.

```
lpadmin -p myepson  -u allow:all   deny:justin
```

lpoptions

The `lpoptions` command lets you set printing options that govern how your print jobs will be printed. For example, you can set the color or page format to be used with a particular printer. Default settings for all users are maintained by the root user in the `/etc/cups/lpoptions` file, and each user can create their own configurations, which are saved in their `.lpoptions` files. The `-1` option lists current options for a printer, and the `-p` options designates a printer (you can also set the default printer to use with the `-d` option).

```
lpoptions -p myepson -l
```

Printer options are set using the `-o` option along with the option name and value, `-o option=value`. You can remove a printer option with the `-r` option. For example, to print on both sides of your sheets, you can set the `sides` option to `two-sided`:

```
lpoptions -p myepson -o sides=two-sided
```

To remove the option, use -r:

```
lpoptions -p myepson -r sides
```

To display a listing of available options, check the standard printing options in the CUPS Software Manual at www.cups.org.

enable and disable

The `enable` command starts a printer, and the `disable` command stops it. With the `-c` option, you can also cancel all jobs on the printer's queue, and with the `-r` option, you broadcast a message explaining the shutdown.

```
disable myepson
```

accept and reject

The `accept` and `reject` commands let you control access to the printer queues for specific printers. The `reject` command prevents a printer from accepting jobs, whereas `accept` allows new print jobs.

```
reject myepson
```

lpinfo

The `lpinfo` command is a handy tool for letting you know what CUPS devices and drivers are available on your system. Use the `-v` option for devices, and the `-m` option for drivers.

```
lpinfo -m
```

The Line Printer Server: LPRng

LPRng is an enhanced version of the Berkeley Line Printer Daemon (LPD) `lpd` and associated `lpr` applications. It features a wide range of capabilities that include security measures and access to remote printers. Many of the commands are the same as those used by LPD on a standard Unix system. The Linux printer server program is called `lpd`, the line printer daemon. Printers are installed to run under `lpd`, which then handles print jobs for them both locally and from remote sources. Though `lpd` is called the line printer daemon, it is designed to manage any kind of printer, not just line printers. You should think of it as a general-purpose print server capable of handling laser, inkjet, PostScript, and dot-matrix printers. LPRng also features a companion IFHP filter package, which provides hardware-level support for postscript, PCL, and text printers, among others (see www.astart.com/lprng).

The `lpd` daemon is installed and configured on your Linux system during installation. `lpd` is run as a standalone process by the `lpd` startup script in the `/etc/rc.d/init.d` directory. You can use the `service` command on this script to start, stop, and restart the daemon:

```
service lpd restart
```

`lpd` makes use of two configuration files: `lpd.conf` and `lpd.perms`. `lpd.conf` contains general `lpd` configuration commands. You use `lpd.perms` to set up rules with which you can restrict access to the `lpd` server. Here, you can deny access by certain hosts, users, or even networks.

Requests to print documents are performed by print clients such as `lpr`. When a document is submitted for printing, it becomes a print job that is placed on a queue for the printer it was sent to. While the job is on the queue waiting to print, you can check its status and even remove it from the queue, canceling the job. The `lpq` client lets you check a print queue, `lpc` allows you to make changes to it, and `lprm` is used to remove a print job from a queue.

LPRng Print Clients

You can use any of several LPRng print clients to manage the printing jobs on your printer or printers, such as Klpq and several command-line print clients like `lpr` and `lpq`. Klpq is a KDE desktop utility and is labeled the Print Job Administration tool. With Klpq, you can list the print jobs for a printer, remove a print job, and move a print job to the top of the queue. You can also disable printing for a printer. To have the print queue listing automatically updated, you can set an update frequency in the Options menu.

printcap File

The `/etc/printcap` file holds entries for each printer connected to your system. A `printcap` entry holds information, such as the pathname for a printer's spool directory and the device name of the printer port the printer uses. The first field in a `printcap` entry is a list of possible names for the printer. These are names you can make up yourself, and you can add others if you want. Each name is separated by a | symbol. You use these names to identify the printer when you enter various printer commands or options, such as the `-P` option. These names are also used for special shell variables, such as the `PRINTER` variable, used in many initialization scripts.

The fields following the list of names set different fields for your printer. The fields are separated by colons and assigned a value using the = symbol. Three of the more important fields are `lp`, `sd`, and `of`. The `lp` field is set to the device name the printer uses. The `sd` field is set to the pathname of the spool directory, and `if` is set to the particular filter used for this printer. Some fields have Boolean values and simply list the field name with no assignment, which indicates a value of "true." You can find a complete listing of the `printcap` fields in the `printcap` man pages: `man printcap`. An example of a `printcap` entry follows:

```
myprinter|myepson:\
:sh:\
:ml=0:\
:mx=0:\
:sd=/var/spool/lpd/myprinter:\
:lp=/dev/lp0:\
:lpd_bounce=true:\
:if=/usr/share/printconf/mf_wrapper:
```

To install a remote (network or remote host-attached) printer, you place remote entries for the printer host and device in the printer's `/etc/printcap` file entry. An `:rm` entry identifies the remote host that controls the remote printer, and an `:rp` entry specifies the device name of the remote printer. In the following example, the remote printer is located at `rabbit.mytrek.com`, and is called `lp1`:

```
:rm=rabbit.mytrek.com
:rp=lp1
```

Configuring lpd

LPRng allows you to configure your `lpd` server, setting global defaults or controlling printer access. There are only two configuration files to manage, and both are heavily commented. Your distribution will normally provide basic versions for both. An extensive set of features are available, letting you create servers with powerful and complex capabilities.

lpd.conf

The general configuration for the `lpd` print server is handled in the `/etc/lpd.conf` file. Here, you can specify features that apply to all printers and print management. You should think of these more as default features, as any of them can be overridden in a printer's `printcap` entry. The `lpd.conf` file installed with LPRng contains an extensive list of configuration parameters. They are all commented out, prefixed with # signs. Each parameter is preceded by a comment describing the parameter. The entry itself lists the default value given to the parameters, preceding the entry with the term `default`. The entry for the `connect_timeout` parameter is shown here:

```
# Purpose: connection timeout for remote printers
# default connect_timeout=10 (INTEGER)
```

To create your own timeout entry, it is best to add your own entry below, as shown here. Notice that the preceding # and the term `default` are missing from the new entry. The connection timeout for remote printers is now set at 20. This can be overridden by a printer's `printcap` file entry.

```
# Purpose: connection timeout for remote printers
# default connect_timeout=10 (INTEGER)
connect_timeout=20
```

Parameters can also be flags that you can turn on or off. An off flag is noted with an attached @ sign. In the following example, the `allow_user_logging` parameter is a flag that allows users to request login information. By default, it is turned off. The following example turns it on:

```
# Purpose: allow users to request logging info using
lpr -mhost%port
# default allow_user_logging@ (FLAG off)
allow_user_logging
```

LPRng Access Controls: lpd.perms

LPRng provides access control rules for controlling how remote users access your print server, and thereby the printers it controls. These rules are placed in the lpd.perms file and can be used to refuse print services to specific hosts or users. Such rules consist of an action and a set of keys. The keys specify criteria to be met, and if they are met, their associated action is taken. In each rule, you have one action and one or more keys. If there are several keys, all their criteria must be met for the action to take place. An example of a key would be to specify the IP address of a host. In addition, you have to specify the kind of service that is being requested, such as a printing or connection request. The action is usually either ACCEPT or REJECT. Keys operate as flags or variables. To specify a host, you assign the address to the HOST key, using an assignment operator. For a user, you use USER, and for IP addresses, IFIP. The kind of service is specified by the SERVICE key. For a printing request, the value you assign is the lpd code P. The following example specifies a host as the key and will REJECT any request from that address:

```
REJECT SERVICE=P HOST=192.168.0.57
```

The lpd.perms file consists of a set of rules that are sequentially evaluated until a match is found. The DEFAULT action rule should be the last rule and is normally one to accept any requests. In other words, any request that is not matched by the previous rules is accepted. Normally, you would set up rules to reject certain requests, such as requests for specific hosts. Most requests would not match these rules and should fall through to the DEFAULT action, which would ACCEPT them.

SERVICE key values differ depending on the type of request submitted. These can range from a simple connection request by a remote server to a removal of a print job. The print clients such as lpr, lpq, lprm, and lpc make different kinds of service requests. lpq makes a request for queue information that has the key value Q for SERVICE. lprm issues a removal request indicated by a key value M.

LPRng Print Clients

LPRng uses the same command line print clients as described for CUPS. These include the lpr, lpc, lpq, and lprm commands. Check the man pages for each for detailed options. Certain features, like encryption, are only available with CUPS versions.

8

Chapter 9

Kernel Administration

The *kernel* is the operating system, performing core tasks such as managing memory and disk access, as well as interfacing with the hardware that makes up your system. For example, the kernel makes possible such standard Linux features as multitasking and multiuser support. It also handles communications with devices like your CD-ROM or hard disk. Users send requests for access to these devices through the kernel, which then handles the lower-level task of actually sending instructions to a device. Given the great variety of devices available, the kind of devices connected to a Linux system will vary. Kudzu detects these devices automatically at boot time, and the kernel is appropriately configured when Linux is installed. However, if you add a new device, you may have to enable support for it in the kernel. This involves creating a modified version of the kernel, which is often referred to as *building* or *compiling the kernel*. In addition, new versions of the kernel are continuously made available that provide improved support for your devices, as well as a smoother running system. You can download and install these new versions on your system.

Kernel Versions

The version number for a Linux kernel consists of three segments: the major, minor, and revision numbers. The *major number* increments with major changes in the kernel. The *minor number* indicates stability. *Even numbers* are used for stable releases, whereas *odd numbers* are reserved for development releases, which may be unstable. New features first appear in the development versions. If you're concerned about stability, you should wait for the stable version. The *revision number* refers to the corrected versions. As bugs are discovered and corrected, new revisions of a kernel are released. A development kernel may have numerous revisions. For example, kernel 2.4.20 has a major number of 2 and a minor number of 4, with a revision number of 20. Distributions often add another number that refers to a specific set of patches applied to the kernel. For example, for Red Hat 9, the kernel is 2.4.20-8, where 8 is the patch number. On distributions that support RPM packages, you can use an RPM query to learn what version is installed, as shown here:

```
rpm -q kernel
```

You could have more than one version of the kernel installed on your system. To see which one is running currently, you use the uname command with the -r option.

```
uname -r
```

New kernels are released on two different tracks, a stable track and a development track. Stable kernels have an even revision number, whereas development kernels use an odd number. The stable kernel would be 2.4, and its development kernel would be 2.5. Although they are unstable, development kernels often include support for the most recent hardware and software features. However, unless you are experimenting with kernel development, you should always install a stable version of the kernel.

The Linux kernel is being worked on constantly, and new versions are released when they are ready. Distributions may include different kernel versions. Red Hat includes the most up-to-date kernel stable in its releases. Linux kernels are kept at kernel.org. Also, RPM packages for a new kernel are often available at distribution update sites. You may need to upgrade your kernel to provide support for new hardware or for features not supported by your distribution's version. For example, you may need support for a new device not provided in your distribution's version of the kernel. Certain features may not be included in a distribution's version because they are considered experimental or a security risk.

TIP *You probably don't need to install a new kernel just to add support for a new device. Kernels provide most device support in the form of modules, of which only those needed are installed with the kernel. Most likely, your current kernel has the module you need; you simply have to compile it and install it. For this task, see the "Installing New Modules for the Kernel" section in Chapter 7.*

- You can learn more about the Linux kernel from `kernel.org`, the official repository for the current Linux kernels. The most current source code, as well as documentation, is there. Your distribution web site will also provide online documentation for installing and compiling the kernel on its systems. Several Linux HOW-TOs also exist on the subject. The kernel source code software packages also include extensive documentation. Kernel source code files are always installed in the `/usr/src/linux-version` directory, where *version* is the kernel version, as in `/usr/src/linux-2.4`. In this directory, you can find a subdirectory named `/Documentation`, which contains an extensive set of files and directories documenting kernel features, modules, and commands. The following listing of kernel resources also contains more information.

- **kernel.org**   The official Linux kernel web site. All new kernels originate from here.

- **www.linuxhq.com**   Linux headquarters, kernel sources, and patches.

- **kernelnewbies.org**   Linux kernel sources and information.

- **www.tldp.org**   Linux Documentation Project.

Kernel Tuning: Kernel Runtime Parameters

Several kernel features can be turned on or off without compiling and installing a new kernel or module, such as IP forwarding or the maximum number of files. These tunable parameters are controlled by the files in `/proc/sys` files. The proc file system is described in Chapters 5 and 7. You can use the redhat-config-proc tool to assign values to these parameters. redhat-config-proc is accessible from the More System Tools menu as Kernel Tuning. redhat-config-proc lists headings for Networking, File System, Virtual Memory, Kernel, and Hardware. Networking lets you control features such as IP forwarding, ICMP broadcast messages, and TCP time stamping. The File System option lets you set the maximum number of files. The Kernel option enables you to control logging, shared memory, and certain security features such as disabling debugging. The Hardware option lets you control RAID speeds.

Parameters that you set are saved in the `/etc/sysctl` `.conf` file. Red Hat installs this file with basic configuration entries such as those for IP forwarding and debugging control. The redhat-config-proc tool overwrites this file, replacing it with entries for assigning values to different `/proc/sys` files. Changes to the `/proc/sys` file are not made until you click the Activate Saved Configuration button. For example, if you turn on IP forwarding in the Networking IP panel, the content of `/proc/sys/net/ipv4/ip_forward` is set to 1, once you save and activate the proc values.

Instead of using redhat-config-proc, you could use the `sysctl` command directly. The `-p` option causes `sysctl` to read parameters from the `/etc/sysctl.conf` file (you can specify a different file). You can use the `-w` option to change specific parameters. You reference a parameter with its key. A key is the parameter name prefixed with its `proc` system categories (directories), such as `net.ipv4` `.ip_forward` for the `ip_forward` parameter located in `/proc/sys/net/ipv4/`. To display the value of a particular parameter, just use its key. The `-a` option lists all available changeable parameters. In the next example, the user changes the domain name parameter, referencing it with the `kernel.domainname` key (the `domainname` command also sets the `kernel.domainname` parameter):

```
# sysctl -w kernel.domainname="mytrek.com"
```

The following example turns on IP forwarding:

```
# sysctl -w net.ipv4.ip_forward=1
```

If you use just the key, you display the parameter's current value:

```
# sysctl net.ipv4.ip_forward
 net.ipv4.ip_forward = 1
```

Installing a New Kernel Version

To install a new kernel, you need to download the software packages for that kernel to your system. You can install a new kernel either by downloading a binary version from your distribution's web site and installing it or by downloading the source code, compiling the kernel, and then installing the resulting binary file along with any modules. For Red Hat, the binary version of the kernel is provided in an RPM package. You can install a new kernel, just as you would any other RPM software package.

The easiest way to install a new kernel on Red Hat is to use the Red Hat Network update agent (the Red Hat Network is now a subscription service you need to pay for). The update agent automatically downloads, updates, and installs a new kernel. The Red Hat Network does not automatically select kernel files for download. Although they are listed, you have to explicitly select them to be downloaded and installed.

If you want to download kernel RPM packages directly from Red Hat, keep in mind that the complete kernel installation usually includes a series of RPM packages, all beginning with the word *kernel*. There are also other packages you may need, which contain updated system configuration files used by the new kernel. You can use the packages already installed on your system as a guide. Use the `rpm` command with the `-qa` option to list all packages and then pipe that list through the `grep` command with the `kernel` pattern to display only the kernel packages:

```
rpm -qa | grep kernel
```

The source code version is available for download from distribution FTP sites and is included on distribution CD-ROMs. You can also download the latest source directly from www.kernel.org. Wherever you download a kernel version from, it is always the same. The source code downloaded for a particular kernel version from a distribution site is the same as the one for www.kernel .org. Patches for that version can be applied to any distribution.

Red Hat Kernel Packages

As an example, the kernel packages for Red Hat are listed here. You should install only one of the `kernel-version-ix86` and `athlon` packages This will suffice for standard single processor computers. The others are optimization, support, or configuration packages that you may need depending on the hardware configuration of your PC, namely for multiprocessor, laptop, and computers with memory larger than 4GB.

```
kernel-2.4.20-8.athlon.rpm
kernel-2.4.20-8.i586.rpm
kernel-2.4.20-8.i686.rpm
kernel-doc-2.4.20-8.i386.rpm
kernel-bigmem-2.4.20-8.i686.rpm
kernel-pcmcia-cs-3.1.31-13.i386.rpm
kernel-smp-2.4.20-8.i686.rpm
kernel-smp-2.4.20-8.athlon.rpm
kernel-utils-2.4.20-8.i386.rpm
kernel-source-2.4.20-8.i386.rpm
kernel-BOOT-2.4.20-8.i686.rpm
```

CPU Kernel Packages

Red Hat provides different kernel packages optimized for various popular CPUs. Choose the appropriate one for your machine. Each package is named `kernel`, but has a different qualifier. Red Hat 9 includes three different kernel packages: one for Athlon and Duron CPUs; one for Pentium 2, 3, and 4 CPUs; and one for the older Pentium, AMD K6 CPUs, and other older systems. Each package will have a CPU reference in its file name: `athlon` for

Athlon and Duron; `686` for Pentium 2, 3, and 4; and
`586` for Pentium, K6, and other systems.

```
kernel-2.4.20-8.athlon.rpm
kernel-2.4.20-8.i686.rpm
kernel-2.4.20-8.i586.rpm
```

In addition, if you are installing on a laptop computer or a
system that uses PCMCIA cards, you also need to install
the `pcmcia-cs` package.

```
kernel-pcmcia-cs-3.1.31-13.i386.rpm
```

If your computer has more than 4GB of RAM memory, you
will need to also install the `bigmem` package.

```
kernel-bigmem-2.4.20-8.i686.rpm
```

If your system supports multiple CPU processors, you
will also need to install the `smp` package instead of the
standard `cpu` ones. Red Hat provides packages for Athlon
and Pentium computers.

```
kernel-smp-2.4.20-8.athlon.rpm
kernel-smp-2.4.20-8.i686.rpm
```

9

TIP *The `kernel-BOOT` package is a smaller version
of kernel and is meant to be used for floppy installation
disks only.*

Support Packages

In addition, if you are planning to customize your kernel,
you should download the `source` package. The `doc` package
provides updated documentation. The `utils` package
contains various hardware monitoring tools like `smardctl`
for hard drives, along with user-mode Linux (UML) tools.

```
kernel-source-2.4.20-8.i386.rpm
kernel-utils-2.4.20-8.i386.rpm
kernel-doc-2.4.20-8.i386.rpm
```

Installing Kernel Packages: /boot

You will not need all of these packages. For example, for
a simple kernel upgrade for a basic Pentium computer
(Pentium 3 or 4 with less than 4GB memory, single

processor, and no customization) you would only need the following package:

```
kernel-2.4.20-8.i686.rpm
```

For an Athlon or Duron system, you would use:

```
kernel-2.4.20-8.athlon.rpm
```

For a more complete upgrade, you would include the pcmcia, source, doc, and utils packages.

```
kernel-2.4.20-8.i686.rpm
kernel-pcmcia-cs-3.1.31-13.i386.rpm
kernel-utils-2.4.20-8.i386.rpm
kernel-source-2.4.20-8.i386.rpm
kernel-debug-2.4.20-8.i386.rpm
```

To make sure a kernel RPM package was downloaded without any errors and to verify its authentication, you can use the rpm command with the -K option (to authenticate the package, you need the Red Hat public key):

```
rpm -K *rpm
```

You can now install the kernel. As a safety precaution, you should preserve your old kernel in case the new one does not work out for some reason. This involves installing with the install (-i) option instead of the update (-U) option, creating a separate RAM disk for the new kernel, and then modifying grub.conf to have GRUB start up using the new kernel.

```
# rpm -ivh kernel-2.4.20-8.i686.rpm
# rpm -ivh kernel-pcmcia-cs-3.1.31-13.386.rpm
# rpm -ivh kernel-smp-2.4.20-8.i686.rpm
```

If your system has a SCSI controller or any other specialized hardware, RPM will also create a RAM disk to hold appropriate support modules (you can create a RAM disk manually with the mkinitrd command, see Chapter 6). The RAM disk is named initrd-*kernel-version*.img and is located in the /boot directory, as in /boot/initrd-2.4.20-8.img.

TIP *redhat-config-packages do not support kernel package installation. You have to install the kernel package manually using the* rpm *command in a terminal window.*

If you are customizing the kernel, installing the source code and headers for the kernel is also essential. You need the source code to generate any modules and to tailor the kernel to your own needs. For example, you can use the source code to generate modules containing device drivers for any uncommon devices you may have installed, as shown here:

```
# rpm -Uvh kernel-source-2.4.20-8.i386.rpm
```

On most distributions, kernels are installed in the `/boot` directory. Performing an `ls -l` operation on this directory lists all the currently installed kernels. A file for your old kernel and a file for your new one now exist, as well as a link file called `vmlinuz` that links to the new kernel file. If you took the precautions described in the previous section, you may have already renamed the older kernel. If you are using a boot loader such as GRUB, you needn't change its configuration file (`grub.conf`) because the entry to invoke the kernel still references the `/boot/vmlinuz` link, which now points to the new kernel. The kernel boots using the `/boot/vmlinuz` link to the kernel file. In your `grub.conf` file, the kernel line for the kernel file references this link. You also need to include a line for the RAM disk, `initrd`.

```
kernel /boot/vmlinuz-2.4.20-8 ro root=/dev/hda3
initrd /boot/initrd-2.4.20-8.img
```

TIP *Although it is not included with Red Hat 9, user-mode Linux (UML) is an optional version of the kernel designed to run as a stand-alone program separate from the kernel. In effect, it creates a virtual machine with disk storage implemented on a user file. UML is often used to test software or experiment with kernel configurations, without harming the real system. You can also use UML to implement virtual hosting, by running several virtual machines on one physical host. With a virtual machine, you can control the access to the host system, providing greater security. You can find out more about user-mode Linux at user-mode-linux.sourceforge.net.*

Precautionary Steps for Modifying a Kernel of the Same Version

If you want to modify your kernel configuration, and build a new one, you should retain a copy of your current kernel. In case something goes wrong with your modified version, you can always boot from the copy you kept. You do not have to worry about this happening if you are installing a new version of the kernel. New kernels are given different names, so the older one is not overwritten.

To retain a copy of your current kernel, you can make a backup copy of it, letting the original be overwritten. An installed version of a kernel makes use of several files in the `/boot` directory. Each file ends with that kernel version's number. These include the `vmlinuz` file, which is the actual kernel image file, along with several support files, `System.map`, `config`, and `module-info`. This `System.map` file contains kernel symbols needed by modules to start kernel functions. For example, the kernel image file is called `vmlinuz-version` where `version` is the version number attached, as in `vmlinuz-2.4.20-8`. The `System.map` file for this kernel called `System.map-2.4.20-8`. Here are the kernel files for version `2.4.20-8`:

```
/boot/vmlinuz-2.4.20-8
/boot/System.map-2.4.20-8
/boot/module-info-2.4.20-8
/boot/config-2.4.20-8
```

The `vmlinuz`, `System.map`, and `module-info` files for a particular kernel also have symbolic links using those names without the version number. For example, `vmlinuz` is a link to the current kernel image file, in this case, `vmlinuz-2.4.20-8`, and `System.map` is a link to the current `System.map` file, `System.map-2.4.20-8`. When you install a new kernel, the links are changed to that kernel. So if you installed a new version, such as 2.4.21-10, the `/boot/vmlinuz` would then link to that kernel's `vmlinuz` file, `/boot/vmlinuz-2.4.21-10`.

```
/boot/vmlinuz              /boot/vmlinuz-2.4.20-8
/boot/System.map           /boot/System.map-2.4.20-8
/boot/module-info          /boot/module-info-2.4.20-8
```

If, on the other hand, you are creating a modified version of the same kernel, the kernel file, here called `vmlinuz-2.4.20-8`, will be overwritten with the new kernel image file, along with the `System.map` and `module-info` files. To keep your current working version, you first have to make a copy of these files. You would make a copy of the `/boot/vmlinux-2.4.20-8` file, giving it another name, as shown here:

```
cp /boot/vmlinuz-2.4.20-8 /boot/vmlinuz-2.4.20-8.old
```

You would also make a backup of the `System.map` and `module-info` files. The `System.map` file is a symbolic link to the `System.map-2.4.20-8` file. You should also back up your modules located in the `/lib/modules/`*version* directory, where *version* is the version number of the kernel. Otherwise, you will lose the modules already set up to work with the original kernel. For version 2.4.20-8, the libraries are located in `/lib/modules/2.4.20-8`. If you are compiling a different version, those libraries are placed in a new directory named with the new version number.

Boot Loader

If you are using a boot loader, you should create a new entry for the old kernel in the boot loader configuration file. You can then make an entry for the new kernel. Leaving the entry for the old kernel is advisable in case something goes wrong with the new kernel. This way, you can always reboot and select the old kernel. For example, in the `grub.conf,` add a new entry, similar to the one for the old kernel, which references the new kernel in its image line. The `grub.conf` entry would look something like the following code. You could then select the entry with the title "Old Linux (2.4.20-8.old)" at the GRUB menu to launch the old kernel.

```
title Old Linux (2.4.20-8.old)
 root (hd0,2)
 kernel /boot/vmlinuz-2.4.20-8.old root=/dev/hda3
 initrd /boot/initrd-2.4.20-8.old.img
```

If you use a label for the boot partition, the `root` option
for the `kernel` statement would look like this for a boot
partition labeled `/`.

```
kernel /boot/vmlinuz-2.4.20-8.old ro root=LABEL=/
```

Boot Disk

You should also have a boot disk ready, just in case
something goes wrong with the installation (normally, you
created one during installation). With a boot disk, you
can start your system without using the boot loader.
You can create a boot disk using the `mkbootdisk` utility.
To create a boot disk, you need to know the full version
number for your kernel. You can, in fact, have several
kernels installed, and create boot disks for each one (your
`grub.conf` file lists your kernel version number). If the
kernel version is 2.4.20-8, use it as the argument to
the `mkbootdisk` command to create a boot disk for your
system:

```
mkbootdisk 2.4.20-8
```

If you want to make a boot CD-ROM, you can use the
`--iso` option with the `--device` option to specify the CD
image file. You can then burn the image file to a CD-ROM
disk. In the next example, the user creates a CD-ROM image
file, called `myimage.iso`, for a boot CD-ROM of the
2.4.20-8 kernel:

```
mkbootdisk --iso --device myimage.iso  2.4.20-8
```

Compiling the Kernel from Source Code

Instead of installing already compiled binary versions
of the kernel, you can install the kernel source code on
your system and use it to create the kernel binary files

yourself. Kernel source code files are compiled with the
`gcc` compiler just as any other source code files are.
One advantage to compiling the kernel is that you can
customize its configuration, selecting particular devices
you want supported by the kernel or the kind of networking
support you want. You can have more control over exactly
what your operating system can support. The 2.4 kernel
is described here.

Installing Kernel Sources: Kernel Archives and Patches

You can obtain a recent version of the kernel source
code from your distribution. It will have the name
`kernel-source`. New versions can be downloaded with
your distribution update agent, or by directly accessing
the distribution's FTP site. As noted previously, you
simply install them as you would any RPM package.

```
# rpm -ivh kernel-source-2.4.20-8.i386.rpm
```

The source files are placed in the `/usr/src` directory,
within the subdirectory that has the prefix `linux`
and a suffix consisting of the kernel version, as in
`linux-2.4.20-8` for kernel 2.4, revision 20, patch 8.
The full directory will be `/usr/src/linux-2.4.20-8`.
When you download and install a new kernel, a separate
subdirectory is created for it. For example, the 2.4.20-8
kernel is placed in `/usr/src/linux-2.4.20-8`. A link
is created called `/usr/src/linux-2.4` that links to the
most recent kernel source directory that you installed.
You can use this link to access your most recent kernel
source. Originally, this would link to `/usr/src/`
`linux-2.4.20-8`. If you later installed the 2.5.67 kernel,
this would link to `/usr/src/linux2.5.67`.

You can also obtain the most recent version of the source
code from www.kernel.org These versions are normally
much more recent than those available on your distribution
site, but may not have been thoroughly tested on the
distribution platform. The kernel source is in the form of
compressed archives (`.tar.gz`). They have the prefix
`linux` with the version name as the suffix. You decompress

and extract the archive with the following commands. First, you change to the `/usr/src` directory and then unpack the archive. It creates a directory called `linux` where the source files are placed. The following example extracts the 2.4.20 kernel:

```
cd /usr/src
tar -xzvf linux-2.4.20.tar.gz
```

Be sure to unpack the archive in the `/usr/src` directory. The archive extracts a directory named `linux` that holds the source code files. This way, the files are located in the `/usr/src/linux` directory. You should rename this directory adding the kernel version, as Red Hat does, `/usr/src/linux-2.4.20-8`.

TIP *If you are using the original kernel source, you should also check for any patches.*

Configuring the Kernel

Once the source is installed, you must configure the kernel. Configuration consists of determining the features for which you want to provide kernel-level support. These include drivers for different devices, such as sound cards and SCSI devices. You can configure features as directly included in the kernel itself or as modules the kernel can load as needed. You can also specifically exclude features. Features incorporated directly into the kernel make for a larger kernel program. Features set up as separate modules can also be easily updated. Documentation for many devices that provide sound, video, or network support can be found in the `/usr/share/doc` directory. Check the `kernel-doc` package to find a listing of the documentation provided.

```
rpm -ql kernel-doc
```

NOTE *If you configured your kernel previously, and now want to start over from the default settings, you can use the* `make mrproper` *command to restore the default kernel configuration.*

Kernel Configuration Tools

You can configure the kernel using one of several available configuration tools: `config`, `menuconfig`, or `xconfig`. You can also edit the configuration file directly. These tools perform the same configuration tasks, but use different interfaces. The `config` tool is a simple configure script providing line-based prompts for different configuration options. The `menuconfig` tool provides a cursor-based menu, which you can still run from the command line. Menu entries exist for different configuration categories, and you can pick and choose the ones you want. To mark a feature for inclusion in the kernel, move to it and press the SPACEBAR. An asterisk appears in the empty parentheses to the left of the entry. If you want to make it a module, press M and an M appears in the parentheses. The `xconfig` tool runs on a window manager and provides a window interface with buttons and menus. You can use your mouse to select entries. A menu consists of configuration categories that are listed as buttons you can click. All these tools save their settings to the `.config` file in the kernel source's directory. If you want to remove a configuration entirely, you can use the `mrproper` option to remove the `.config` file and any binary files, starting over from scratch.

```
make mrproper
```

You start a configuration tool by preceding it with the `make` command. Be sure you are in the `/usr/src/linux-`*version* directory. The process of starting a configuration tool is a `make` operation that uses the Linux kernel makefile. The `xconfig` tool should be started from a terminal window on your window manager. The `menuconfig` and `config` tools are started on a shell command line. The following example lists commands to start `xconfig`, `menuconfig`, and `config`:

```
make xconfig
make menuconfig
make config
```

xconfig

The `xconfig` tool opens a Linux Kernel Configuration window listing the different configuration categories. Buttons at the right of the screen are used to save the configuration or to copy it to a file, as well as to quit. Clicking an entry opens a window that lists different features you can include. Three check boxes to the left of each entry enable you to choose to have a feature compiled directly into the kernel, created as a separate module that can be loaded at runtime, or not included at all. As a rule, features in continual use, such as network and file system support, should be compiled directly into the kernel. Features that could easily change, such as sound cards, or features used less frequently, should be compiled as modules. Otherwise, your kernel image file may become too large and slower to run.

Important Kernel Configuration Features

The `xconfig` and `menuconfig` tools provide excellent context-sensitive help for each entry. To the right of each entry is a Help button. Click it to display a detailed explanation of what that feature does and why you would include it either directly or as a module, or even exclude it. When you are in doubt about a feature, always use the Help button to learn exactly what it does and why you would want to use it. Many of the key features are described here.

- **Loadable Module Support**   In most cases, you should make sure your kernel can load modules. Click the Loadable Module Support button to display a listing of several module management options. Make sure Enable Loadable Module Support is marked Yes. This feature allows your kernel to load modules as they are needed. Kernel Module Loader should also be set to Yes, because this allows your daemons, like your web server, to load any modules they may need.

- **Processor Type And Features** The Processor Type And Features window enables you to set up support for your particular system. Here, you select the type of processor you have (486, 586, 686, Pentium III, Pentium IV, and so forth), as well as the amount of maximum memory your system supports (up to 64GB with the 2.4 kernel).

- **General Setup** The General Setup window enables you to select general features, such as networking, PCI BIOS support, power management, as well as support for ELF and `a.out` binaries. Also supported is `sysctl` for dynamically changing kernel parameters specified in the `/proc` files. You can use redhat-config-proc (Kernel Tuning tool in the System Tools menu) to make these dynamic changes to the kernel. In the additional device driver support menu, you can enable specialized features like Crypto IP Encapsulation (CIPE) and accelerated SSL.

- **Block Devices** The Block Devices window lists entries that enable support for your IDE, floppy drive, and parallel port devices. Special features, such as RAM disk support and the loopback device for mounting CD-ROM image files, are also there.

- **Multidevice Support (RAID and LVM)** The Multidevice Support window lists entries that enable the use of RAID devices. You can choose the level of RAID support you want. Here you can also enable Logical Volume Management support (LVM), which lets you combine partitions into logical volumes that can be managed dynamically.

- **Networking Options** The Networking Options window, lists an extensive set of networking capabilities. The TCP/IP Networking entry must be set to enable any kind of Internet networking. Here, you can specify features that enable your system to operate as a gateway, firewall, or router. Network Aliasing enables support for IP aliases. Support also exists for other kinds of networks, including AppleTalk and IPX. AppleTalk must be enabled if you want to use NetTalk to connect to a Macintosh system on your network.

9

- **ATA/IDE/MFM/RLL Support**   In the ATA/IDE/MFM/RLL Support window, you can click on the "IDE, ATA, and ATAPI Block Device" button to open a window where you can select support for IDE ATA hard drives and ATAPI CD-ROMs. Included here are IDE chipsets such as HTP366 used for ATA66 drives.

- **SCSI Support**   If you have any SCSI devices on your system, make sure the entries in the SCSI Support window are set to Yes. You enable support for SCSI disks, tape drives, and CD-ROMs here. The SCSI Low-Level Drivers window displays an extensive list of SCSI devices currently supported by Linux. Be sure the ones you have are selected.

- **Network Device Support**   The Network Device Support window lists several general features for network device support. There are entries here for windows that list support for particular types of network devices, including Ethernet (10 or 100Mb) devices, token ring devices, WAN interfaces, and AppleTalk devices. Many of these devices are created as modules you can load as needed. You can elect to rebuild your kernel with support for any of these devices built directly into the kernel.

- **Multimedia Devices**   Multimedia devices provide support for various multimedia cards as well as Video4Linux.

- **File Systems**   The File Systems window lists the different types of file systems Linux can support. These include DOS, VFAT (Windows 95/98), and ISO9660 (CD-ROM) file systems. Network file systems—such as NFS, SMB (Samba), and NCP (NetWare)—HFS (Macintosh), and NTFS are also listed.

- **Character Devices**   The Character Devices window lists features for devices such as your keyboard, mouse, and serial ports. Support exists for both serial and bus mice.

- **Sound**   The Sound window lists different sound cards supported by the kernel. Select the one on your system. For older systems, you may have to provide the IRQ, DMA, and Base I/O your sound card uses.

These are compiled as separate modules, some of
which you could elect to include directly in the kernel
if you want.

- **Bluetooth Devices**   Support for Bluetooth enabled
  peripherals, listing drivers for USB, serial, and PC
  card interfaces.

- **Kernel Hacking**   The Kernel Hacking window lists
  features of interest to developers who work at the
  kernel level and need to modify the kernel code. You
  can have the kernel include debugging information,
  and also provide some measure of control during
  crashes.

Once you set your options, save your configuration. Save
and Exit option overwrites your `.config` configuration
file. The Store to Configuration File option lets you save
your configuration to a particular file.

TIP   *Red Hat Linux 9 incorporates support for the Native
POSIX Thread Library (NPTL), an updated version of
Linux POSIX threads, providing for more efficient use of
high-end processors. Though this feature is designed to
be backward compatible, some older modules may prove
incompatible and may need to be recompiled with the
new kernel.*

9

Compiling and Installing the Kernel

Now that the configuration is ready, you can compile your
kernel. You first need to generate a dependency tree to
determine what part of the source code to compile, based
on your configuration. Use the following command in
`/usr/src/linux-2.4`:

```
make dep
```

You also have to clean up any object and dependency files
that may remain from a previous compilation. Use the
following command to remove such files:

```
make clean
```

You can use several options to compile the kernel (see Table 9-1). The `bzImage` option simply generates a kernel file called `bzImage` and places it in the `arch` directory. For Intel and AMD systems, you find `bzImage` in the `i386/boot` subdirectory, `arch/i386/boot`. For a kernel source, this would be in `/usr/src/linux-2.4/arch/i386/boot`.

```
make bzImage
```

The previous options create the kernel, but not the modules—those features of the kernel to be compiled into separate modules. To compile your modules, use the `make` command with the `modules` argument.

```
make modules
```

To install your modules, use the `make` command with the `modules_install` option. This installs the modules in the `/lib/modules/version-num` directory, where `version-num` is the version number of the kernel. You should make a backup copy of the old modules before you install the new ones.

```
make modules_install
```

The `install` option generates both the kernel files and installs them on your system as `vmlinuz.`, incorporating the `make bzImage` step.

```
make install
```

Option	Description
zImage	Creates the kernel file called `zImage` located in the `/usr/src/linux/arch` or `arch/i386/boot` directory.
install	Creates the kernel and installs it on your system.
zdisk	Creates a kernel file and installs it on a floppy disk (creates a boot disk).
bzImage	Creates the kernel file and calls it `bzImage`.
bzdisk	Creates the kernel and installs it on a floppy disk (creates a boot disk).

Table 9-1. Compiling Options

If you are booting Linux from DOS using `loadlin`, you will need to copy the `bzImage` file to the `loadlin` directory on the DOS partition where you are starting Linux from.

The commands for a simple compilation and installation are shown here:

```
make dep
make clean
make bzImage
make modules
make modules_install
make install
```

If you want, you could enter these all on fewer lines, separating the commands with semicolons, as shown here:

```
make dep; make clean; make bzImage; make modules
make modules_install; make install
```

A safer way to perform these operations on single lines is to make them conditionally dependent on one another, using the `&&` command. In the previous method, if one operation has a error, the next one will still be executed. By making the operations conditional, the next operation is run only if the previous one is successful.

```
make dep && make clean && make bzImage
make modules
make modules_install &&  make install
```

Installing the Kernel Image Manually

To install a kernel `bzImage` file manually, copy the `bzImage` file to the directory where the kernel resides and give it the name used on your distribution, such as `vmlinuz-2.4.20-8`. Remember to first back up the old kernel file, as noted in the precautionary steps. `vmlinuz` is a symbolic link to an actual kernel file that will have the term `vmlinuz` with the version name. So, to manually install a `bzImage` file, you copy it to the `/boot` directory with the name `vmlinuz` and the attached version number such as `vmlinuz-2.4.20`. You then create a symbolic link from `/boot/vmlinuz` to `/boot/vmlinuz-2.4.20`.

```
make bzImage
cp arch/i386/boot/bzImage /boot/vmlinuz-2.4.20
ln -s /boot/vmlinuz /boot/vmlinuz-2.4.20-8
```

TIP *The* `bzImage` *option, and those options that begin with the letter b, create a compressed kernel image. This kernel image may not work on older systems. If not, try using the* `zImage` *option to create a kernel file called* `zImage`*. Then, install the* `zImage` *file manually the same way you would with* `bzImage`*. Bear in mind that support for* `zImage` *will be phased out eventually.*

You will also have to make a copy of the `System.map` file, linking it to the `System.map` symbolic link.

```
cp arch/i386/boot/System.map
                        /boot/System.map-2.4.20
ln -s /boot/System.map /boot/System.map-2.4.20-8
```

The following commands show a basic compilation and a manual installation. First, all previous binary files are removed with the `clean` option. Then, the kernel is created using the `bzImage` option. This creates a kernel program called `bzImage` located in the `arch/i386/boot` directory. This kernel file is copied to the `/boot` directory and given the name `vmlinuz-2.4.20-8`. A symbolic link called `/boot/vmlinuz` is created to the kernel `vmlinuz-2.4.20-8` file. Then create the modules and install the modules:

```
make dep
make clean
make bzImage
make modules
make modules_install
cp arch/i386/boot/bzImage /boot/vmlinuz-2.4.20-8
ln -s /boot/vmlinux-2.4.20-8 /boot/vmlinuz
cp System.map /boot/System.map-2.4.20-8
ln -s /boot/System.map-2.4.20-8 /boot/System.map
```

Kernel Boot Disks

Instead of installing the kernel on your system, you can simply place it on a boot disk and boot your system from

that disk. In that case, you just have to create a boot disk
using the `bzdisk` option. This option installs the kernel
on a floppy disk placed in your floppy drive. The kernel
resides on the floppy disk, and to use that kernel, you boot
your system from the floppy (the kernel is not installed on
your root partition as it is with the `install` option).

```
make bzdisk
```

Be sure you have a floppy disk in the floppy drive. The
`make bzdisk` command copies the image directly to the
floppy disk. You still have to create and install your modules.
Be sure that the `bzImage` file is small enough to fit on a
floppy disk. If not, you will have to reconfigure your kernel,
compiling as many features as possible as modules instead
of as part of the kernel.

```
make clean
make bzImage
make bzdisk
make modules
make modules_install
```

TIP   *If you are experimenting with your kernel
configurations, it may be safer to put a new kernel version
on a boot disk or boot CD-ROM, rather than installing it
on your system. If something goes wrong, you can always
boot up normally with your original kernel still on your
system (though you can always configure your boot loader
to access previous versions).*

9

Boot Loader Configurations

If you are using a boot loader such as GRUB or LILO, you
can configure your system to enable you to start any of
your installed kernels. As seen in the "Precautionary
Steps for Modifying Kernels" section, you can create an
added entry in the boot loader configuration file for your
old kernel. As you install new kernel versions, you could
simply add more entries, enabling you to use any of the
previous kernels. Whenever you boot, your boot loader
will then present you with a list of kernels to choose from.

For example, you could install a developmental version of the kernel, along with a current stable version, while keeping your old version. In the image line for each entry, you specify the filename of the kernel. You can create another boot loader entry for your older kernel.

GRUB Configurations

In the next example, the /etc/grub.conf file contains entries for two Linux kernels, one for the kernel installed earlier, 2.4.18-4, and one for a more recent kernel, 2.4.20-8. With GRUB, you only have to add a new entry for the new kernel.

```
# grub.conf generated by anaconda
#
#boot=/dev/hda
default=0
timeout=30
splashimage=(hd0,2)/boot/grub/splash.xpm.gz
title New Linux (2.4.20-8)
        root (hd0,2)
        kernel /boot/vmlinuz-2.4.20-8 ro \
                    root=/dev/hda3 hdc=ide-scsi
        initrd /boot/initrd-2.4.20-8.img
title  Old Linux (2.4.18-4)
        root (hd0,2)
        kernel /boot/vmlinuz-2.4.18-4 ro \
                    root=/dev/hda3 hdc=ide-scsi
        initrd /boot/initrd-2.4.18-4.img
title Windows XP
        rootnoverify (hd0,0)
        imakeactive
        chainloader +1
```

LILO Configurations

If you are using LILO, you can configure your system to enable you to start any of your installed kernels. As seen in the "Precautionary Steps" section, you can create an added entry in the lilo.conf file for your old kernel. As you install new kernel versions, you simply add more entries to your LILO configuration file. Whenever you add

a new entry, be sure to execute the `lilo` command to
update LILO. Whenever you install the kernel on Red Hat
using the RPM kernel package, the `/boot/vmlinuz` link
is automatically changed to the new kernel. You can still
create another LILO entry for your older kernel. In the
next example, the `lilo.conf` file contains entries for two
Linux kernels, one using the standard `/boot/vmlinuz`
link, as well as windows.

```
boot = /dev/hda
install = /boot/boot.b
message = /boot/message
prompt
timeout = 200
default = linux
image = /boot/vmlinuz
        label = linux
        root = /dev/hda3
        read-only
image = /boot/vmlinuz-2.2.16
        label = linux-2.2
        root = /dev/hda3
        read-only
other = /dev/hda1
        label = win
        table = /dev/hda
```

Module RAM Disks

If your system uses certain block devices unsupported by
the kernel, like some SCSI, RAID, or IDE devices, you will
need to load certain modules when you boot. Such block
device modules are kept on a RAM disk that is accessed
when your system first starts up (RAM disks are also used
for diskless systems). For example, if you have a SCSI
hard drive or CD-ROMs, the SCSI drivers for them are
often held in modules that are loaded whenever you start
up your system. These modules are stored in a RAM disk
from which the startup process reads. If you create a new
kernel that needs to load modules to start up, you must
create a new RAM disk for those modules. You only need

to create a new RAM disk if your kernel has to load modules at startup. If, for example, you use a SCSI hard drive, but you incorporated SCSI hard drive and CD-ROM support (including support for the specific model) directly into your kernel, you don't need to set up a RAM disk (support for most IDE hard drives and CD-ROMs is already incorporated directly into the kernel).

If you need to create a RAM disk, you can use the `mkinitrd` command to create a RAM disk image file. The mkinitrd command incorporates all the IDE, SCSI, and RAID modules that your system uses, including those listed in your `/etc/modules.conf` file. See the man pages for `mkinitrd` and RAM disk documentation for more details. `mkinitrd` takes as its arguments the name of the RAM disk image file and the kernel that the modules are taken from. In the following example, a RAM disk image called `initrd-2.4.20-8.img` is created in the `/boot` directory, using modules from the 2.4.20-8 kernel. The 2.4.20-8 kernel must already be installed on your system and its modules created.

```
# mkinitrd /boot/initrd-2.4.20-8.img 2.4.20-8
```

You can select certain modules to load before or after any SCSI module. The `--preload` option loads before the SCSI modules, and `--with` loads after. For example, to load RAID5 support before the SCSI modules, use `--preload=raid5`:

```
mkinitrd --preload=raid5 raid-ramdisk 2.4.20-8
```

In the `grub.conf` segment for the new kernel, place an `initrd` entry specifying the new RAM disk:

```
initrd /boot/initrd-2.4.20-8.img
```

Appendix

Service Management Tools: chkconfig and redhat-config-services

On Red Hat, redhat-config-services and the `chkconfig` command provide simple interfaces you can use to choose what servers you want started up and how you want them to run. You use these tools to control any daemon you want started up, including system services such as `cron`, the print server, remote file servers for Samba and NFS, authentication servers for Kerberos, and, of course, Internet servers for FTP or HTTP. Such daemons are referred to as *services*, and you should think of these tools as managing these services. Any of these services can be set up to start or stop at different runlevels.

These tools manage services that are started up by scripts in the `/etc/rc.d/init.d` directory. If you add a new service, both `chkconfig` and redhat-config-services can manage it. As described in the following section, services are started up at specific runlevels using startup links in various runlevel directories. These links are connected to the startup scripts in the `init.d` directory. Runlevel directories are numbered from 0 to 6 in the `/etc/rc.d` directory, such as `/etc/rc.d/rc3.d` for runlevel 3 and `/etc/rc.d/rc5.d` for runlevel 5. Removing a service from a runlevel only changes its link in the corresponding runlevel `rc.d` directory. It does not touch the startup script in the `init.d` directory.

A

TIP *The KDE The System V Init Editor features a GUI interface to enable you to manage any daemons on your system easily—Internet servers as well as system daemons, such as print servers.*

255

redhat-config-services

With the Red Hat redhat-config-services utilities, you can simply select from a list of commonly used services the ones that you want to run when your system boots up. You can access redhat-config-services from the Services icon in the Server Settings window or menu. redhat-config-services lets you start, stop, and restart a server, much like the `service` command. redhat-config-services provides a Gnome GUI interface for easy use. It displays a list of your installed servers, with checked checkboxes for those currently chosen to start up. You can start, stop, or restart, any particular service by selecting it, and choosing either Start Service, Stop Service, or Restart Service from the Action menu.

You can also set startup runlevels for services, just as you can with `chkconfig`, though you are limited to levels 3, 4, and 5. The list of checked entries differs depending on the runlevel you choose from the Edit Runlevel menu. In effect, you are choosing which services to start at a given runlevel. The default is runlevel 5, the GUI startup level. You may want a different set of services started or stopped for runlevel 3, the command-line startup level. In that case, you would select Runlevel 3 from the Edit Runlevel menu to display the services with selected checkboxes for runlevel 3.

chkconfig

You can specify the service you want start and the level you want to start it at with the `chkconfig` command. Unlike other service management tools, `chkconfig` works equally well on standalone and on `xinetd` services. Though standalone services can be run at any runlevel, you can also turn `xinetd` services on or off for the runlevels that `xinetd` runs in. Table A-1 lists the different `chkconfig` options.

Option	Description
`--level` *runlevel*	Specifies a runlevel to turn on, off, or reset a service.
`--list` *service*	Lists startup information for services at different runlevels. `xinetd` services are just `on` or `off`. With no argument, all services are listed, including `xinetd` services.
`--add` *service*	Adds a service, creating links in the default specified runlevels (or all runlevels, if none are specified).
`--del` *service*	Deletes all links for the service (startup and shutdown) in all runlevel directories.
service `on`	Turns a service on, creating a startup link in the specified or default runlevel directories.
service `off`	Turns a service off, creating shutdown links in specified or default directories
service `reset`	Resets service startup information, creating default links as specified in the `chkconfig` entry in the service's `init.d` startup script.

Table A-1. chkconfig Options

Listing Services with chkconfig

To see a list of services, use the `--list` option. A sampling of services managed by `chkconfig` are shown here. The on or off status of the service is shown at each runlevel. `xinetd` services and their status are also shown.

```
chkconfig -list
dhcpd   0:off 1:off 2:off 3:off 4:off 5:off 6:off
httpd   0:off 1:off 2:off 3:off 4:off 5:off 6:off
named   0:off 1:off 2:off 3:off 4:off 5:off 6:off
lpd     0:off 1:off 2:on  3:on  4:on  5:on  6:off
nfs     0:off 1:off 2:off 3:off 4:off 5:off 6:off
```

```
crond  0:off 1:off 2:on  3:on  4:on  5:on  6:off
xinetd 0:off 1:off 2:off 3:on  4:on  5:on  6:off
xinetd based services:
      time:         off
      finger:       off
      pop3s:        off
      swat:         on
```

Starting and Stopping Services with chkconfig

You use the `on` option to have a service started at certain runlevels, and the `off` option to disable it. You can specify the runlevel to effect with the `--level` option. If no level is specified, `chkconfig` will use any `chkconfig` default information in a service's `init.d` startup script. Red Hat installs its services with `chkconfig` default information already entered (if this is missing, `chkconfig` will use runlevels 3, 4, and 5). The following example has the Web server (`httpd`) started at runlevel 5:

```
chkconfig --level 5 httpd on
```

The `off` option configures a service to shut down if the system enters a specified runlevel. The next example shuts down the Web sever if runlevel 3 is entered. If the service is not running, it remains shut down:

```
chkconfig --level 3 httpd off
```

The `reset` option restores a service to its `chkconfig` default options as specified in the service's `init.d` startup script.

```
chkconfig httpd reset
```

To see just the startup information for a service, you use just the service name with the `--list` option:

```
chkconfig --list httpd
httpd   0:off  1:off 2:off 3:on 4:off 5:on 6:off
```

Enabling and Disabling xinetd Services with chkconfig

Unlike redhat-config-services, `chkconfig` can also enable or disable `xinetd` services. Simply enter the `xinetd` service with either an `on` or `off` option. The service will be started up or shut down, and the disable line in its `xinetd` configuration script in the `/etc/xinetd.d` directory will be edited accordingly. For example, to start `swat`, the Samba configuration server, which runs on `xinetd`, you simply enter:

```
chkconfig swat on
chkconfig --list swat
    swat              on
```

The `swat` configuration file for `xinetd`, `/etc/xinetd.d/swat`, will have its disable line edited to no, as shown here:

```
disable=no
```

If you want to shut down the swat server, you can use the `off` option. This will change the disable line in `/etc/xinetd.d/swat` to read "disable=yes".

```
chkconfig swat off
```

The same procedure works for other `xinetd` services such as the POP3 server, and `finger`.

Adding and Removing Services with chkconfig

If you want a service removed entirely from the entire startup and shutdown process in all runlevels, you can use the `--del` option. This removes all startup and shutdown links in all the runlevel directories.

```
chkconfig --del httpd
```

You can also add services to `chkconfig` management with the `--add` option. `chkconfig` will create startup links for the new service in the appropriate startup directories, `/etc/rc.d/rcn.d`. If you have previously removed all links for a service, you can restore them with the `add` option.

```
chkconfig --add httpd
```

INDEX

261

INTERNATIONAL CONTACT INFORMATION

AUSTRALIA
McGraw-Hill Book Company Australia Pty. Ltd.
TEL +61-2-9900-1800
FAX +61-2-9878-8881
http://www.mcgraw-hill.com.au
books-it_sydney@mcgraw-hill.com

CANADA
McGraw-Hill Ryerson Ltd.
TEL +905-430-5000
FAX +905-430-5020
http://www.mcgraw-hill.ca

GREECE, MIDDLE EAST, & AFRICA
(Excluding South Africa)
McGraw-Hill Hellas
TEL +30-210-6560-990
TEL +30-210-6560-993
TEL +30-210-6560-994
FAX +30-210-6545-525

MEXICO (Also serving Latin America)
McGraw-Hill Interamericana Editores S.A. de C.V.
TEL +525-117-1583
FAX +525-117-1589
http://www.mcgraw-hill.com.mx
fernando_castellanos@mcgraw-hill.com

SINGAPORE (Serving Asia)
McGraw-Hill Book Company
TEL +65-6863-1580
FAX +65-6862-3354
http://www.mcgraw-hill.com.sg
mghasia@mcgraw-hill.com

SOUTH AFRICA
McGraw-Hill South Africa
TEL +27-11-622-7512
FAX +27-11-622-9045
robyn_swanepoel@mcgraw-hill.com

SPAIN
McGraw-Hill/Interamericana de España, S.A.U.
TEL +34-91-180-3000
FAX +34-91-372-8513
http://www.mcgraw-hill.es
professional@mcgraw-hill.es

UNITED KINGDOM, NORTHERN,
EASTERN, & CENTRAL EUROPE
McGraw-Hill Education Europe
TEL +44-1-628-502500
FAX +44-1-628-770224
http://www.mcgraw-hill.co.uk
computing_europe@mcgraw-hill.com

ALL OTHER INQUIRIES Contact:
McGraw-Hill/Osborne
TEL +1-510-420-7700
FAX +1-510-420-7703
http://www.osborne.com
omg_international@mcgraw-hill.com